Black Education in Alabama, 1865–1901

Black Education in Alabama, 1865–1901

Robert G. Sherer

THE UNIVERSITY OF ALABAMA PRESS
Tuscaloosa

∞
The paper on which this book is printed meets the minimum requirements of American National Standard for Information Science–Permanence of Paper for Printed Library Materials, ANSI Z39.48-1984.

Library of Congress Cataloging-in-Publication Data

Sherer, Robert G.
Black Education in Alabama, 1865–1901.

Bibliography: p.
Includes index.
1. Blacks—Education—Alabama—History. I. Title.

LC2802.A2S47
370'.9761
75-44050

Manufactured in the United States of America

Contents

Acknowledgments

Because this study grew out of the research for my dissertation, I owe my primary appreciation to my advisor, George B. Tindall, and to Joel Williamson who worked with me for one year during Dr. Tindall's leave of absence. The encouragement and support of George Breathett at Bennett College and Calvin S. White at Alcorn State University made publication of this study possible. I am also very appreciative of the assistance I received from the staff members at the following institutions: Library of Congress, Congregational Library, Amistad Collection, Duke University, University of North Carolina, University of Alabama, Selma University, Atlanta University, Howard University, Alabama State University, Alabama A & M University, Alabama State Department of Archives and History, Brown University, Yale University, and Oberlin College.

Of the many individuals who helped me locate fugitive materials or who read and commented on parts of this study I must especially thank J. T. Alexander, G. Murray Branch, Raymond Gavin, Walter B. Weare, Stephen Channing, and the families of John W. Beverly and William Burns Paterson. My typist, Linda Awad, put far more time and care into preparing the final manuscript than any typist I have ever known. Finally, my wife, Ann, and my children, Robbie and Ann Marie, gave up much family time to enable me to finish this study. Ann's suggestions and support were always helpful throughout the preparation and many revisions of this study.

Introduction

Many Americans from the Puritans of the 1600's to the student protesters and educational reformers of the 1960's have believed education to be vitally important in society. It is somewhat surprising, therefore, to realize that historians have made comparatively few studies of education in the United States apart from chapters in general works of social history, quick analyses as part of a call for educational reform, or uncritical studies of particular educational institutions (usually by a faculty member).

This omission is even more glaring in the case of the education of black Americans.[1] While there are very few general or specific studies of black schools, most of the studies that do exist deal primarily with the political actions of white legislatures to segregate and discriminate against black public schools.[2] The main recent social history of black public education and white philanthropic aid to black schools in the South, Henry Allen Bullock, *A History of Negro Education in the South* (New York: Praeger Publishers, 1970), deals primarily with the period since 1901.

Subordination or Liberation? explains and describes the development of black private and public, elementary, secondary, normal, and collegiate education in Alabama from emancipation to 1901. A state study is large enough for synthesis and small enough to permit detailed analysis. All public schools are in state systems. Since most graduates of black private colleges before 1915 taught in state schools or followed their professions in the state where they received their education, state studies are important for private schools. Many other social groups such as teachers' associations, professional organizations, churches, and lodges are largely statewide bodies. Many black public schools began as private schools, which philanthropic organizations turned over to the states as they agreed to support these schools. Since little has been written until recently about developments within the black community in Alabama, a state study of all black education in Alabama will provide some of the information about black leaders and institutions so badly needed in both black studies, Alabama, Southern, and American history courses and textbooks.[3]

The study of education in Alabama is especially important in understanding black education throughout the United States since the most famous black school, Booker T. Washington's Tuskegee Institute, is located in Alabama and began as a state teachers' training school. A history of black education in Alabama provides a test case of the frequently assumed dominance of Booker T. Washington and his plan of "industrial" or vocational training in black education.[4]

Subordination or Liberation? begins by describing the way Alabama whites sought to use black schools as part of the web of subordination they wished to continue to maintain over blacks even after emancipation. Since white dominance of blacks was not total immediately after the Civil War, blacks sought to use education as a means of escaping their subordinate status. With Booker T. Washington, Tuskegee Institute, and its offshoots representing one pole (industrial training) and the leaders and schools of the American Missionary Association representing the other pole (collegiate, liberal arts education like that available in white schools), the leaders of Alabama's black schools followed different strategies in trying to use education to help blacks to achieve their proper, equal place in the American social, economic, and political systems.

Washington's political influence after Theodore Roosevelt became the President of the United States in 1901 and Washington's inside contacts with white philanthropists who founded the General Education Board in 1901 made Washington and his educational theories very influential in the early twentieth century. But the principles that were to guide the development of black education in the black public and private schools and colleges were established in the decades immediately after emancipation, 1865–1901. During this period most black schools emphasized liberal arts, collegiate education for black leaders. This tradition never disappeared, even during the worst years of white suppression of blacks, 1890–1915, or during Washington's most influential years, 1901–1915.

Black Education in Alabama, 1865–1901

For

Robert Glenn, Sr. and Esther Lee

Ann, Robert Glenn III, and Ann Marie

the heritage of the past, the hope of the future

1

THE WEB OF SUBORDINATION

All education has two basic parts—the teaching of basic skills and information and the transmission of social values. Southern slaveowners clearly understood the social uses of education. In 1832 Alabama denied formal education to all blacks to discourage revolts.[1] This attempt to keep the slaves illiterate did not mean that the planters did not try to educate their slaves. Many planters gave their slaves some manual instruction. The plantation system also included an elaborate, informal curriculum designed to indoctrinate the slaves for their "proper place" in society. Christian education on plantations sought to ensure the submission as well as the salvation of the slaves.

So defenders of Southern slavery such as Ulrich Bonnell Phillips are correct in asserting that the plantation was a school for blacks. The curriculum or aim of this school, however, was subordination not civilization. While modern scholars from Stanley Elkins to John Blassingame differ markedly in their judgment of the *effectiveness* of this instruction, they agree with Kenneth Stampp that the *intent* of the planters was "To Make [the slaves] Stand in Fear."[2]

When the Civil War ended, the planters had lost two of the instruments with which they sought to inculcate subordination in blacks, black chattel slavery and the white-dominated churches which slaves had to attend. While the whites still had political and economic weapons to enforce black subordination, they needed an institution to teach it.

During the transitional period immediately after the Civil War, several forces converged to overcome Alabama's whites' thirty-year-old tradition of opposition to formal black education. Some impoverished whites needed jobs so desperately that they wanted to teach in black schools. Many whites were concerned about illiterate blacks voting after 1867–1868. A few white educators such as Jabez Lamar Monroe Curry were committed to universal education for blacks and whites.[3]

Alabama's blacks did all they could to persuade whites to allow and to support black schools. Many blacks perceived the importance of education and began working to establish schools immediately after the Civil War ended. On November 20, 1865, a convention of fifty-six black men from towns throughout Alabama met in Mobile to discuss the implications of their new freedom. This convention passed several resolutions including one stating "That we regard the education of our children and youths as vital to the preservation of our liberties . . . and shall use our utmost endeavors to promote these blessings in our common country."[4] In December, 1865, several of Selma's black leaders used the local newspaper to appeal to their friends and their former masters for aid in obtaining teachers and schools. Playing on the whites' fear of outside intervention, the blacks shrewdly pointed out that "if you stand back, strangers will take the money from under your hands."[5]

Upon obtaining their freedom, most blacks of all ages sought education as a panacea for their troubles and flocked to any school available. Some plantation owners took advantage of this black craving for education by establishing schools on their plantations to keep the freedmen from leaving.[6]

Where no schools were available blacks frequently succeeded in bringing pressure on the whites to open public schools, which the blacks then helped build and sustain. For example, the first public school for blacks in Mobile, Alabama, began only after the local blacks held a mass meeting and twice sent a representative to the local school board to present their request for a school.[7]

Blacks also worked closely with the Freedmen's Bureau after 1867 by offering to furnish schoolhouses and to board teachers if the Bureau would send them a teacher and pay his salary. Some blacks used the Homestead Act to buy land for schoolhouses. Black leaders in Selma tried to buy land near the town for a schoolhouse. Blacks in Huntsville raised money to send someone to Superintendent Charles W. Buckley to find out how they could find a teacher and build a schoolhouse. So great was the blacks' desire for education that the pupils of one school in 1866 selected some of their own classmates to continue the school during the summer when the white missionaries returned to the North for a vacation.[8] Blacks played an influential role in some of the decisions of missionary associations about locating their schools. The American Missionary Association sometimes responded to well-organized local blacks' requests for aid in beginning schools.

The main pressure on Alabama's whites to establish black schools came from Northern missionaries who followed the Union Army into north Alabama and established a black school in 1863. These missionaries and Union chaplains taught the newly freed blacks such "alien" values as equality, brotherhood, and citizenship for all, along with the traditional three R's. These teachers also strongly emphasized moral and religious training or "character building" in all their schools.

While several missionary societies established and maintained various black schools in Alabama, the American Missionary Association (AMA) had become the dominant society through a series of mergers by 1867–1868. Besides the AMA only two societies established schools in Alabama during Reconstruction and maintained them after 1874—the Presbyterian General Commission for Freedmen's Affairs (after 1883, the Presbyterian Board of Missions for Freedmen) and the Freedmen's Aid Society of the Methodist Episcopal Church.[9]

The missionary societies received the support of the Freedmen's Bureau from 1865 to 1870. Although almost all of the missionaries were white, by 1866 the Bureau began using blacks as teachers and principals "wherever possible." The Bureau turned to black teachers primarily out of necessity and expediency. The great demand for teachers could not be met by the Northern white missionaries alone. The Bureau often chose black teachers because it discovered it could get away with paying them less than it had to pay whites. The Bureau also sought to spare its schools any possible trouble from Southern whites who believed they could influence black teachers more easily than they could Northern white missionaries. Still, most of the early schools met for safety near Army posts.[10]

According to the Bureau's records, its work in Alabama black schools reached a peak in 1866–1867 when the term ended with 175 schools, 14 permanent schoolhouses, 150 teachers, and 9,799 pupils.[11] The Bureau's expenditures in Alabama rose from $6,633.62 in 1865–1866 to $45,237.55 in 1866–1867. The Bureau usually provided buildings, while the aid societies paid the teachers' salaries. In 1866 and 1867, however, the societies sent an insufficient number of teachers to Alabama, so the Bureau paid $33,762.25 for salaries. Evidently Alabama was the only state where this occurred and the Bureau discontinued the practice in 1867.[12]

According to the Bureau's reports, black education in Alabama under the Bureau declined seriously in 1867–1868. Political excitement due to the Constitutional Convention and elections (in both of which Bureau officials and missionaries took active parts) caused some whites to burn schoolhouses and to turn out the teachers who were boarding with them. The year's poor crops gave few blacks even the minimal tuition needed for school. By this time the immediate postwar enthusiasm in the North was fading and the aid societies found it increasingly difficult to raise funds.

In 1868 Alabama's new Board of Education (established by the Reconstruction Constitution of 1868) passed a law whereby the Bureau would continue furnishing schoolhouses by renting buildings or building new ones and would pay the teachers' transportation to the schools, the aid societies would select the teachers and pay their transportation from the field, and the state would pay the teachers' salaries. This system seldom worked very well. The Conservatives refused to cooperate. The new superintendents were unfamiliar with their jobs and many of them were incompetent. The funds which the Board of Education provided were insufficient.

By 1868 the Bureau sensed that its time was short and persuaded many of those from whom it rented buildings to use the money to build new schoolhouses that could be used when the Bureau could no longer pay. In this way, and through direct appropriations for building and repairing schoolhouses, the Bureau provided school buildings "adequate in size and nature" in most of the key locations in Alabama, "and smaller buildings suitable to the wants of the communities" in the remaining areas.

Black education suffered from 1868 to 1870 because of inadequate funds from the state and the administration's inability to enforce the new educational laws. The best efforts of N. B. Cloud, the Republican Superintendent of Education, could not prevent many county and township officials from flouting the law prohibiting discrimination against blacks in the schools.[13] Despite all these difficulties, black education in Alabama recovered in 1868 and began to flourish modestly under the 1868 Reconstruction Constitution by 1871.[14]

On June 30, 1870, General Oliver Otis Howard ordered the Bureau to conclude its educational work in Alabama by July 15. From October, 1865 until February, 1870, the Bureau spent $156,941.10 for black education in Alabama.[15] Along with its relief work, the Bureau made its main quantitative contribution in Alabama in education.[16]

The quality of the Freedmen's Bureau schools in preparing former slaves to be citizens, however, is another matter. Charles W. Buckley, the Bureau's Superintendent of Education for Alabama, knew that Alabama's whites first tried to prevent black education and then decided to support black schools only upon recognizing their inevitability. The Bureau's General Superintendent of Education, John W. Alvord, sought white Alabama teachers for black schools in 1866 and reported in 1867 that he had not had much trouble finding them.[17]

While comparatively few Southern whites taught black schools, the willingness of the Freedmen's Bureau and the "Radical" Republicans to allow these Southerners to teach showed only minimal concern for *what* the schools taught or *who* taught in them. Northern "Radicals" did urge integration of the schools, but few said much about the loyalty, competency, or degree of racism of these teachers. White Southerners, however, sensitized to ideology by seeing the structures of pro-slavery and secessionist thought toppled by the Civil War, protested vigorously against Northern teachers in black Southern schools.

While the "Radicals" went to great lengths to try to ensure that the proper persons would lead the South politically, they evidently ignored these white teachers in black schools who were helping lead the South in education. These teachers did not have to take any oaths. Perhaps few "Radical" Republicans saw the problem of education in political terms. Obviously, the North did not have the will to carry out such a program of testing teachers for long, if it ever could have been established; but there was no indication that the Bureau even attempted such testing in Alabama.

This lack of concern with the social values transmitted in education, this considering education a neutral commodity which a former secessionist and slaveowner could distribute as well as a Unionist, this failure even to try to reconstruct education, this surrender of the ideological field to white Southerners (both in hiring teachers by the Bureau and in conducting the public school system later)—combined to help make Southern education for whites and blacks what it became and to help build the intellectual basis of the solid South. For the North did not seriously interfere with the Southern white teachers and school officials who, before and after the war, transmitted the tradition and culture of the antebellum, slave society and who molded the minds of the coming generations.

All these pressures slowly pushed Alabama's white leaders toward accepting and even supporting black schools.[18] This movement was uneven. While in 1865 many whites showed their opposition to black schools by burning buildings and threatening teachers, by 1866 most leading whites accepted black education. During the political struggles of 1867–1868, many whites showed their displeasure with Congressional Reconstruction by attacking black schools verbally or physically. Once the reconstruction government established free black public schools in 1868,[19] Alabama's Conservative leaders at first refused to cooperate with the leaders of these schools. Just as the Anti-Federalists accepted the new United States government of 1789 and strove to gain control of it, the Alabama Conservatives gradually accepted the existence of black public schools after 1868 and sought to get control of them.

The issue of control was always basic. Some Alabama whites, including several religious denominations, came to support black education in 1866 when they realized that the Selma blacks' newspaper appeal of 1865 had been prophetic—if the local whites did not provide black schools, Northern missionaries would. One Alabama white admitted that many whites who supported black education in 1866 did so "with the provision that Northern teachers shall not be sent."[20] In addition to wishing to keep Northern teachers out, Alabama's whites supported black education to control it. A newspaper in Greensboro, Alabama candidly urged whites to support black schools because, "the more interest the whites take in Negro education the better they will be able to control their former slaves for good."[21] The "good," of course, would be the good of the whites.

Many whites who aided black education really saw themselves as benefactors. They believed they had a responsibility to society to ensure that blacks received the "proper" education. Later white reaction against black education came not only because of black and missionary political activity, but also because the Southern whites found that educating free men was not the same thing as indoctrinating slaves. Thus, many whites who aided black schools immediately after the Civil War felt betrayed by their efforts. The trouble with education was that it *did* affect blacks the same way it did whites, i.e., it increased the students' qualifications and desires for upward social mobility. Therefore, if Alabama was to be segregated with the whites dominant, the whites had to provide for two kinds of education—white and black. While specifically "black," that is, industrial, academically inferior education did not become the aim of state law until 1887–1891, the basic idea was behind the aid to black schools which Southern whites so "generously" gave immediately after the Civil War.

While the Conservative Southern whites could not control public education during Congressional Reconstruction, 1868–1875, one unique educational feature of Alabama's Constitution of 1868 hampered the development of public education. Unlike most Southern states, from 1868 to 1875, Alabama divided its control of education between the legislature and a Board of Education. This board managed the schools and could pass educational legislation which remained in effect unless the legislature repealed it or the governor vetoed it. The legislature resented this invasion of its prerogative and frequently overturned the board's acts. The unpopularity of the board and the intra-governmental struggles it provoked aided the Conservatives by stifling educational innovation and by helping to make many Alabamians oppose the Constitution of 1868.[22]

In addition to strife between the Board of Education and the legislature, political changes from 1868 to 1875 hindered education. Republicans controlled the Board of Education, 1868–1874, but they lost the House of Representatives and the offices of governor and state superintendent of education to the Democrats, 1870–1872. The reports of the state superintendents of education—N. B, Cloud, Republican, 1868–1870; Joseph Hodgson, Democrat, 1870–1872; Joseph H. Speed, Republican, 1872–1874; and John Martin McKleroy, Democrat, 1874–1876—were largely concerned with justifying their actions and attacking those of their predecessors. This wrangling was most pronounced over the amount of money given to the schools. Each superintendent excused his failings by placing the blame on the corruption and incompetence of the man before him. Although the 1868 Constitution theoretically provided sufficient funds for the schools, it was almost impossible to tell how much of this money the schools actually received.[23]

While most of the debate and public attention focused on the local, common schools, black higher (secondary) education also began during Congressional Reconstruction in Alabama.[24] On August 11, 1868, the Reconstruction Board of Education first provided for public normal schools in Alabama by establishing normal classes in eleven towns and cities.[25] In 1869, Alabama's Superintendent of Education, N. B. Cloud, reported that nine normal classes with a total of three hundred students had successfully been operated in six towns during the preceding year.[26] The 1868 act had not required racially separate classes, but in 1869 the board provided for four normal schools, each of which was to have one department for white and one department for black students.[27]

In its 1870 session the Board of Education abolished the normal schools and established thirteen new ones, seven for whites and six for blacks. Governor Robert Lindsay, a Democrat, refused to approve the bill. This "abandonment of the schools" caused the Department of Education to lose $5,371.85 in 1869 and $16,582.10 in 1870.[28]

The actual number of normal schools in existence in 1870–1871, if any, cannot be determined.[29] On December 20, 1871, the Board of Education appropriated $4,750 to establish normal schools for blacks at Montgomery, Huntsville, Marion, and Sparta.[30] In December, 1872, another act appropriated $3,250 for the black normal schools at Marion, Huntsville, and Sparta and made the Marion school's appropriation permanent.[31] In December, 1873, the Board of Education provided annual appropriations for the only two black normal schools to survive the end of Reconstruction. On December 5, 1873, the board established a "state normal school and university for colored teachers and students" at Marion with an annual appropriation of $2,000.[32] On December 8, 1873, the board repealed its act of 1871, thereby leaving the Marion school, which had a white president, as the only black normal school in Alabama. On the next day, December 9, 1873, however, the board established another school at Huntsville with an annual appropriation of $1,000.

The last acts of the Reconstruction Board of Education dealing with black normal schools came in 1874 when the Democrats had gained control of the board. The Democratic Board of Education appointed black Democrats to replace the black Republicans on the Board of Trustees of the Negro Normal School and University and raised the school's annual appropriation to $4,000.[33] The Democratic legislature, in the Code of 1876 and 1877, reenacted the 1873–1874 legislation of the Board of Education concerning normal schools.[34] After establishing Tuskegee Institute in 1881, on February 28, 1887, the Alabama legislature established a black normal school in Greene County and provided an annual appropriation of $2,000 per year for the school.[35] The Alabama legislature established no additional black normal schools in the nineteenth century.

By the end of Reconstruction Alabama's black and white normal schools theoretically received equal appropriations, $5,000 total to Marion and Huntsville and $5,000 to Florence. Actually, Florence always received its full quota while the total sum Marion and Huntsville finally received varied from $3,000 to $5,000.[36] This discrepancy increased as time passed. In 1879 Florence's appropriation rose to $7,500. New white normal schools began in 1883 at Jacksonville and Livingston at $2,500 each and at Troy in 1887 at $3,000. The appropriations at the black normal schools, however, remained at $4,000 for Marion, $2,000 for Huntsville, and $3,000 for Tuskegee (established in 1881).[37] During the decade after the Compromise of 1877, Alabama moved from theoretically equal appropriations to black and white normal schools to a surplus annual appropriation to white normal schools of $4,500 ($15,500 white, $11,000 black).

White discrimination against black education in Alabama was much more severe than even these figures indicated. The case of the State Normal School and University for Colored Teachers and Students provided the best example of white subordination of blacks. On December 5, 1873, the Board of Education accepted the donation of the American Missionary Association's Lincoln Normal School in Marion (established in 1866) on the condition that Alabama would make the school into a black normal school and university "to provide for the liberal education of the colored race in the same manner as is already provided for the education of the white race in our Universities and Colleges."

In contrast to Mississippi, which established Alcorn University with an appropriation equal to the University of Mississippi, Alabama provided an annual appropriation of only $2,000 for the Marion school when the University of Alabama received $24,000 annually and the Alabama Agricultural and Mechanical College at Auburn (opened in 1872) received the entire income from Alabama's share of the Morrill Land Grant Act, 240,000 acres ($20,280 annually). Although Alabama raised Marion's appropriation to $4,000 in 1874, the legislature never appropriated building funds to the school. The University of Alabama, however, received $60,000 in 1883 for buildings in addition to the cancellation of indebtedness for a $30,000 loan for building in 1878.[38] Marion did not receive other special appropriations from Alabama while Auburn's annual income from Federal and state funds increased from around $20,000 in 1874–1875 to $65,000 in 1890–1891 in addition to special legislative appropriations for buildings. Auburn also received more of Alabama's share of the money from the Second Morrill Land Grant Act of 1890 than did Alabama Agricultural and Mechanical College at Huntsville-Normal.[39] From 1873 to 1887, except for the name, University, some empty promises, and a small normal school appropriation, Alabama increasingly betrayed its pledge to the AMA and to blacks to provide them a university.[40]

In addition to this discrimination in higher education, three important precedents established during Congressional Reconstruction later aided the Conservatives in shaping segregated, discriminatory primary education for blacks. On January 28, 1868, the Mobile Board of School Commissioners directed its secretary to determine the amount of school taxes paid by blacks and to give this amount to schools for black pupils.[41] Thus, the first money an Alabama public agency granted for educating blacks established the principle of segregating school funds by race. Since blacks had lower incomes than whites, this meant that black schools would receive substantially less money than white schools did. This action by the city that led Alabama in education before the Civil War gave Alabama's blacks a clear preview of what they could expect from the "best" white leaders in Alabama.

Black members of Alabama's Constitutional Convention in 1867 succeeded in blocking an article requiring racially separate schools. They insisted that they did not particularly want black and white pupils in the same school so long as the black and white schools were equal. They did not want "separate" in the Constitution so that the Board of Education could always use the threat of mixed schools to ensure that the schools would, in fact, remain equal.[42]

Despite Democratic demagoguery, segregation was never a real issue in nineteenth century Alabama. In 1868 the much-abused "radical" Republican Board of Education established *de facto* segregation in Alabama's public schools by requiring separate schools for whites and blacks unless the parents at a school gave unanimous consent for integration. In 1874 the board reaffirmed its segregation policy.[43]

Betrayed by Republicans and Conservatives, Alabama's blacks next confronted a discriminatory precedent begun by a philanthropic agency. George Peabody established the Peabody Fund to aid education in the South without mentioning racial discrimination. Under the leadership of Barnas Sears, however, the Fund discriminated against black schools from the beginning. In 1869 Sears suggested that the trustees adopt a scale by which black schools received two-thirds the amount granted white schools under the same circumstances. In 1870–1871, the trustees adopted this discriminatory scale.[44] With these precedents of segregation and discrimination to guide them the Conservatives took control of Alabama's government, 1874–1875, and drew up a new constitution to embody their ideas.

These ideas can be best understood by employing the image of a web of restrictions which the whites spun around black schools to ensure black subordination within the Southern social system. The constitutional provisions of 1875 and the discriminatory legislation during the next quarter of a century are the strands of the web which whites wove ever more tightly around black schools. The major strands in this web were segregation and discrimination, both in the kind of higher education provided for blacks and whites and in the ever increasing gap between the appropriations to black and white colleges and schools.

Like all webs, these restrictions contained some holes. The holes remained because the restraining web stretched between the two poles of the American Creed of equality and opportunity and the Christian faith, which emphasized the brotherhood of all mankind. These two liberating ideals prevented the full development of a Southern caste system. This is not to minimize the severity of white restrictions, but to emphasize that they were not absolute. Some room did exist in black schools for the development of skills, aspirations, and a black middle class-leadership elite which would begin to tear loose some strands of the web in the twentieth century.[45]

The first strand in the web of subordination was racial segregation within the schools. While *de facto* segregation existed from the beginning of Alabama's public school system, the Constitution of 1875 made segregated schools part of Alabama's basic law.[46]

The first state financial segregation went into effect in Alabama in 1877, when a law provided that poll taxes should be separated and distributed by race.[47] The legislature moved further toward separating taxes by race when it passed a bill in 1885 providing that the marshall of Auburn in Lee County would keep his lists of property assessments separate by race. On February 22, 1887, the legislature carried this idea to its logical conclusion by establishing an Opelika school district where tax funds collected from whites went to white schools and tax funds collected from blacks went to black schools.[48]

In 1887 the Alabama Supreme Court ruled that taxing power could be given to a school district only if it were a municipal corporation.[49] This decision further widened the gulf between city and rural schools by prohibiting local taxation for school purposes in rural areas. Again this was an indirect blow to blacks since most of them lived in rural areas at this time.[50]

Black higher education in Alabama also faced a series of crises in 1887.[51] Of the three black normal schools, only Tuskegee emerged unscathed.

In two separate incidents, first William Hooper Councill and then some of the students at his Huntsville school, were ejected when they attempted to sit in the "white" car on a train. The resultant uproar after the second incident was so great that Councill had to resign as principal to keep the school from being abolished. The wave of support for Councill during the next year persuaded the whites to allow Councill to resume leading the school in 1888.[52] Alabama, thus, proved itself less bigoted than Atticus Greene Haygood, Agent of the Slater Fund, who refused to grant the school any additional money as soon as he heard that Councill had been restored.[53]

While the Huntsville school only lost its president for one year, the Marion normal school and university lost its home and almost lost its life because of racial strife. In 1887 an incendiary fire destroyed the school's main building. The trouble grew out of conflict between the black college students and white students at the Baptist school, Howard College, then located in Marion. Early in 1887 some Howard College cadets attacked a crowd of black children who fled to the home of Mrs. Henrietta Curtis. When she threatened to shoot, the cadets left. This inspired several merchants in Marion to work openly to drive the black school out of town. The blacks retaliated with a boycott which drove the merchants Mason, Drake, and Irpy into bankruptcy. The whites won when the Alabama legislature decreed that none of the school's buildings could ever again be used for black education and that the school could "be located anywhere except at Marion."[54]

Governor Thomas Seay (1886–1890) then further angered Alabama blacks, especially the black press, by appointing only whites to the school's Board of Trustees. The editor of the Huntsville *Gazette* could not "see the justice or equity or policy in appointing . . . only white trustees." He believed it was obvious that an all black or at least a mixed board "would be better adapted to such an institution, would know its wants and needs better, and therefore be the better able to manage its affairs successfully."[55] While many blacks probably felt that they should have some representation, Jesse Duke, editor of the Montgomery *Herald*, outspokenly called for at least a majority of blacks on the board.[56]

One of the new white trustees, Thomas Goode Jones, Speaker of the House of Representatives, who helped lead the fight to even have a black college, summed up the "liberal" white attitude about the necessity of having an all white Board of Trustees.

> The protection of our wives and children from insult rests on something mightier and nobler than whether a Negro shall learn algebra or have a particular school [in Montgomery].
>
> The absolute control of the Trustees over the institution ought to convince anyone that it could never become a hot bed of rudeness and insult. Education controlled and directed by our own people will repress not merely the expression but thought like [editor of the Montgomery *Herald*] Duke's and produce on the contrary, politeness, good will, respect for authority and good deportment.[57]

Throughout the summer of 1887, the board tried to decide where to locate the school. Whites in the two most likely sites, Birmingham and Montgomery, worked diligently to keep the school out. With some white support, blacks in Birmingham obtained subscriptions for three thousand dollars and six acres of land. Montgomery citizens offered five thousand dollars and three acres of land. "The great bulk of donations offered by both cities was voluntary subscriptions by the colored people." Montgomery blacks encouraged subscriptions for the school by holding mass meetings in every black church in town.[58]

Instead of working for one city, Booker T. Washington and his supporters worked openly and secretly against locating the school in Montgomery where it might compete with nearby Tuskegee.[59] On July 8, 1887, most of Tuskegee's faculty and six preachers appeared before the board opposing Montgomery.

In a letter to the Huntsville *Gazette*, Washington wrote that the largest number would benefit if the state schools were "scattered over the state." He was also personally concerned that the bill might

> pave the way for the state appropriation of $3,000 to the Tuskegee Normal School to be withdrawn and thus cripple to some extent an institution that has been built up by the colored people themselves . . . (My [Washington's] reason for fearing the loss of the state appropriation I will not here state.)

Washington then said that he did not fear losing students to the new school and that he was not opposed to the university *per se*. If it had to be in Montgomery, he would work for it. The Montgomery correspondent for the Huntsville *Gazette* responded that Washington did "not like the idea of a school so near his doors. But the more the merrier, and the greater the competition the better the schools will be made."

While Washington and the Birmingham blacks were working to get the school in Birmingham, a petition "numerously signed by the white people of Birmingham was presented opposing the location of the University at that city." The Huntsville *Gazette's* editor sarcastically remarked that these whites were "relics of a decayed era and . . . strangely out of place in a progressive town such as the Magic city boasts itself to be."[60]

Faced by all these pressures the board delayed its final decision until its second meeting in July, although the governor, the superintendent of education, and the board initially preferred Birmingham. At this meeting, someone noted that Howard College was considering moving to Birmingham and said that the people of Birmingham were afraid Howard College might go elsewhere if the board put the black school there. At this point in the meeting, "there was a change of views on the part of most of the trustees; and when the matter again came up, Montgomery was chosen by a unanimous vote."[61]

To those white citizens of Montgomery who were concerned about the black school moving there, the local trustee, T. G. Jones, issued the assurance that the white board would totally control the school and that the school would be "an industrial school." Whereas as late as 1876 the superintendent of education could say that the school was to give blacks "collegiate and University education," by 1887 a definite change had occurred. According to Jones, the purpose of the school was "'that the students may be taught in the best manner possible, the things they are to *live by;* preferring always the English language and the industries to an education for culture only.'"[62]

But even this was too much for some of Montgomery's whites. William E. Elsberry and Alexander Troy took their request for an injunction to prevent the location of the black university in Montgomery to the Alabama Supreme Court. In *Elsberry v. Seay*, February, 1888, the court ruled that the law establishing the black university was unconstitutional since the school was not under the state superintendent of education. This meant that the school was not a part of the public school system so it was not entitled to receive school funds. As a result of this decision the only money the school received in 1887–1888 was $500 from the Peabody Fund and $2,500 of the $7,500 granted it by the 1887 law. In 1888–1889 the school's president, William Burns Paterson, continued the school without any state support.[63]

With this decision the hypocrisy of Alabama in dealing with black higher education reached its apogee. From the beginning Alabama had called the school a university while providing it with the income of a normal school. Now the court was using the name, "university," to destroy it. The court never considered the other alternative—recognizing that the school was legally Alabama's "separate but equal" black university and forcing the state to grant it a university's funding. Alabama, thus, dropped all pretense and betrayed all promises to its black citizens and the legal contract with the AMA to furnish university education to blacks as it had furnished university education to whites since 1831. Not until the third decade of the twentieth century did Alabama begin to redeem this pledge.

Alabama did not completely abandon this school. Through the influence of men like T. G. Jones and Thomas Seay, on February 23, 1889, the Alabama Legislature created the State Normal School for Colored Students to be located in Montgomery with an annual appropriation of $7,500.[64] As the new title indicated, State Normal was not to offer collegiate work, but could only give secondary classes and teacher training.[65]

The actions of the Alabama Legislature and Supreme Court, 1887–1889, clearly showed their changing attitude toward black education. Beginning in 1889, Alabama formally declared itself in favor of special education for blacks, not only separate and unequal from white education, but also of a different kind. Black public education had lost its capstone—collegiate and university training. This decision, the consequences that followed from it, and the 1891 Apportionment Act indicated a basic reorientation of white Alabama. "Black education" was to be special education for second-class citizens who could not have university education if they were to remain subordinated within a segregated society.

Faced with a constantly declining per capita state educational appropriation ($3.35 in 1874–1875, $2.29 in 1889–1890) and unable to pass local taxes in some instances, white legislators in 1888 decided to divert the money allotted for black schools to white schools. This further betrayal of the blacks came through a compromise between representatives of Black Belt and predominantly white counties in December, 1888. Black Belt representatives opposed a bill to raise the state's school appropriation by $100,000 because they did not want this money to go to blacks. The Black Belt representatives blocked the bill on December 3, 1888, but on the next day the bill passed without a record vote.[66] The white counties got the increased appropriation "as a result of an understanding that the Black Belt counties could use more of their school fund for white education."[67]

This "understanding" bore bitter fruit for Alabama's blacks with the passage of the Apportionment Act of 1891. Since Reconstruction, Alabama law had directed the state superintendent of education to apportion the school fund between the races on the basis of the number of children of each race in school. Black common school children actually should have received a slightly higher per capita amount because the funds for the normal schools came out of the common school fund before the superintendent sent the money to the local officials and the white normal schools received larger grants than did the black normal schools.[68]

In his 1890 report, Alabama's Superintendent of Education, Solomon Palmer, called for a change in this method of apportioning school funds. He believed the superintendent should apportion the fund to the various school boards "without regard to race," leaving it up to the local officials to determine how to divide the money. While there had been no attack on the Alabama law since Reconstruction, Palmer claimed that he opposed segregating taxes for schools by race because "such a law . . . would be declared unconstitutional."

Palmer hypocritically claimed that he had "no sympathy with those who would deprive the colored race of an equal participation in the benefits of the school fund." He revealed his true attitude when he explained why many whites wanted to change the law. The whites believed that (1) blacks in the Black Belt received "all of the money while paying no taxes" (2) blacks were not sufficiently mentally advanced to need the same kind of education whites received. Palmer rhetorically refused to debate the validity of these ideas, but he did believe that the present law caused whites "peculiar hardships that can be . . . remedied by a different and more simple form of apportionment."

Soon after the Alabama Legislature met, Mr. Steel introduced Palmer's plan in the House where it passed 65–0 with no real debate. On the next day, February 3, 1891, a Colored Convention convened in Montgomery to try to moderate anti-black legislation then being considered. At the convention, Booker T. Washington made what a reporter described as a "bitter speech" against the apportionment law and a pending House bill to segregate railroad cars.[69] The convention sent a delegation to Governor Thomas Goode Jones to discuss legislation affecting blacks. Jones's assurances that the educational bill would not discriminate against blacks satisfied most of the delegation.

Although the apportionment bill passed the House unanimously, it encountered some opposition in the Senate. The defeated amendments showed the true intent of the bill. One proposed amendment would have excluded eighteen white counties from the provisions of the bill. Another attempted to insert "and for the equal benefit of the children thereof." The Senate was careful, however, to protect itself from charges of *de jure* segregation in the language of the bill. By a vote of 19–8 all proposed amendments failed and the bill passed without a record vote.

The old law required the superintendent to "apportion the educational funds . . . *between the races* . . . so that all children who attend the public schools established for them shall receive *equal benefit* from such fund." Apportionment of the public school fund under the 1891 law was "according to the entire number of children of school age . . . *the township trustees* . . . shall apportion to each school . . . such an amount . . . *as they may deem just and equitable*."[70]

Alabama's Attorney-General further illustrated the intent of the bill—to permit local racial discrimination—when he ruled that equal per capita payment was not necessary for equal educational opportunity. He said that trustees met the "equal benefit" provisions of the constitution if they provided schools for the two races "equally suited to the educational wants of the children of each race."[71]

After 1891, the reports of the superintendent of education did not list the school appropriations by race. This omission might have been due to a desire to cover up growing inequities,[72] or might merely show that the superintendent of education no longer apportioned funds by race and, therefore, reported only what his office granted to the local officials. Although the state reported distributing the school fund fairly equitably as late as 1888–1889, when the superintendent of education did resume reporting the distribution of funds by race in 1908, blacks made up forty-four percent of the school population but they only received twelve percent of the school fund.[73]

Although Alabama did not print the figures for state appropriations of the school fund by race from 1891 to 1908, Table I shows the average monthly pay of teachers by race for some of these years. These figures show progressive discrimination against black teachers. Since teachers' salaries were ninety-six percent of the school fund, these figures are a good indication of trends in the distribution of the school fund in the 1890's.

TABLE I

Teachers' Average Monthly Salary by Race[74]

Year	*White*	*Black*	*Difference*
1889–1890	$22.04	$21.05	$ .99
. . .	. . .	. . .	. . .
1894–1895	24.03	18.71	5.32
1895–1896	23.96	18.29	5.67
1896–1897	22.97	17.70	5.27
1897–1898	24.09	18.44	5.65
1898–1899	25.05	17.66	7.39
. . .	. . .	. . .	. . .
1900–1901	32.25	22.59	9.66
1901–1902	32.50	22.38	10.12
. . .	. . .	. . .	. . .
1908–1909	50.92	25.23	25.69

After 1891, the salaries and length of terms in the black schools diminished. The number of black teachers declined while the number of white teachers grew. Horace Mann Bond, author of the classic study of Alabama's legislation on black education, concluded that the Act of 1891 "irretrievably doomed the Negro schools of the Black Belt to an inferiority which widened constantly as the years passed."[75]

Although Alabama's Constitution of 1901 represented an overall advance in education for white schools by permitting local taxation for schools, in education as in suffrage the constitution was a setback for blacks. A comparison of the education sections of the 1875 and 1901 Constitutions shows the extent of the whites' subordination of blacks. The only mention of equality in the 1901 Constitution came in a provision that school districts and townships would "provide, as nearly as practicable, school terms of equal duration." The 1875 Constitution's requirement that public schools were to be for the "equal benefit of the children" gave way to the pointed provision of education for the "benefit of the children." While both Constitutions provided separate black and white schools, after 1901 the law decreed that "no child of either race shall be permitted to attend a school of the other race."[76] The 1901 Constitution also included the essential features of the Apportionment Act of 1891. The Constitutional Convention of 1901 adopted these educational sections without debate. None of the other sections of the article on education contained any essential changes in black education except for a provision that receipts from the poll tax were to be divided by race and township.[77] With the adoption of these discriminatory sections of the new constitution, Alabama's legislation on black education reached a "definite climax."[78] White Alabama had now finished weaving the basic strands of its web of subordination around black education although the whites did continue to tighten some of the strands of the web by increasing the amount of discrimination between funds allotted to black and white schools and colleges.

PART I Seeking a Way Out: Public Schools

2

TEACHERS INSTITUTES AND THE STATE TEACHERS ASSOCIATION

In studying education most scholars have focused on what whites were doing to blacks, on the developing web of subordination and its three main strands of separate, unequal, and different education for blacks. It is impossible to understand this period, however, without also studying the ways black leaders sought to free black students to play a fuller role in society. As William Edward Burghardt DuBois ultimately realized, education alone was not enough. Blacks also needed economic and political power. But neither DuBois nor most other black leaders ever denied the critical importance of education, especially for black leaders, in helping blacks attain their just place in the American economy, society, and politics. Having come "up from slavery," blacks also busied themselves with "finding a way out" of the web of subordination.[1] Alabama blacks sought to use primary and secondary public schools along with private schools and colleges as one way out of the web. While educational strategies differed, the goal remained the same. Alabama left the control of local public education almost entirely in the hands of local officials. Considering the effects of the Apportionment Act of 1891 and the disfranchising Constitution of 1901, this meant that the local schools faced more discrimination and white domination than did the state normal schools.

But there were openings in the web of subordination even in the local schools. As recent studies of slavery have shown, emancipated blacks had a long tradition of sustaining certain elements of their culture despite white pressures.[2] Also, compared to today's schools, black public schools in the nineteenth century were functionally private schools.[3] For most black families to allow a child to attend school, they had to give up a field hand for several months each year and raise the money for registration or tuition, books, supplies, and clothes.[4] For black families living at a subsistence level this sacrifice was comparable to that of middle-class whites who sent their children to more expensive private schools. This quasi-private nature of black public schools meant that economic class and level of education began to coalesce. It also meant that black parents tended to have a high interest in the conduct and activities of the schools since they had a substantial stake in them.

As letters to Booker T. Washington from teachers in black public schools indicated, these schools appeared private from the teachers' perspective. Unlike modern teachers who take a job in an established school, these early teachers often had to establish their own school and find sources of support either in the community or elsewhere. These teachers usually referred to the parents of their pupils as "patrons." Since only four percent of the state school fund could be used for anything but the teacher's salary, even teachers in established schools had to spend much of their time soliciting funds to maintain, administer, and provide books and equipment for the school even if they did not have to raise funds for the building.

The black community as a whole also had a special interest in the school. Either on their own or with solicited white donations, the blacks usually bought the land, built their schoolhouse or used a church building, furnished, equipped, and maintained it, and then held benefits to sustain the school, augment the extremely low state salary of the teacher, or extend the school term beyond the two to three months provided many county schools by the state. This support meant that the teacher had to answer to the black community for his conduct of the school as well as to the white supervisor who hired him and paid him from the public school fund.[5]

This community involvement sometimes had negative as well as positive effects on the schools. If a group of parents became dissatisfied with a teacher (for religious or denominational reasons), they could seriously undermine or destroy the school. Another negative effect of this necessary community support of schools was that the gap between the funds received by black and white schools was much greater than even the discriminatory school fund figures indicated since the blacks' relative poverty kept them from supporting their schools to the extent that whites could support theirs.[6]

Blacks were also able to resist total subordination through their participation in the educational institutions between the local school and the state normal school—the state teachers institutes (one week seminars on teaching methods) and the State Teachers Association. While teachers institutes began in Alabama in 1854 and 1856, the first mention of institutes for black teachers came when the 1878–1879 legislature turned the control of the institutes over to the county boards of education, required that the boards hold not less than three institutes annually for each race, and provided that teachers could attend only those institutes for their race.[7] After the Peabody Fund granted $500 to Alabama for teachers institutes, the legislature provided for centralized administration of the institutes in each congressional district in 1887. The legislature also agreed to pay the institutes' expenses up to $500 if the sum spent in any year did not exceed the fund contributed for that year for institutes by the Peabody Fund.[8]

Two Huntsville black educators, W. H. Councill, president of the state normal school, and A. W. McKinney, president of a private normal school, conducted most of the institutes in north Alabama.[9] Booker T. Washington helped the state superintendent of education find persons to conduct the institutes in central Alabama.[10]

In 1895 the Peabody Fund decided to give its money for Alabama to normal schools entirely, rather than funding both normal schools and teachers institutes. This action virtually killed the institutes for the next decade since the state appropriation had been a matching sum for the Peabody grant. Legislation in 1907 raised the state's maximum grant to institutes to $1,200 and deleted references to the Peabody Fund. In 1911, another act provided $5,000 for white and $1,000 for black institutes and revived the institutes in twentieth century Alabama.[11]

These institutes encouraged the development of several county institutes (Madison County blacks, however, had been holding county institutes even before the state institutes developed) and aided in the growth of the [Black] State Teachers Association (STA) by holding elections for delegates to the STA at the institutes. The institutes also provided black teachers an opportunity to meet and discuss problems and matters of concern. In addition to discussing teaching methods these county and state teachers institutes had a strong moralistic orientation, as can be seen in the temperance meetings held in the evenings in conjunction with the institutes. Some institutes passed temperance resolutions, petitioned the legislature about pending educational legislation (the Hundley Amendment), requested monthly instead of quarterly pay for black as well as white teachers, and urged all blacks to be sure to pay their poll taxes.[12] The institutes also frequently passed resolutions threatening to punish absent teachers or asking the state superintendent of education to revoke the licenses of teachers who did not attend as provided by state law.[13] When the institutes declined after 1895, black educators continued to meet in county institutes and at the annual meetings of the State Teachers Association to seek ways to deal with their educational problems.

The State Teachers Association grew out of a meeting of sixty teachers of black schools in Selma on April 6–7, 1882.[14] The delegates heard papers on education, established a permanent organization, adopted a constitution, and elected officers. The first president was William Burns Paterson, President of the Lincoln Normal School and University in Marion. The STA pledged itself "to advance the interests of the profession of teaching along moral and intellectual lines . . . [and] to bring the teachers together in a social way." Any teacher "of good moral standing" could join by paying a membership fee of fifty cents.[15]

George Milton Elliott, pastor of the Reformed Presbyterian Church and

Principal of the Geneva Academy in Selma, was the STA's second president. Elliott stressed "Thoroughness of Scholarship coupled with Christian Education," during his term in office. His vice-president, Booker T. Washington, succeeded Elliott as President of the STA after being elected unanimously. Washington served longer than any other STA President and emphasized industrial education.[16]

While Washington ran the STA during the late 1880's and early 1890's, his successors (like his predecessors) emphasized liberal education over industrial training. Nathan Benjamin Young, Sr., the STA's fourth president, graduated from Talladega College and Oberlin College. During his presidency, Young emphasized "Higher Education for Our Race."[17] The STA's fifth president, Richard Byron Hudson, graduated from Selma University (Baptist) and studied at the College of Liberal Arts in Chautauqua, New York. Hudson urged the STA to seek "More Money for Teachers of Alabama and Longer Terms Both in County and City."[18] The STA's president, 1900–1901, was John William Beverly, a graduate of the Lincoln Normal School and University at Marion and Brown University. Beverly emphasized "Self-Reliance with Thorough Preparation for Leadership."[19]

In addition to the usual educational topics, the papers at the STA Conventions dealt with denominational schools, making "the Women of Our Race Stronger," the role of teachers in encouraging people to own their homes, "The Moral Training of Youth," and "The Need of Educated Labor in the South."[20] In 1889 G. M. Elliott moved toward dealing with corruption when he asked Washington to give a paper on "some method of breaking up the abominable habit of [Township] Superintendents requiring teachers to give them part of their salary."[21]

Many of the STA's resolutions dealt more with moral or political issues than with purely educational issues. Representative resolutions condemned excursions, the Colored World's Exhibition, and the convict lease system; urged prohibition; and required that teachers should be "examined and admitted [to the STA] only upon their proving themselves competent and morally qualified." In 1890 the STA scheduled "a private council" of educational leaders "to consider important points bearing on the 'race problem' and what are the best means to be used in its solution?" The Negro Convention of 1891 in Montgomery grew out of this teachers' meeting.[22]

In 1892 the issue of race within the STA erupted. The STA had always included black and white teachers of black schools. Its first two presidents had been white. There had been no real conflict until W. H. Councill used Paterson's being white against him in the contest for the Morrill Land Grant Fund. So Paterson and several of his supporters refused to attend the 1892 STA convention in Huntsville (the site of Councill's school).

Paterson (one of the founders and the first President of the STA) also threatened to drop out of the organization. In an exchange of letters with Paterson, Washington reminded him that he had worked fruitfully within the STA up to that point and urged Paterson not to withdraw.[23] Evidently Paterson was reconciled to the STA by 1900, when his associate and successor at Alabama State, John W. Beverly, accepted the Presidency of the STA.

But the race issue involved more than just a personal, professional quarrel between Councill and Paterson. In 1892, some STA delegates, without authorization wrote letters saying that "the Association passed resolutions calling on the State to have [only] colored teachers in all the State colored public and Normal Schools." Washington wrote the recipient of one of these letters that such a statement was "untrue and misleading."[24]

Despite this conflict in the STA in 1892, the 1893 meeting went smoothly. Governor T. G. Jones invited the STA to meet in the Hall of the Alabama House of Representatives. The 1893 meeting was the most representative ever and one of the most cordially received by the townspeople. The meeting featured academic and industrial exhibits by Talladega and Tuskegee in addition to the usual speeches, papers, and resolutions. Since its organization in 1882, the STA had met in Selma, Montgomery, Tuskegee, and Birmingham twice each, and in Marion and Huntsville once each.[25]

By 1899 the STA had moved toward an emphasis on academic, rather than industrial education. The convention chose to reprint only a paper emphasizing the need for academic training after "ringing addresses were made in its favor." The speakers agreed that some industrial training was still needed, but they believed that black leaders needed academic training. One speaker remarked that industrial school graduates were "just a little above the masses and experience is showing that they won't do."[26]

Throughout the last two decades of the nineteenth century, the STA did try "to advance the interests of the profession of teaching along moral and intellectual lines." Washington's long presidency indicated that many teachers either greatly admired him personally, appreciated his organizational ability, or agreed with his educational philosophy stressing industrial training. The more academic, liberal arts orientation of his successors and of meetings in the late 1890's also suggested that many teachers of black schools believed that the "interests of the profession" would be best served by emphasizing higher, liberal arts education over industrial training. That the STA took this position even after Washington's famous speech at Atlanta in 1895 also indicated that Washington was less influential in black education even in Alabama than has previously been believed.

Although Alabama's black public normal schools faced many of the problems and even worse discrimination in fund allocation than did the local schools, the normal schools were less constrained by the web of subordination. True, Alabama segregated these schools almost from the first, gave them an ever decreasing share in the total normal school funds, never provided separate funding like that given the University of Alabama and Auburn, and abolished the black state university in 1887. But these schools were almost totally free of local white control and were less constrained by local black influence. While their trustees were usually whites, these men felt at least a paternalistic interest in promoting the well-being of the school and shielded it both from state and local influence to some degree. Their appropriations, though less than the white normal schools', were substantially larger than those of any local school.

The normal schools also had the advantage of being established early (1873–1881) and having only one president each from their founding until after 1900. Since they were better known, these schools' presidents could appeal to a wider, wealthier group of patrons. Being in urban centers sometimes aided the Huntsville and Montgomery schools. Also, instead of having a well-developed educational plan for these schools, the Alabama legislature varied and shifted its opinion of the proper kind of secondary education for blacks. This openness, indifference, or indecisiveness of Alabama's legislators gave the leaders of the black normal schools substantial leeway in developing their schools' programs.

Given this limited freedom to develop their schools as they saw fit, the heads of the three black normal schools each stressed a different kind of education to offer their students the best way out of the web of subordination.[27] The development of each of these schools was closely related to the life and ideas of the man who guided it for the first one third of a century of its existence—William Burns Paterson (1878–1915) at Marion (1873–1887) then Montgomery, William Hooper Councill (1875–1887 and 1888–1907) at Huntsville (1875–1891) then Normal, and Booker T. Washington (1881–1915) at Tuskegee. A brief study of the lives of these three men and the development of their schools provides an overview of the basic characteristic of public black, normal school education, its pluralism. Each school sought to develop its own program. No one educational philosophy or mode of development was dominant.

3

WILLIAM BURNS PATERSON— LIBERAL EDUCATION

William Burns Paterson was the president of the state normal school at Marion—Montgomery from 1878–1915.[1] Paterson's career had been "strange and chequered" when he so described it in 1872; and so it was to be until his death in 1915. He was born in Tullibody, Clackmannshire, Scotland on February 9, 1849. When poor health forced him out of school after three years, he began working as a gardener on the nearby estate of Lord Abercrombie.[2]

Driven by a desire "to see the world," Paterson left Scotland and came to the United States in 1867. From New York he traveled through all but five of the states working at a wide variety of jobs—mail boy, railroad laborer, deck hand, clerk, salesman, farmhand, carpenter, hod-carrier, and teacher. In 1870 he became a labor contractor in Hollow Square, Hale County, Alabama.[3]

Until 1871, Paterson's story resembled that of thousands of other immigrants who flocked to America and spent a few years working at odd jobs to make money as they could and finally settled down in one place. Although the economic opportunity and equalitarian social structure of America favorably impressed Paterson, the political corruption[4] and violence[5] in his new home appalled him. A decent, law-abiding man, Paterson was courageous and active against extra-legal violence, especially that perpetrated by the Ku Klux Klan.[6]

Between 1870 and 1873 a transformation took place in Paterson's life. He forsook the frenetic search for fame to teach—sometimes without the promised state support—in a black school. The reasons that impelled Paterson to this change can only be inferred. His interest in education drove him to continue reading and studying even during his rambling around the United States, 1867–1870. Not understanding the Southern white ostracism of teachers in black institutions, Paterson sought status in becoming the head of his own school. While he knew that he could never have climbed above his father's social rank in Scotland, he believed that he could be judged on his own merits in the United States. In Tullibody, Scotland he would always be called "Juck, Wull . . . or at best . . . Wellum." In Greensboro, Alabama he was "Mr." and by teaching his own school, he would become "Professor." In describing a newspaper story about the closing exercises of his school, Paterson wrote, "You would have been pleased I have no doubt at the eulogistic remarks on *Professor* [*sic*] Paterson." Thus the approval of his family in Scotland, which respected teachers highly, would counterbalance the social slights Paterson would later receive from Alabama whites. Finally, perhaps Paterson's organizing urge, thwarted in his earlier attempt to organize a Scottish colony in Alabama, asserted itself in his efforts to build a school.[7]

Still, Paterson's decision to teach a black school was largely accidental. He first began teaching black workmen in the ditching crew during their lunch hour while he was working with a dredging crew on the Black Warrior River.[8] When he moved to Hale County in 1870, Paterson made friends with the McFaddens who owned a large plantation. At the McFaddens' urging, Paterson started a school on the plantation to encourage the blacks to remain there.[9] In this school, started for a purely economic reason (to enable a plantation owner to retain his labor force), converged all the factors which shaped the rest of Paterson's life: his love of learning, his equalitarian attitude toward opportunity, his interest in leadership and organizing, his desire for appreciation of his abilities and for status, his opposition to political corruption and violence, and his first-hand experience of the overwhelming need and desire of the freedmen for an education.[10]

In 1871 Paterson left the plantation, moved to Greensboro, and established his own school, Tullibody Academy, named for his home town in Scotland. Some whites in Greensboro opposed this school, especially if a white man conducted it. "'Let the Negroes educate themselves,' they said." The McFaddens and other "plantation owners and leading citizens" supported the school and overt opposition finally dissipated.[11]

Paterson drove himself hard at Tullibody. In 1875 he wrote that he had not taken a holiday in three and one half years. In addition to teaching common school on weekdays, he taught normal school on Saturdays and Sunday School "for two hours . . . besides attending church two or three times that day." He also taught night school for six months each year and attended to other unspecified business.[12] Like most instructors in the nineteenth century, Paterson taught a wide range of subjects. In September, 1873, he planned to teach reading, writing, arithmetic, geometry, music, drawing, Latin, Greek, German, French, Spanish, Hebrew, chemistry, and philosophy.[13]

The local whites respected Paterson and his school. In 1873, Southern University (Birmingham-Southern after 1918), the Methodist college in Greensboro, offered him a professorship, but "for a whim of [his] own" he refused it.[14] In 1877, the [Greensboro] *Alabama Beacon* thought that Tullibody Academy was "among the better Negro schools." It was "a well graded, well organized school with a faculty of four teachers and the principal, and its curriculum included Latin, Greek, geometry, grammar, and natural philosophy."[15]

In 1878 Paterson left Tullibody to become president of the Lincoln Normal School in Marion. The American Missionary Association began supporting this school in 1867. In 1871, it offered its first normal courses with the aid of a grant of $1,250 from Alabama. In December, 1873, the AMA deeded the school to Alabama in return for the state's promise to make it a normal school and university for blacks.[16] As was often the case in the transfer of missionary schools, Lincoln's becoming a state school caused a drop in enrollment at first, from 300 pupils in 1872 to 188 pupils in 1874. The Sabbath School's enrollment during this period, by contrast, rose from 72 to 145.[17]

On December 15, 1874, the Alabama legislature passed an amendment to the 1873 law reaffirming its rhetorical commitment to university education for blacks at Marion. These acts created, at least on paper, "the oldest state institution in America established for the function of teacher education and liberal-arts education [for blacks]." The earlier black state schools—Lincoln University of Missouri (1866) and Alcorn College (1871) were land-grant colleges.

The Conservative Democrats who came to power in Alabama in 1874, continued the charade that the Marion school was "to become a university." In 1876, State Superintendent of Education, John M. McKleroy, said that Marion was "so liberally endowed by the state and furnished with a competent faculty as to afford to the colored race opportunities for acquirement of collegiate and University education."[18]

In 1878 Professor George W. Card, Marion's principal since 1874, retired and W. B. Paterson took his place.[19] During Paterson's first year as principal, Marion's four teachers taught 127 pupils. The physical plant was only a two-story building with four rooms. The curriculum was classical only. "There was no provision for industrial work, athletic training and other Departments of Culture that add to literary development. . . ." Marion's main emphases were "vocal music and literary training."[20]

On June 5, 1879, Paterson added a permanent teacher to his staff when he married Margaret Bingham Flack. After graduating from Oberlin, "Maggie" joined hundreds of other "Yankee schoolma'ms" by coming south to teach.[21] "Maggie" doubtlessly strengthened Paterson's commitment to black education. She joined the faculty just in time to help teach the school's first graduating class of three young men and three young ladies in 1880.[22]

Although Marion offered no industrial work as late as 1879–1880, "within the next four years . . . [it] began to develop the industrial feature of its work. . . ."[23] The industrial work in 1885 consisted of Mr. Davis teaching "a little carpentry" to the male students in "a small shop."

In addition to the shop, Marion's 1885 physical plant consisted of a main building, a small dormitory, and Paterson's home. There were ten faculty members, nine white men and women and the black head of the Industrial Department. One of the students later remembered that the teachers and students "usually worked well together." In 1885, counting the eighteen female students who boarded at Paterson's home and about one hundred other boarders, the school's full enrollment slightly exceeded three hundred. Seventeen of these graduated in 1885, becoming doctors, carpenters, and farmers. In his annual report in November, 1885, Paterson summed up Marion's situation: "the time is at hand when one of the objects of the school . . . to be a state 'university for colored students' . . . will have to be recognized and sufficient support given to carry out this object."[24]

Instead of growing into a university, Marion was to spend the next few years fighting for its very existence. In 1887 the Alabama Legislature banished it from Marion. In 1888 the Alabama Supreme Court declared it unconstitutional.[25]

Alabama's black press rallied to the school's defense. The most outspoken advocate of a black university was Jesse Duke, editor of the Montgomery *Herald*. His articles and editorials so angered many whites, however, that "enemies of the university" used "the objectionable utterances of the *Herald* as ammunition to blow up our Colored University." "Initial," the Montgomery correspondent of the Huntsville *Gazette*, bitterly condemned the attempts of Montgomery and Birmingham whites to keep the school out of their cities. When the school's all white board of trustees chose Montgomery as the school's new site, "Initial" labeled the further attempts of Montgomery whites to keep the school out as "revolutionary." Their actions were "unwise because the premises upon which said opposition is based are simply shallow, hollow pretects [*sic*] seized upon by unreasoning prejudice to accomplish its ends." The correspondent claimed that most blacks in Montgomery and throughout Alabama "and the voice of the colored press almost unanimously have spurned the sentiments attributed to Duke [Editor of the Montgomery *Herald*], add [*sic*] protested against being held responsible for them." After condemning William E. Elsberry and Alexander Troy for filing an injunction to prevent the board from locating the school in Montgomery, "Initial" praised Governor Thomas Seay and Speaker of the House Thomas Goode Jones (also a trustee of the school) for their support of the school. The Montgomery white press, however, was so bitterly anti-black during the university controversy that "Initial" finally began to wonder if black emigration were not necessary. "Is the Negro wanted in this part of Alabama? It seems not."[26]

Against this background of white opposition and legal conflict, in the summer of 1887, Paterson came to Montgomery to try to establish a school.[27] He met with "some of the leading citizens of the city," then called a mass meeting in the "Old Ship" A.M.E. Zion Church where he announced that the state would build the school if the people of Montgomery would buy the land and donate it to the state. This meeting was well attended and "much interest manifested in the proposition since at that time the Public Schools and the Montgomery Industrial School [for girls], with a few Independent Schools, were the only means for an education for the colored children [in Montgomery]." Weekly mass meetings began in the churches of the city to arouse interest and to raise the necessary funds.

Paterson decided to try to open the school at once and began seeking a temporary location. He accepted Rev. William Jenkins' offer of his church, the Beulah Baptist Church for a chapel and assembly room. He obtained classrooms by renting seven houses "and two buildings once used as stores." Blacks showed their eagerness for education by renting one room of their homes for a classroom.

Students registered for the new school in the basement of the Dexter Avenue Baptist Church. On October 3, 1887, the opening day of the Alabama Colored People's University, "about four hundred children together with their parents and friends gathered within the walls of 'Beulah.'"[28] In addition to Paterson, the first faculty consisted of nine teachers.

At first the faculty in Montgomery "labored at a great sacrifice, receiving little or no salary," since the students could not pay much tuition. The strain was especially severe in 1888–1889 when the Alabama Supreme Court denied the school its share of the common school fund so that the teachers were totally dependent upon tuition. During this period the school existed on public donations and "private tuition of one dollar per capita per month." The teachers and students gave entertainments to raise the money to buy an organ, "the first musical instrument purchased for the school." Teachers also raised money by selling the products of the girls' classes in plain sewing and fancywork.[29]

During the first term in Montgomery, Paterson grouped the 358 students into Grammar Grades and four classes in the Normal Department. Despite the legal setback, by 1888 the enrollment grew to five hundred students in the Normal, Preparatory, and Industrial Departments. Paterson planned a Collegiate Department, but "no students presented themselves of sufficient attainments to profit by a college or university course of study." The lack of funds in 1888–1889 did not keep Paterson from beginning a primary department, the Model School, to relieve the public schools' "congested conditions." Paterson acquired four houses for this department and hired Miss Bridgeman, who had special training in primary work, to direct it.[30]

Although the school act of 1889[31] redirected black education by betraying Alabama's commitment to provide university education for blacks, State Normal needed funds so desperately that the news of even this assistance from the state touched off a celebration among the faculty and students. An 1893 graduate recalled what happened "when the news reached us in 'Beulah Bottom.'" The teachers quickly summoned all the students from the recitation rooms, "small houses of two rooms each," to assemble in the chapel, Beulah

Baptist Church. When Paterson officially announced the forthcoming state aid, "scenes of the wildest excitement and exhibitions of unbounded joy and happiness were for a time indulged in." The music teacher, Miss Faunstalk, played "the familiar song, 'Hallelujah, 'tis done: I believe on the Son, and etc.,' led by Mrs. Paterson. . . . Prayers were offered, addresses were delivered and what had been a morning of serious study was now turned into a holiday of celebration and thanksgiving."[32]

After the legislature established the State Normal School in 1889, the state board of trustees met with an elected, local, advisory board of blacks to select a site for the school. This advisory board consisted of three pastors, four businessmen, and one man in public service, "all men of high ideals, ability and sterling character, whose worth to the community could not be gainsaid." On May 8, 1889, the state board formally accepted the Montgomery black community's donation of $3,300 in cash and a campus site of six and one half acres of land in Montgomery.[33]

This money and land represented the efforts of blacks outside Montgomery also. Early in January, 1889, H. V. Cashin of Decatur and A. A. Garner, a Montgomery attorney, went to Birmingham to work for the school. Andy Beard, a Birmingham grocer, donated four lots worth $3,000. The Birmingham churches also held meetings for the benefit of the school. Cashin then planned to help build the college with the aid of men like Alfred Billingslea and Andy Beard and to name one wing of the school, the Andy Beard Hall.[34]

The trustees were not able to finish the new college buildings that summer, so the fall term, 1889, began again in "Beulah Bottom." Mr. Garrott, Head of the Industrial Department, and some of the male students helped complete minor work such as installing desks. State Normal then moved into its new quarters "a few weeks" after the term began. The curriculum consisted of "a Normal course only, but a very liberal one"; whereas, before the court abolished the State Normal School and University, "the course included a full college course, or rather was so intended."[35]

Despite Mrs. Paterson's missionary background, Paterson's school evidently was not so involved in community uplift projects as were the other black normal schools. The school did, however, sponsor the Alabama Literary Society and the Mechanicsville Literary Society, which were important in Montgomery's black society. Meeting in churches, these societies presented programs to inspire students and townspeople. Many of Montgomery's leading blacks took part in the activities of the societies. The influence of the societies extended beyond Montgomery since the students at other colleges often attended the societies' meetings when they were home for vacations and holidays.

The first graduating class of the State Normal School for Colored Students at Montgomery, six young men and two young ladies, finished in 1890. Due to the uncertainties during the move to Montgomery, there had been no graduating classes in 1888 or 1889.[36] (See Table II.)

TABLE II

Number of High School Graduates of Alabama State College, 1880–1901[37]

Year	*Male*	*Female*	*Total*
1880	3	3	6
1881	5	3	8
1882	2	6	8
1883	8	3	11
1884	6	3	9
1885	9	3	12
1886	8	12	20
1887	15	4	19
1888–1889	Moved to Montgomery from Marion. No graduating classes.		
1890	6	3	9
1891	3	10	13
1892	7	4	11
1893	2	6	8
1894	1	6	7
1895	2	4	6
1896	4	2	6
1897	3	5	8
1898	3	4	7
1899	4	7	11
1900	9	7	16
1901	2	9	11

In 1890 Paterson and Booker T. Washington sought the money from the Second Morrill Act for their schools, but the prize went to W. H. Councill's school in Huntsville. Washington and Paterson remained on good terms after the fight, but Paterson intensely disliked Councill thereafter for his use of the race issue in the struggle.[38]

Paterson's ideas about education are important. Not only did he shape the school during most of its formative years, but only one other man, Hooper Councill Trenholm (1925–1963) has exceeded or even closely approached Paterson's tenure as head of the school. Unfortunately, a fire early in the twentieth century destroyed most of the school's records and nothing Paterson wrote after the 1870's has survived, except some of his reports to the state superintendent of education. It is clear, however, that Paterson believed that blacks should have a liberal arts education and that they deserved and needed university education just like that Alabama's whites received. He offered classical, liberal arts courses at Tullibody in Greensboro and at Lincoln in Marion. He constantly prodded the legislature to provide funds for true collegiate education for blacks. Only after the legislature pointedly omitted any provision for university-level work in the school's charter in 1889 did Paterson cease planning for collegiate and university education for blacks.

Paterson did begin industrial work at his school around 1883, evidently to get support from the Slater Fund, but he never allowed this part of his school to dominate the others. Although he had worked at a wider variety of jobs than had the heads of the other two normal schools, Paterson did not constantly preach the importance of manual labor to his students as did Booker T. Washington. One of Paterson's fellow teachers for twenty years recalled, "He said little to the students about work, but could be seen doing something almost daily. The boys who were not afraid to work enjoyed laboring with him."[39]

Paterson was especially interested in educational methodology and kept up with current trends in the field. Not long after Francis W. Parker (the "father of progressive education" according to John Dewey) made his school in Quincy, Massachusetts famous, Paterson gave a paper on "The Quincy Plan" at the 1882 organizational meeting of the Alabama State Teachers Association in Montgomery.[40] In his annual report in 1899, he deplored the exclusive discussion of the *what* (industrial versus liberal arts) of education, if this made people overlook the importance of the *how* or manner of education.[41]

While Paterson's school always received more state money than either of the other black normal schools, Tuskegee's total budget from all sources was much larger during the 1890's. Paterson's belief that blacks deserved the same kind of education as whites permitted his school to be as successful as Alabama's white normal schools in producing teachers. In 1902 Paterson's school, like the white normal schools, had 56 percent of its graduates still teaching. Although Tuskegee and Normal had produced more graduates (Tuskegee—734; Normal—736; Montgomery—229) in terms of the percentage of those teaching in 1902 they lagged far behind (Tuskegee—22 percent; Normal—25 percent).[42]

Paterson's interest in liberal arts education and teacher training did not mean that he had an "ivory tower" opposition to business. On the contrary, soon after he successfully reestablished his school in Montgomery, Paterson capitalized on his lifelong interest in growing flowers by establishing a florist's shop which became quite successful.[43]

In addition to his school work, Paterson worked with blacks in other ways. He helped organize and served as the first President of the State Teachers Association. A coworker, Mary Frances Terrell, remembered that Paterson aided in some way "every church (colored) in [Montgomery]." Larger churches received donations, smaller ones got specifically needed items, from chandeliers to heaters. "His purse was always open toward 'Old Ship' [A.M.E.Z.] Church, for he said, 'The school had its birth there.'" Mrs. Terrell reported that Paterson was also concerned about individuals, especially his students, and he helped each one who was "reported to him." Paterson revealed his paternalism somewhat more openly than did other teachers by calling the younger pupils his " 'buds of promise.' "

At Commencement Paterson most looked forward to the Alumni Reunion when he could learn what his former pupils were doing. On one of these occasions he remarked, "'My prayer is Lord, make it fifty years.'" In the same vein he wanted his epitaph to be, "'He taught Negroes fifty years.'" Paterson was only five years short of his goal when he died on March 14, 1915.[44] Hooper Councill Trenholm, Secretary of the State Teachers Association and President of State Teachers College, 1925–1963, in 1931 claimed that Paterson was "the pioneer as well as the Apostle of Negro Education in Alabama."[45]

4

WILLIAM HOOPER COUNCILL—LIBERAL AND INDUSTRIAL EDUCATION

William Hooper Councill, head of the Huntsville normal school, never completely embraced liberal arts education for his school as did Paterson nor did he totally endorse industrial training as did Booker T. Washington. Councill was born a slave in Fayetteville, North Carolina on July 12, 1848. In 1857 his master sold the Councill family to slave traders who took them to Huntsville, Alabama and sold them to Judge David C. Humphreys.[1] Humphreys took the Councills to Stevenson, Jackson County, Alabama where Councill worked in the corn and cotton fields until emancipation.[2]

When Councill later described the hardships of slavery, he focused on the poor clothes and housing he had to endure.[3] Despite the hardships of slavery, Councill found time to raise his own corn, cotton, and vegetables and take them to his mother nineteen miles away to sell. He also made baskets and brooms out of wheat straw and horse collars and foot mats out of the shucks of corn. His master also allowed him to raise his own hogs.[4]

Although he could not receive formal education as a slave, Councill studied "grasses, weeds, trees and other things of my world. I knew the variegated colors of the pebbles and stones." Councill also had a chance to look at some books when he served as a baby's nurse. With one hand he rocked the baby; with the other hand he "turned the pages of an old magazine, showing to my unlettered mind, combats between men and animals."

Slavery, itself, awakened an intense desire for education in the hearts and minds of slaves like Councill by holding one idea always before them, the division of society into "the master and the slave. . . . To us, everything that would tend to make us know more, would bring to us the unearned ease and comfort, which we thought we saw exhibited in the life of the master. . . ."[5]

This yearning for education led Councill into one of the first schools in north Alabama, established by an Army chaplain, a Quaker named Walton, in Stevenson. Councill attended this school for three years before a lack of funds forced him to drop out and to begin teaching his own school in Jackson County. Councill never again was able to attend a school, but he continued to study with private tutors often at considerable sacrifice. He once plowed three days to get a Greenleaf's Arithmetic. For three years he studied at night by the light of split cedar, which he later called his "Cedar College." He "walked eight miles, three times a week, for three lessons . . . in Physics and Chemistry and paid a learned professor fifty cents for each lesson." In 1869 he moved to Huntsville and opened Lincoln School, the first black rural school in Madison County, about four miles west of Huntsville.[6]

In Huntsville, Councill became active in Reconstruction politics and won election as enrolling clerk in the Alabama Legislature, 1872–1874.[7] There Councill helped secure the passage of a bill on December 9, 1873, to establish a state normal school at Huntsville with an annual appropriation of $1,000.[8] Councill also obtained the appointment as principal of the school. To prepare himself for this position, Councill took private lessons from five "prominent white men" in Huntsville. When the normal school did not open in 1874, Councill turned this tutoring to good advantage by taking and winning "a competitive examination with college taught men" to become principal of the Huntsville City School. On May 1, 1875, Councill became principal of the state normal school and, except for one year, remained in that position for the rest of his life.[9]

By 1874 Councill and several other black politicians became disenchanted with the Republican Party. Believing that the Conservative Democrats were going to sweep the next elections, these black politicians scheduled a meeting with Mr. Clanton, a Democratic leader, to throw their support to his party. Such a switch was a decisive step for blacks in 1874. Most blacks were staunch Republicans and would bitterly censure any black man who became a Democrat. Becoming a Democrat would also mean the loss of federal appointments even if the Democrats did control the state offices.

At the appointed time, only Councill met with Clanton, became a Democrat, and campaigned actively for the Democratic gubernatorial candidate, George Smith Houston. While many whites applauded this switch, most Alabama blacks bitterly condemned Councill. "During this time Councill's life was threatened and many attempts were made to do him bodily harm but always he escaped without any serious injury."[10]

Councill always strenuously denied charges that he had sold out. In campaigning for the Democrats among blacks, Councill emphasized his belief that the race should not be tied to just one party. In a political debate, Professor A. W. McKinney, head of Rust College in Huntsville, reminded Councill that the Democrats were "not doing much to help our people. As quick as lightning came the reply, 'How can a man help you when you are trying to kill him?'"[11]

This fear of alienating whites dominated Councill's early political thought. In one of his most famous speeches at Tuscumbia in 1880, Councill warned the black audience not to always oppose whites as a group. If they did, within twenty-five years the whites would "come into power and take from you the ballot which you continue to cast against them."[12] Councill warned that whites of both parties would desert the blacks. "The republican party will grow tired of you . . . and like the bat who was disowned by the beasts and not recognized by the birds, you will find favor with neither democrats or republicans."[13] From 1874 until his death in 1909, Councill strove constantly to conciliate and placate whites. His life provides an excellent example of what happened to blacks who explicitly trusted Southern whites to fulfill their promises of just treatment of blacks.

In 1875 President Ulysses S. Grant appointed Councill Receiver-General of the Land Office of the Northern District of Alabama. This effort to get Councill back into the Republican Party failed as Councill sacrificed the post to remain a Democrat.[14]

Councill remained active in politics for almost a decade after his switch to the Democrats in 1874. From 1877 to 1884, he edited and published the Huntsville *Herald* to spread his political views. During this time he studied law and was admitted to the bar in Alabama in 1883, although he never practiced law. Councill actively encouraged blacks to become Democrats "until about 1882." In that year the only Madison County black to serve in the Alabama Legislature after Reconstruction cosponsored a bill to abolish Councill's school.[15] This might have intimidated Councill. Perhaps the legislature's chartering of Tuskegee Institute in 1881 discouraged him. Whatever the reason, after 1884 Councill stopped trying to convert blacks to the Democratic Party, withdrew from electoral politics, and concentrated on building up his school.

On September 5, 1885, Councill married Maria Howard Weeden. Their daughter, Ida, married Walter S. Buchanan, Councill's successor as Normal's president after Councill's death in 1909. Buchanan later recounted some of Councill's salient characteristics. He enjoyed reciting for the students in chapel. He "liked to laugh and to make others laugh." Like Washington, Councill was especially fond of Shakespeare. Councill did not read Shakespeare just for improving his speaking style and occasional quotes, but memorized several portions of the plays, "especially the dialogues between Portia and Shylock, and between Romeo and Juliet." He enjoyed singing and listening to classical and martial music.[16] The plantation melodies, however, were "serious worship with him." Councill's love of music led him to hire the great jazz composer, William Christopher Handy, to lead the band and work with the school's music program.[17]

In 1895 Councill made a speaking tour of Europe and examined the school systems there. On this trip he spoke in several famous London churches and received private audiences with leaders like William E. Gladstone in England and King Leopold of Belgium who "cordially received him."[18]

After this trip Councill's poor health caused him to turn to writing. In 1898 he published his longest book, *Lamp of Wisdom*, a survey of black history in question-and-answer form. He weakened the value of the book as history by including at the end a disorganized, unrelated listing of "Miscellaneous Race Facts" and "Greatest Things on Earth." Councill also published *The Negro Laborer—A Word to Him*, *Bright Side of The Southern Question* (1903), *The Young Negro of 1864: The Young Negro of 1904: The Problem Then: The Problem Now* (1904), and a pamphlet, "Negro-Brute," (1906 or after). Councill wrote several articles for magazines. In recognition of his writings, Morris Brown College in Atlanta awarded him the degree, Doctor of Philosophy.[19]

While all the heads of black normal schools sacrificed for their schools, W. H. Councill led his teachers in returning part of their salary to build up the school. By 1881 the rented buildings housing the school were clearly inadequate, but only four percent of the school fund could be used for anything but salaries and Alabama refused to give Councill's school any additional money for a building. Councill and his faculty then signed a contract to "surrender part of the salary they were getting to purchase a school site to be deeded to the state for a Normal school for Negroes." With this pledge, the Commissioners of the school bought some property and repaired the building there.[20] Councill also used his own money to equip shops and to subsidize students' board, lodging, and washing.[21] During the year he was forced out of the presidency of Normal, Councill wrote Booker T. Washington that he was facing financial disaster. 'I suppose that you know that I foolishly put *all* [*sic*] of my money in the work here. Now, I have not ten dollars."[22] The extent to which Normal was *Councill's* school showed most clearly after his death. When the Madison County Probate Court rendered its final judgment, "most of William Hooper Councill's private property belonged to his school."[23]

For one so devoted to a school, "it was the disappointment of his life" that Alabama did not "rescue . . . [A. & M.] during his failing years." While A. & M. did receive $4,000 annually out of the school fund after 1885, and from $11,000 to $18,000 annually from the United States Government's Morrill Fund, A. & M. never received "a special appropriation for debts or buildings or to buy stock, or equipment." In 1907 A. & M. desperately needed $30,000 to repair its buildings. Councill, then "confined to a wheel chair most of the time and requir[ing] careful watching all the time . . . , asked the state for $10,000. . . . He got nothing." Buchanan, Councill's successor, concluded a bit rhetorically that Councill died two years later, in April, 1909, "a diabetic, we know, but perhaps with a broken heart."[24]

Councill was largely responsible for the school's success and longevity. Huntsville was the only black normal school that was established during reconstruction under a black principal to survive under Conservative Democrats. By cooperating with Republicans Councill received the appointment as principal. By becoming a Democrat he preserved his position and the very existence of the school.

Washington, coming into Alabama in 1881, could afford to be a nominal Republican and still remain Tuskegee's president largely because of the good will Councill had built up by sacrificing some of his personal opportunities for the good of his school and his race. As the first black head of a black normal school in Alabama, Councill paved the way for Washington.[25] Councill's example also showed Washington the danger of too much state control of a school and helped direct him to seek aid from another direction, the Northern philanthropists.

Councill opened his school in "a little shanghai building" on Eustice Street in Huntsville on May 1, 1875, with an assistant, Rev. Alfred Hunt, and sixty-one students. By 1878 C. R. Donegar joined the staff in teaching an average of sixty-six pupils per month. The school spent $1,102.50 in 1878. On February 6, 1879, the legislature increased the school's appropriation from $1,000 to $2,000 per year. The average attendance for 1878–1879 decreased to fifty-one,[26] but when Washington began Tuskegee in 1881, Councill's school enrolled 133 pupils, with an average attendance of ninety-four. Excepting bookkeeping, there was no evidence that Councill espoused industrial education at any time during his six years as president of a normal school before Washington came to Alabama.[27]

Lacking the contact with Northern philanthropists enjoyed by Washington, Councill and his early faculty members built the buildings of the school through self-sacrifice. In 1881 Councill took the school's glee club on a tour of the country to raise money for land and buildings and to attract new students. By these means, augmented by private donations, $500 from the Peabody Fund, and "the strictest frugality in the application of the State's appropriation," the Board of Commissioners, in September, 1882, bought a lot for $3,000 and deeded it to the State. The Commissioners also remodeled a two-story building on the lot for use as a school building. Before this purchase the school rented several houses since it owned no property. The Commissioners also began collecting books for a library and reading room. Private individuals, Departments at Washington, and several Northern publishing firms "contributed to the project."[28]

The 1882 enrollment of 200 increased to 268 in 1883 and to 302 by 1888. Since Councill sent many who enrolled in the primary and intermediate departments to the Huntsville public school, there was a big difference in the figures listed for total enrollment and for average attendance, 268 and 142 respectively in 1883.[29]

In 1883 the Alabama legislature raised Tuskegee's annual appropriation from $2,000 to $3,000. This put Tuskegee ahead of Huntsville, which had been receiving $2,000 a year since 1879. Councill and his Board of Commissioners went to work and by February 17, 1885, persuaded the legislature to double Huntsville's appropriation from $2,000 to $4,000.[30] From 1885 until 1896, when Tuskegee won the agricultural experiment station, Huntsville received $1,000 a year more from Alabama than did Tuskegee.

Along with the increased appropriation in 1885, the Huntsville school also received a new name, "The Huntsville State Colored Normal and Industrial School." This addition of "industrial" to the title of the school indicated a basic change in purpose from the original bill in 1873, to establish "a normal school for the education of colored teachers." The legislature did not add such a provision for industrial training to Tuskegee's charter until 1893.[31]

Since 1868 all legislative provisions for a school at Huntsville, Marion (1873), and Tuskegee (1881) had specified that the schools were to be normal schools. As late as 1881, the Alabama legislature saw a normal school (or at Marion, a normal school and university) as the kind of secondary school that should be established for blacks. Legislation adding "industrial" to Huntsville's name in 1885 and to Tuskegee's in 1893, was a recognition of an existing situation rather than planning for the future.

The location of the schools in Huntsville and Tuskegee had a bearing on industrial education. Whereas Washington bought land in the country within a year after he began Tuskegee, from 1875 to 1882 Councill had to conduct his school in rented houses in Huntsville. This more urban setting and tenant status of the school undoubtedly made the development of industries more difficult at Huntsville than at Tuskegee, where the first "industry," farming for food for the school, was soon followed by making bricks and building housing for the students. Still, according to one of Councill's first students, by 1882 Councill taught carpentry, printing, mattress-making and horticulture for boys and plain sewing, fancy sewing, millinery, and domestic science for girls.[32]

While Councill might have begun some industrial work by or before 1882, he announced plans late in 1883 to add an industrial department to the school in January, 1884. There was no mention of an industrial department in Councill's 1884 report to the Alabama Superintendent of Education, but in 1885 Councill reported (for the school year 1884–1885) that his school had a "new feature," the Slater Industrial Department. With the $1,000 given to the school by the Slater Fund's general agent, Dr. Atticus Greene Haygood, Councill conducted industrial training for fifty-five students in carpentering, painting, printing, sewing, and horticulture. Councill thanked Huntsville's citizens for contributing work, tools, and money to the new department. While admitting that the classes were small, Councill insisted that "the work was thorough in all respects." Councill promised further development of the industrial department if the school continued to receive aid from the Slater Fund.[33]

This statement and Councill's beginning industrial work about 1884 suggest that Councill might have begun this department to get badly needed money from the Slater Fund. If so, Councill's commitment to industrial education would be quite ironic. While Washington got ever increasing amounts from the Slater Fund, by 1888 Councill had lost favor with Haygood. On June 5, 1888, Haygood wrote Rutherford Birchard Hayes, "I believe we can make better use of the $600. Councill's use of the money in his day was not satisfactory."[34]

Huntsville and Tuskegee began offering printing at about the same time. Tuskegee began printing the *Southern Letter* in 1885. Although Huntsville did not begin publishing a paper until November, 1885, the school did offer two classes in printing during the 1884–1885 session. *The Normal Index* was a six-column weekly folio, dedicated to "the education of the hand head and heart."[35]

In 1887 Councill gave a speech to the State Teachers Association urging industrial education for blacks in Alabama. Washington preceded Councill in this area. At the organizational meeting of the STA in Selma in 1882, Washington "spoke with much force, it is said, on 'Industrial education.'"[36] By the late 1880's both Councill and Washington were pushing for industrial education, while other teachers felt that blacks should have the same kind of education as the whites.

On April 27, 1885, Councill became involved in a "shooting affray" with Blount McCravy at the State Normal School. McCravy had accused Councill of raping his niece, Martha Mary Ellen Clay, a mentally retarded, twelve-year-old student at the school. She said that Councill had attacked her, but several other students who were nearby when the alleged incident occurred denied that anything of the kind had taken place.[37] Since there was a poor case for the rape charge, the only charge brought against Councill was "assault with intent to kill Blount McCravy."

On May 23, 1885, several blacks in Huntsville called a mass meeting to discuss the Councill case with the Commissioners of the State Normal School. Those attending the meeting asked the Commissioners to remove Councill as president of the school and asked the A.M.E. church to remove Councill from his position as Superintendent of the Sunday School. Rev. Goodloe, pastor of the A.M.E. church, and the Church Board strongly supported Councill by refusing to receive the committee that the mass meeting sent them. When the grand jury met, it refused to give any indictments against Councill for rape or for assault.

Despite all the pressure that was brought to bear against them to remove or to refuse to reappoint Councill, the Commissioners of the State Normal School late in July, 1885, reelected Councill and all the school's teachers except A. A. Garner.[38] So Councill came through his first serious crisis virtually unscathed. He was not always to be so lucky.

In 1887 Councill and his students made mistakes that almost destroyed the school and did cost Councill the presidency for one year. In two separate incidents Councill and Normal students sat in a "white" railroad car. The incident involving just Councill might have caused no real trouble by itself because it occurred on a train from Tennessee to Atlanta. The incident with the students, however, occurred in Alabama and immediately stirred up a hornets' nest.[39]

Actually, the first incident was far more significant outside Alabama, for it led to the first case decided by the newly created Interstate Commerce Commission. In the summer of 1887, while riding in a first-class car from Tennessee to Atlanta, Councill was handled roughly and evicted.[40] Councill sued for $25,000 damages and $1,500 lawyers' fee in *William H. Council* [sic] *v. The Atlantic Railroad Company*. The Interstate Commerce Commission received the case on July 23, 1887, and handed down its decision on December 3, 1887. The ICC refused to rule on damages, but, using the dictum of separate but equal, ruled that Councill had not been treated equally (since he had been refused first-class service for a first-class ticket) and directed the railroad to provide equal if separate service in the future.[41]

Then on June 4, 1887, several of Councill's students entered the first-class car on the train from Huntsville to Decatur. One of these students, H. C. Hopkins, later recalled, "the affair was an entirely innocent one on the part of all concerned . . . I don't think one of us had thought about the matter at all. I know I had not." Councill was busy loading the students' baggage on the train and two lady teachers were helping some girls get on another car, so they knew nothing about what was going on. The students did not realize the seriousness of their action until they returned from Decatur. Some of the students went to Councill and "told him . . . of a little friction with the porter and the conductor [that] took place when we attempted to put some girls in the first class coach." Hopkins remembered finding Councill in his office, "his face buried in his hands and crying as if his very heart would break. . . . He raised his head from his hands, and said to me in agony, 'Well, you all have ruined me.'"

The outcry against Councill and his school was so great after this incident that Councill submitted a letter of resignation.

> The charge that I, with some of my teachers and pupils who were leaving the city, entered the ladies car on the M. & C. R. R. at our depot on June 4th, for the purpose of forcing social equality, has created so much unjust and unreasonable prejudice against me as to threaten the abolition of the school by the next Legislature, if I am retained as Principal, therefore for the love I have for my race and the cause of education, I hereby tender my resignation.

The commissioners accepted his resignation and appointed Peter H. Clark of Ohio as principal.

Immediately the commissioners began receiving petitions for Councill's restoration from churches, Sunday Schools, teachers institutes, and other religious, educational, and fraternal organizations. Letters and petitions came from other states bearing notes of sympathy and support and sometimes containing donations to further the work of the school. This outpouring of support for Councill persuaded the commissioners to restore him as principal.[42]

Knowing the precariousness of his position, Councill began an extensive campaign to improve the school and to regain favor with Alabama's leading whites.

In 1889, just one year after Councill regained his job as principal, the black Primitive Baptists attacked Councill for not hiring a member of their denomination as a teacher. The Indian Creek Association of Primitive Baptists sent a petition to Solomon Palmer, Alabama's Superintendent of Education, claiming that Councill, alone, (not the Board of Commissioners) kept Primitive Baptists from teaching. Palmer forwarded the petition to Councill, who refused to hire a Primitive Baptist as such, but he publicly announced that the faculty then had members of five denominations and that any qualified person would be considered when an opening occurred. Evidently the commissioners supported Councill in this matter, since the Primitive Baptists soon organized their own school under W. H. Gaston.[43]

Black advocates of higher education also attacked Councill. At the 1889 meeting of the National Educational Association in Nashville, Tennessee, Dr. William Sanders Scarborough, Professor of Latin and Greek at Wilberforce University, charged Councill with trying to raise blacks "through 'favoritism' . . . [and] of attempting to disparg [*sic*] higher education" for blacks. Scarborough agreed that blacks needed industrial education to keep "their present vantageground in the labor market of the South," but he believed that Councill did not properly understand the issue. Scarborough denied that black schools were "throwing into the community many young people educated beyond the ability of effectual assimilation." The real problem was that too many graduates of black schools were "half-educated and ill-prepared for the work of life." These graduates caused trouble, not "the so-called over-educated class."[44]

Despite all this criticism, ranging from the head of the Slater Fund to Huntsville black Primitive Baptists, Councill was still able to win one last major political victory. In 1891, only four years after being forced out of his job for supposedly advocating "social equality," Councill defeated both a white man, W. B. Paterson, and Booker T. Washington in the contest for the black share of the money Alabama received under the second Morrill Land Grant Act.

In 1890 the Alabama legislature appointed a special commission to visit the three black normal schools and then to recommend the best school to receive the land grant money.[45] Considerations other than quality of instruction alone were important. After a brief attempt at cooperation, the heads of the three black normal schools began serious political competition for the funds upon learning that all the money would have to go to one school. In this game, Tuskegee seemed to hold most of the high cards. Of the three schools, only Tuskegee had had no serious disturbances. Although its appropriation from Alabama was lowest, Tuskegee had the largest total income (largely from Northern philanthropists), the most buildings, and the most students.

Tuskegee also had the support of Alabama's Senators, James Lawrence

Pugh and John Tyler Morgan. In 1890 Pugh introduced an amendment to the Morrill Act to permit the land grant funds to go to schools which did not have "college" in their names.[46] Senator Morgan was even more specific. Ignoring Councill's school altogether, Morgan said that there were two black normal schools in Alabama. The Montgomery school was "a fine literary college . . . with a fine faculty," but Tuskegee had "done more good for the youthful colored population in that State than can be claimed by almost any other State in the South." Without Pugh's amendment, the money would go to the Montgomery school. Morgan believed it was "necessary therefore . . . [to] avoid the feature of the bill which gave [the money] to colleges of like kind and give it to another institution which is called a normal agricultural and mechanical school at Tuskegee."[47]

There are two basic explanations for Councill's being able to jerk the land-grant award out of Washington's eagerly outstretched hand. Since 1874, Councill had carefully cultivated Alabama's white leaders. He had intensified this campaign of conciliation after his restoration as Normal's head in 1889. His board of commissioners consisted of former Confederate officers while Washington's included many Northerners. Councill sought most of his school's funds in the South while Washington went North for Tuskegee's main support. Also, Councill had been a Democrat since 1874, while Washington was a nominal Republican. This does *not* mean that Councill "could out-Booker Booker, and he frequently did."[48] Both men shaped their rhetoric and developed their schools to please whites: Washington—Northern industrialists, Councill—Southern politicians. Councill's error was betting on the wrong horse, not gambling.

But it might be more accurate to say that Washington lost the land-grant money as much as Councill won it. In a speech to a Colored Convention in Montgomery on February 3, 1891, Washington attacked the 1891 school fund apportionment law and the practice of providing separate railroad cars for blacks.[49] The inflammatory report of this speech in the local paper probably ensured that Tuskegee would not get the land-grant money when the legislature awarded it ten days later, February 13, 1891.

This did not explain why Paterson at Montgomery did not get the money. In the conflict with Paterson, Councill showed no scruples. Washington carefully instructed his lobbyist, Warren Logan, not to fight for the money "if we could not get it without ['passing' crossed out, 'drawing' written in] the color line. . . . Do not go into the dirt with Paterson even if we lose the money."[50] Councill, however, was more desperate for funds and urged the Alabama Legislature not to grant the funds to a black school headed by a white man. Evidently Councill knew his men, for he won the grant.

Upon receiving the grant, Councill decided to move his school to a better location for teaching agriculture and industry. The school's commissioners sold the land in Huntsville and bought a plot of land four miles north of Huntsville on the Elora branch of the N. C. & St. L. Railroad. The town, Normal, grew up around the school in its new location.[51]

Before the Civil War this plot of land had been the site of a race course, an inn, a distillery, a grog shop, several slave cabins, and stables for the race-horses. Like Tuskegee, Normal used many of the old buildings that were still standing for faculty homes, offices, and shops. The "big house" of the plantation was an imposing edifice, built of stone and wood with "cedar shingles, under a heavy coating of moss." This eight-room house, where the planter once entertained Andrew Jackson when he came to bet on the races, became the home of the President of the Huntsville Normal School, William H. Councill, a former slave. After building Palmer Hall, Seay Hall, a barn, and a dairy, Councill opened school at the new location on September 1, 1891.[52]

Soon after the school moved to its new location, Councill began a resettlement plan of his own. First he bought a farm near Normal, between the two railroads on either side of the school. After setting aside part of the land for his own use, Councill offered every other lot to settlers who would agree to "build a specified house, and subscribe to certain other conditions, such as keeping up fences, streets, sidewalks. . . ."[53] While some faculty members did settle there, the city Councill envisaged never materialized because the development of the surrounding land soon boxed in the settlement.[54] Still, this attempt antedated a similar program by Washington and showed Councill's devotion to the black community.

During Councill's successful fight for the Morrill Fund in 1890–1891, his articles in *The Normal Index* continued to praise a "practical education" over a "theoretical one." Since some Southern whites defended lynching by contending that it was necessary to deter black criminals, Councill argued that industrial education was more successful in preventing crime than were "religion, ethical and intellectual culture" if the workmen followed "ethical rules."[55] But at a Chicago meeting of the American Association of Educators of Colored Youth in 1893, he announced his plans to stress literary work more than he had in the past. Without totally ignoring industrial training, he then planned to emphasize "moral and literary [education] . . . to the highest degree. There must first be a good literary and moral foundation or no substantial industrial structure reared—before any honest and intelligent work can be performed."[56]

Councill's shift from industrial training to literary education came when he had lost hope in the promises of white Americans. In a speech in 1893, Councill noted that blacks "had met every condition of civilization to a degree commensurate with [their] opportunities, and yet there are and ever will be limitations to [their] development in this country." White prejudice would keep blacks out of all high political offices. Instead of diminishing this racism, civilization, Christianity, and black education "but intensify it." Councill saw only one viable option—migration to Africa.

> He does not expect to go, nor does he advise his hearers to go en masse, but he advises them to instill into their children that racial spirit that will be satisfied with nothing short of the attainment of every possibility of their natures. This cannot be

in America. It must be in Africa, the home of the Negro, where his mission will be to christianize his own people.[57]

When Councill began urging blacks at least to prepare their children to realize their full potentialities, he also shifted from stressing industrial training to emphasizing literary education. While Councill believed that blacks primarily needed literary education, he had turned to industrial training, 1883–1893, to get money from the Peabody, Slater, and Morrill Funds to keep his school open. From 1874 to 1893, Councill had tried to work with Southern whites, trusting them to accept blacks when they "proved" themselves. By 1893, Councill realized that white racism made this impossible and turned in despair to the "Back to Africa" movement and to emphasizing literary education.

By 1896, Normal was beginning to lose both black and white support. At their annual convention, the Alabama Colored Baptists petitioned the General Assembly to shift the black share of the Morrill Fund to "the centre of Negro population" where it would bring "the greatest good to the largest number."[58] In the same year, 1896, Councill first lost to Washington in the Alabama legislature when Tuskegee began receiving $1,500 per year for an agricultural experiment station.[59] This made the total state appropriation to Tuskegee, $4,500, or $500 more than Normal received.[60]

Tuskegee won this grant, however, only after a spirited contest with Normal in the legislature. In this contest, Tuskegee held all the high cards. Any whites who knew about Councill's "Back to Africa" ideas would have resented them. Undoubtedly the legislators were still impressed by Washington's speech in Atlanta the previous fall, October, 1895. The agricultural experiment station was tied to the U.S. Department of Agriculture and Washington knew the Secretary of Agriculture, James Wilson.[61] Since the Morrill Land Grant fund had been allotted to Normal in 1891, the legislature would have been more disposed to help another school in 1896. Tuskegee was the black normal school closest to the white agricultural school at Auburn.

While this loss was a setback for Councill, it did not represent a total rejection of Councill by the legislature. Councill was able to secure the passage of an act on December 9, 1896, giving Normal the "power and authority to grant diplomas and certificates of proficiency." This act also renamed the State Colored Normal and Industrial School as the Agricultural and Mechanical College for Negroes.[62]

Of the three black, state normal schools, only Councill's failed to increase its income steadily up to 1901 (excepting the period of transfer of Paterson's school from Marion to Montgomery). By 1899 Normal reached its peak income, $34,414.32. In 1900, its income fell to $32,288.73; whereas Tuskegee's income in 1900 reached $197,630.69. Tuskegee passed Normal in enrollment in 1886. Paterson's school in Marion passed Normal by 1885. By 1900 Normal's enrollment was 509 in all departments, compared to 928 at Montgomery and 1,231 at Tuskegee. Normal was the only black normal school in 1900 which did not receive money from either Alabama's Agricultural Fund or from the Peabody Fund, which the legislature usually distributed.[63]

Councill's policy of accommodation, trust, and cooperation with Southern whites had proved, in many ways, to be a failure. The tragedy was not just for Councill and his school, but for the white Southerner; for Councill had trusted the white South's promises of justice and equality for blacks and had shaped his career and the development of his school accordingly.

5

BOOKER T. WASHINGTON—INDUSTRIAL TRAINING

Booker T. Washington, the best-known president of a black normal school in Alabama,[1] was born a slave at Hale's Ford, Virginia in 1856.[2] Soon after the Civil War ended, Washington Ferguson, Washington's stepfather, sent for his family to join him in Malden, West Virginia. Ferguson put Washington to work with him in the salt-furnace, then in a coal mine. Washington next became houseboy for the mine owner's wife, Mrs. Viola Ruffner, who drilled into him almost obsessive habits of orderliness, neatness, and cleanliness.[3]

Washington first became fascinated with education while carrying his master's children's books to school. In Malden he persuaded his mother to buy him a copy of Webster's spelling book and tried to teach himself to read. After prolonged pleading and promising to continue work, Washington persuaded his father to allow him to attend the new school in Malden.

After overhearing some miners discussing a black school in Virginia, Washington decided to go there. He persuaded his mother to allow him to go and set out for Hampton Institute in 1872. He entered Hampton on October 5, 1872 after passing an "entrance examination" of cleaning out a classroom.[4]

Hampton began as an American Missionary Association School in 1868, but General Samuel Chapman Armstrong did not follow the standard missionary school curriculum. He based Hampton's curriculum on that of the missionary school he had known about in Hawaii. This school produced "less advanced but more solid, men" than even the other missionary school in Hawaii. Hampton stressed only English and generally elementary and industrial training. Armstrong intended to teach young people to

> go out and teach and lead their people, first by example, by getting land and homes; to give them not a dollar that they can earn for themselves; to teach respect for

> labor; to replace stupid drudgery with skilled hands; and to these ends to build up an industrial system for the sake of character.[5]

In addition to elementary academic training, Hampton gave its students "practical instruction in agriculture, in housework and in household industries, and drill in teaching." Hampton also drilled its students in the practice of neatness and personal cleanliness. But it was Armstrong's personality that most impressed Washington and, by his own admission, shaped much of his personal and educational philosophy.

Armstrong and the other teachers at Hampton gave Washington a determination to serve others, a paternalistic and moralistic outlook toward his students, a belief in the dignity of even the most menial work, and a commitment to industrial training and elementary education as the best way to inculcate the middle class standards of "character" and the Protestant ethic—the legendary means of "rising" in American society. Washington learned all these lessons well enough to graduate on the Commencement speaker's honor role, June 18, 1875.[6]

After graduating, Washington worked that summer as a waiter in a Connecticut hotel; then he returned to Malden to teach. He taught day school, night school, two Sunday schools, and gave special private lessons to prepare promising students for Hampton. He was a "social worker as well as a teacher," drilling his students in the habits of orderliness and cleanliness his Hampton teachers had emphasized for him.[7]

At Malden, something happened "which, simple though it was, became a guiding light in his subsequent educational enterprises." One beautiful day Washington and the students had been restive before the break. Outside the classroom the dullest student in geography suddenly began to lead the pupils in discovering "along the stream dozens of islands, capes, peninsulas, lakes and what not." All the pupils joined joyfully and enthusiastically in pointing out "the natural divisions of land and water." Washington then discovered for the first time "the real difference between study about things through the medium of books and studying things themselves without the medium of books." Washington later said that this lesson "has remained with me in all of my educational work."

Since this occurred after Washington left Hampton, his adoption of the "project" method of teaching grew out of his own experience rather than from his training at Hampton. Washington went even further than Hampton in integrating academic and industrial training and in insisting that all students must be trained in a specific industry.[8]

In 1878 Washington left Malden to attend Wayland Seminary in Washington, D.C. Although Washington believed he benefitted from his work there, he intensely disapproved of Wayland's stressing literary education to the exclusion of industrial or "practical" training. Washington found Wayland's students "less self-dependent" than Hampton's. He believed that Wayland students, by not "beginning at the bottom, on a real, solid foundation," were more concerned with "mere outward appearances." Washington's study at Wayland intensified his opposition to liberal education and his commitment to industrial training.[9]

Upon leaving Wayland, Washington went on a speaking tour of West Virginia to help the citizens of Charleston secure the capital for their city. When this campaign proved successful, many people urged Washington to go into politics, so he began studying law in Charleston. This career ended abruptly when Washington received letters from Armstrong asking him to speak at Hampton's commencement and then to join Hampton's faculty.

Armstrong put Washington in charge of a new program to educate and train Indians for entry into mainstream American society. This task gave Washington a unique opportunity to observe and to deal with the race problem from another angle since the Indians often quarreled with black students at Hampton. After doing well at this task, Washington took charge of another experiment, the night class, composed of students who worked all day to earn their board and tuition. Washington more than doubled the class and showed its worth so convincingly that Armstrong made it a permanent part of the curriculum.[10]

In May, 1881, Armstrong announced that some men in Alabama had written him asking for the recommendation of a white man to teach a black normal school in Tuskegee. Washington was very surprised when Armstrong asked if he thought he could do the job. Washington replied that he was "willing to try." Armstrong then wrote the Alabamians that he knew no available white men, "but if they would be willing to take a coloured man," he would recommend Washington. A few days later, Armstrong received a telegram. "Booker T. Washington will suit us. Send him at once." After receiving many "very hearty congratulations" from the students and teachers and making a quick trip to Malden, Washington set out for Tuskegee.[11]

Tuskegee began in a political deal between two white office seekers, Wilbur F. Foster and Arthur L. Brooks, and a black leader in Tuskegee, Lewis Adams. In 1880 Adams promised to help deliver the black vote to Foster and Brooks in return for a bill establishing a black normal school in Tuskegee. After Foster and Brooks won their elections, they pushed a bill through the Alabama Legislature on February 12, 1881, appropriating two thousand dollars annually for salaries of the staff of "a Normal School for colored teachers at Tuskegee."[12]

Before Adams and George Campbell, a white Tuskegee merchant and banker, wrote Armstrong they had already brought a white man from another school to Tuskegee to consider the job. When he found that the school "was not yet in existence"; that it had no building, no land, no apparatus, and no students; and "that no money had been voted for any of these purposes"; he "turned his back upon the whole project as hopeless."[13]

When he left for Tuskegee, Washington thought that he would "find there a building and all the necessary apparatus for [him] to begin teaching." When he arrived and found "nothing of the kind," he was bitterly disappointed but he decided to try anyway.

After arriving at Tuskegee in June, 1881, Washington spent that month looking for buildings for the school, "traveling through Alabama, examining into the actual life of the people, especially in the country districts," and announcing the school to "the class of people that [he] wanted to have attend it." Washington found the crude and backward mode of living of most of the people almost overwhelming, but he was firmly convinced that industrial training could reach these people and help them raise their standard of living.

Adams and Campbell, the leaders in starting and developing Tuskegee, understood and agreed with Washington's plans for the school from the beginning. With their support, Washington was eventually able to overcome the opposition of ministers who attacked his nonsectarian curriculum as "godless", blacks who saw all manual labor as a vestige of slavery, and whites who opposed any education for blacks.[14]

Although the legislature had provided no buildings and only four percent of the appropriation could be used for anything but teachers' salaries, Washington decided to open the school as soon as possible. With the aid of Adams, Washington borrowed the African Methodist Episcopal Zion Church and "the dilapidated shanty on its grounds," which had served as the village schoolhouse since the Civil War.[15]

Tuskegee Institute opened July 4, 1881. The thirty students, aged fifteen to forty, were primarily from Macon County and were equally divided by sex. Since Washington admitted only those over fifteen with some prior education, most were teachers, although sometimes both teachers and their former students came. Most of them wanted to get an education so they could earn more money as schoolteachers. Despite all their deficiencies and uneven training, the students were "earnest and willing" as any Washington had ever seen. "They were all willing to learn the right thing as soon as it was shown them what was right." The number of students slowly grew until almost fifty were attending after one month.[16]

About three months after the school opened, the owner of an old, abandoned plantation about a mile from Tuskegee offered to sell the land and buildings for $500, one half down and the balance within a year. J. F. B. Marshall, Hampton's Treasurer, willingly loaned Washington $250 from his own personal funds. Although Washington had no money when he made the loan, he repaid Marshall in three months, and within two months more raised the entire five hundred dollars and received a deed for the one hundred acres of land. Olivia A. Davidson, who arrived to assist Washington in August, 1881, raised the money by visiting most of the black and white families in and around Tuskegee and persuading them to give either cash or articles to be sold in festivals or "suppers." Out of necessity and from having watched Armstrong at Hampton, Washington thus established the policy of buy or build now—

pay later, or at least to request money only to finish a specific project already under way.

With the purchase of the Varner plantation, Tuskegee's physical plant consisted of one hundred acres of land, "a cabin, formerly used as the dining room, an old kitchen, a stable, and an old hen-house." The main house of the plantation had been burned. With the aid of the students, Washington cleaned and repaired the henhouse and the stable and used them as recitation rooms. One of the citizens of Tuskegee donated an old blind horse, the Institute's first livestock.[17]

Once the plantation debt was paid, the first crops planted, and the rundown buildings repaired, Washington began planning for a new building costing $6,000. Since such a sum could not all be raised in Alabama, Miss Davidson went north and solicited funds from the people she knew.[18] On March 30, 1882, Washington conducted the closing exercises for the first term of Tuskegee Institute. The high point of this ceremony was a speech by Hon. Waddy Thompson, county superintendent of education, at the laying of the cornerstone for Porter Hall, the first building erected on the campus.

Washington managed to keep one step ahead of his creditors and finished building and occupied Porter Hall, one of the few buildings at Tuskegee which the students did not build, in the spring of 1883.[19] Washington's phenomenal success in obtaining money to build and to finish buildings soon made Tuskegee's physical plant the best in Alabama, if not in the entire South. (See Table III for a list of the major buildings, 1883–1901.)

In addition to its physical facilities, Tuskegee's success also depended on the faculty Washington assembled. His brother, John H. Washington, served as Superintendent of Industries and Commandant of Cadets, 1885–1919. John supervised the detailed administration of the school and (along with Warren Logan) kept Washington informed about events at Tuskegee during Washington's absences for fund raising.[20]

Washington's three wives also assisted in developing Tuskegee. Fannie Norton Smith (1882–1884) began industrial work for the female students in training sessions in her home. Olivia A. Davidson (1885–1889) graduated from the Normal Training School at Framingham, Massachusetts. One of Washington's first faculty members, she organized Tuskegee's early fundraising drives and persuaded Washington to use some of her Northern contacts and to seek funds primarily from wealthy industrialists in New York and New England. Washington often said that she did more for Tuskegee's early success than any other single person.[21] Margaret James Murray (1893–1925) graduated from Fisk University in 1889. She started Saturday women's meetings in Tuskegee (with parallel meetings for their children) based on the Negro Farmers' Conferences. She also began a rural settlement program on a rundown plantation near Tuskegee. She persuaded Miss Lilla Davis, a Tuskegee graduate, to move into a cabin on the plantation and to teach a day school for the nearby children. In three years, Mrs. Washington was able to raise enough

TABLE III

Main Additions to Tuskegee's Physical Plant, 1883–1901[22]

Date	*Building*	*Facilities in the building*
1883	Porter Hall	Females' dormitory (after 1886, recitation rooms, office, library)
1883	Frame cottage	Males' dormitory
1883	Shop	Carpentry
1886	Alabama Hall	Kitchen, dining room, reception rooms, Dean of Women's apartments, sleeping rooms
1888	Wooden pavilion	Commencement exercises and other public meetings
1888	Armstrong Hall	Printing shop and males' dormitory
1888	Olivia Davidson Hall	Males' dormitory
1892	Cassedy Hall	Mechanical industries (previously in frame buildings scattered around the campus)
1892	Phelps Hall	Bible training school
1893	Science Hall	Laboratories and recitation rooms, third floor—male students' and teachers' rooms (Thrasher Hall by 1905)
1893	Two-story frame cottage	Booker T. Washington's home until about 1900, then a library
1896 (began)	Chapel	Auditorium, ante-rooms, and chaplain's office
1897	Slater-Armstrong Memorial Agricultural Building	Recitation rooms, laboratory, museums, library, and Department of Agriculture Office
1900	Slater-Armstrong Memorial Trades Building	Mechanical industries and electric lighting plant (for school and town)
1900	Farm buildings	Hennery, creamery, dairy-barn, horse-barn, carriage-house, tool-house, piggery, silos, slaughter house (several buildings to minimize loss in case of fire)
1900	Huntington Hall	Brick, females' dormitory
by 1900	Willow Cottage	Wooden, females' dormitory
by 1900	Hamilton Cottage	Wooden, females' dormitory

TABLE III (Continued)

by 1900	Parker Memorial Home	Wooden, females' dormitory and reception room, guest room, dining room, kitchen and laundry
by 1900	Wooden building	Females' hospital
by 1900	Brick house	Booker T. Washington's home
1901	Dorothy Hall	Girls' Industrial Department (previously in small buildings behind Porter Hall). Two of these buildings were on the Varner Plantation when Washington bought it.
1901 (began)	Carnegie Library	Library, librarian's office, study rooms, assembly room, historical room
1901	Children's House	Primary school for blacks in the town of Tuskegee and practice room for Normal Students at Tuskegee Institute

money to buy ten acres of land and to build a three-room house on the plantation, the basis of a miniature Tuskegee.[23]

Several people on Tuskegee's faculty were almost members of Washington's extended family. Washington's early decision to hire only blacks (although the boards of commissioners and trustees always contained whites) helped produce this closely knit, family-like atmosphere at Tuskegee. In the early years, most of the faculty came from Hampton Institute (ten of fourteen in 1884). Gradually, Washington began drawing faculty from among Tuskegee's graduates and seeking faculty, especially for the Academic Department, from schools such as Howard University (Emmett Jay Scott);[24] the Massachusetts Institute of Technology (Robert R. Taylor); Fisk University (Margaret J. Murray Washington); Iowa State Agricultural College at Ames (George Washington Carver);[25] and Atlanta University (Rev. Edgar J. Penney, Rev. John W. Whittaker, and Adella Hunt Logan).[26]

The primary reason for Tuskegee's success was not its physical plant or its faculty, but its leadership—Booker T. Washington—and its philosophy—industrial education. There were several reasons, some contradictory, for beginning industrial education at Tuskegee. Washington agreed with Armstrong that industrial education built character and encouraged students to return to their home districts to serve and raise the standard of living and behavior of the people of that area. Washington wanted to train "practical" men and women like those he had known at Hampton as opposed to the "abstract, theoretical" students he encountered at Wayland Seminary.

Necessity caused the development of some of the early industries. Lacking funds, Washington began farming to provide food for the students and a brickyard to furnish bricks for the buildings. Washington later used the industries at Tuskegee as a means of appealing for funds from businessmen, who were much more willing to give money to further develop the industrial work they saw than they were to donate funds for abstract, academic studies.

Washington and his supporters sometimes contradicted themselves on the motive for beginning the industries. Emmett Jay Scott and Lyman Beecher Stowe wrote that Washington began agricultural work at Tuskegee both because he believed that most blacks lived on farms so they needed this training and because he needed food for the school. They wrote that he began the brickyard to get bricks, but "the brickyard was used as an instrument of education and was never allowed to degenerate into a mere brickyard and nothing more."[27]

Washington and his followers resolved these conflicts—of motive, of the relation of industrial and academic training, and of the advancement of Tuskegee and the black race—by accepting the then current Horatio Alger myth or the Protestant Ethic. The ambiguity in Washington's thinking was inherent in the business ethic which demanded both that any educational program be directly related to a specific need (training in agriculture since most blacks lived on farms) and that an educational program must not be based just on theory (industries began at Tuskegee to meet the needs of the school, not just to provide a certain kind of education).

While the disparate elements of motive fell neatly into place within the Protestant Ethic, the same was not true in the results of applying this theory to the relation of Tuskegee and the black race. Washington desired to develop both his school and his race. He succeeded far better on the former than the latter. The story of Tuskegee was much like that of Horatio Alger. Rich individuals and foundations rewarded Tuskegee's early efforts with lucrative grants which enabled Tuskegee to become outstanding and successful. Washington succeeded at Tuskegee, not primarily by being subservient to Southern whites, but by accepting the prevailing business mythology, shaping his school by the presuppositions of this mind set, and then appealing to businessmen to fulfill their theory of stewardship by aiding Tuskegee.

Washington failed, however, when he applied this ethic to all blacks. Two flaws in the Protestant Ethic made it inapplicable as a racial strategy. The corollary of "anyone can succeed," was "not everyone can succeed," as John D. Rockefeller so graphically portrayed in his speech on the American Beauty Rose, which (like a business, a school, or a people) attained its perfection by the ruthless elimination of lesser buds. Thus, Washington's success with philanthropists often meant that only Tuskegee—not all blacks—got more money. Indeed, Tuskegee sometimes got funds by shutting out other black institutions—a poor strategy for the advancement of an entire race. It was almost impossible for any identifiable group to succeed as a group unless family, religious, or other ties or authority structures gave it a high degree of cohesion.

White racism was the second flaw in Washington's approach. He believed that business in the South was the one area in which blacks could compete effectively with whites. Had this been true, Washington's tactic of training students in the business ethic as well as in a particular trade would have been an effective means of removing discrimination in a society where status was largely determined by wealth. But in a racist society, material success by blacks often led to jealousy and attacks instead of acceptance. Washington's success with Tuskegee made it difficult for him to see that the same tactic would not work for raising all blacks. Washington played the game by the rules as enunciated by the leaders of his day; that he failed was more an indictment of the callous individualism and blatant racism of late nineteenth century America than of Washington.

Washington, himself, must bear the blame, however, for the problems that arose from an excessive concentration on industrial training in black education. While necessity and the current needs of the school largely dictated the order in which industries began at Tuskegee, the integration of each industry into the educational life of the school was in accordance with Washington's utilitarian philosophy of education. All academic training at Tuskegee had to be directly related to the specific trades that students were preparing to follow. Although Tuskegee was a normal (teacher-training) school, the primary focus at Tuskegee was always upon teaching each student a manual trade, for example, carpentry, printing, wheelwrighting.

Washington's idea of education was also simplistic in its opposition to abstraction. He even viewed the commencement exercises as primarily educational. In *My Larger Education*, Washington titled the chapter on commencement programs, "A Commencement Oration on Cabbages." Washington "sometimes reduced his more scholarly teachers to the verge of despair by his insistence that there should be nothing on the program at any exercise to which the public was invited which the every-day man and woman could not understand and appreciate."[28] Washington frequently protested that he was in favor of collegiate training for blacks, but at Tuskegee he seemed totally oblivious to the importance of abstraction, reasoning, and any ideas or study that could not be immediately and directly related to the students' everyday experiences or to a specific trade. This philosophy was Tuskegee's strength and its weakness. Although it created tremendous rapport with nearby farmers and drew the support of Northern and Southern whites, Washington's philosophy also forced him to seek most of his academic teachers from other, more traditional colleges. Of much greater detriment to the long-range development of black education in the United States, however, was the implicit support which the Tuskegee plan gave to the contention of so many whites that the only kind of education that blacks needed or were capable of utilizing was vocational training. Despite frequent disclaimers and against his own desires, Washington thus bartered off quality collegiate training for generations of black leaders for the upbuilding of Tuskegee and his own reputation.

There was a positive side, however, to Washington's utilitarian approach to education. Just as Washington insisted that academic training be directly related to agriculture and industry, he also demanded that Tuskegee be a service institution for blacks in Alabama's Black Belt. The most obvious means of service was the training of students to go out and share what they had learned with others. Most of the teachers who graduated from Tuskegee learned this lesson well and not only practiced lives of service to their community, but also transmitted the gospel of service to their pupils. But Tuskegee did more than train teachers and workers. Margaret Murray Washington began women's and children's conferences and developed a rural settlement program on a rundown plantation near Tuskegee. In 1901 Washington began a Savings Bank Department at Tuskegee and organized the Southern Improvement Company to make land available cheaply and to establish a black colony near Tuskegee.[29] The most famous extension efforts of Washington by 1901, however, were the Bible School and the Farmers' and Workers' Conferences.

Washington often spoke out plainly against the illiteracy and immorality of much of the black clergy. The bitter attacks of many black preachers against Tuskegee as a godless school, since it was not identified with any one denomination, had a good deal to do with Washington's dislike of many black preachers. Instead of just condemning the clergy, Washington decided to change the situation by beginning the Phelps Hall Bible Training School for rural ministers.

Washington opened the Bible School in 1893 to students of either sex and any denomination. Students paid no tuition, only a small entrance fee and eight dollars a month for a furnished room, board, fuel, lights, and washing. Classes met only in the morning so that students could work afternoons to pay their way through school. Many students served as pastors of nearby churches or did missionary work near Tuskegee, some walking up to twenty miles each Sunday to conduct church services. All four pastors of Tuskegee's black churches attended the school. By 1900 the school's enrollment averaged seventy-five.

In 1900 Rev. Edgar J. Penney (Atlanta University and Andover Theological Seminary) directed the instructors and visiting lecturers in the school. The curriculum focused on the English Bible. The school sought to inspire its students to service, "to help in uplifting the race and in teaching right principles." Many students remained at Tuskegee to finish an academic or industrial course also, since few rural churches could afford a full-time preacher. Tuskegee encouraged the preachers to learn another trade, not only to better support themselves, but so that they might furnish "an example of industry and right living to the people in [their] community."[30]

The annual Negro Farmers' and Workers' Conference was Tuskegee's best-known extension program. Washington only had a modest meeting in mind when he began the Negro Conferences in 1892 by inviting about seventy-five farmers, mechanics, school teachers, and ministers to come to Tuskegee to discuss their condition and needs. Washington told those he invited that he did not want formal speeches, only a free discussion of some common problems and what might be done to alleviate them. He was quite surprised when four hundred men and women "of all grades and conditions" attended the first conference.

Washington quickly devised a rough conference agenda similar to the "experience" meeting of many rural black churches.[31] He opened the meeting by encouraging everyone to sing spirituals to develop "a sense of unity and good feeling."[32] He then asked a popular minister to give a prayer. Washington next told of the good and bad homes and farms he had seen on some of his trips, concluding with a striking success story of a farmer who rose from poverty to respectable land-ownership. Turning to the audience, he would call a successful farmer to the platform and ask him a series of "friendly and humorous questions" to draw out the story of his success and, implicitly, to encourage the others to follow his example.[33]

In addition to the power of example in the success stories which he so adroitly drew out of the delegates, Washington also stressed simplicity and positive thinking at the conferences. He invited agricultural specialists and plain, ordinary black farmers to these conferences. As at graduation exercises, he conducted the meetings "for the benefit of the ignorant and not in the interests of the learned."[34]

Washington also limited discussion to problems which the black farmers could remedy themselves. He strictly discouraged "mere negative criticisms and recitations of wrongs." He ensured that the conferences' keynote was "hopeful courage." This simplistic, doggedly optimistic tone of the conferences gave farmers some practical tips on raising their standard of living, but it seriously distorted their understanding of their full situation by ignoring or avoiding all serious problems that could not be solved by applying the proper "technique."

Within this highly restricted framework, the participants at the conferences discussed the educational, moral, and religious conditions of their communities. In the afternoon the discussion turned to possible solutions. Washington tried to steer the participants into deriving solutions through discussions among themselves. After discussing problems and solutions, each conference passed resolutions giving concrete suggestions for improving conditions in the delegates' home communities.[35]

In addition to encouraging economic and moral virtues, Washington intended for the conferences to promote racial reconciliation on the basis of black achievement. He assumed that if blacks were "patient, long-suffering, industrious, economical, and virtuous . . . persistent in efforts that make for progress . . ." they would be rewarded by white acceptance.[36]

By 1895, Mrs. Adella Logan conducted an afternoon meeting for the women whose husbands attended the conference. These women discussed dress, care of children, and agreed on the importance of taking good care of their homes, although some pointed out that their husbands' attitudes forced them to work in the fields.[37]

The day after the Farmers' Conference, Washington conducted a Workers' Conference for the preachers, teachers, local leaders, and heads of schools and colleges who worked with blacks. This conference discussed ways of putting into practice in general terms the lessons they had learned the previous day. Although professional and business men of both races, North and South, attended these conferences, the primary focus was on education.

At the 1895 Workers' Conference, for example, Dr. Hollis B. Frissell, Principal of Hampton Institute, presided over the seventy-five teachers present. Representatives of the various schools spoke out for the kind of education their schools offered—Fisk, Talladega, Berea, and others for "higher collegiate education chiefly or wholly," Hampton and Tuskegee for foundation work and industrial training, and Clark and Alcorn for both. The teachers discussed "practical" education and how to "fit the students for actual life." They sought ways "to keep hold of their graduates and increase their influence on the community, and . . . to overcome race-prejudices, which were acknowledged to exist in both races."[38]

Many of those who attended these conferences organized local conferences of their own, as did most Tuskegee graduates. These local conferences followed the Tuskegee Conferences in agenda and in philosophy. As the conferences spread, Washington hired T. J. Jackson to work full time attending local conferences or farmers' clubs and helping organize new conferences. Jackson stayed close to the farmers, saw the extent to which they put the teachings of the Tuskegee Conferences into practice, and helped decide what subjects should be discussed at the annual gatherings.

One important result of the local conferences was the organization of cooperatives to buy land. Through these cooperatives, black farmers could buy whole plantations (which were frequently sold only as single units) and then subdivide the land among themselves. One such cooperative at Mt. Meigs bought about a thousand acres under this plan.

Sometimes the women of a community formed their own conference if the men were not interested in beginning one. In one community the women "signed an agreement not to wear a mortgaged dress or to eat mortgaged food, and they lived up to the agreement." They also formed a cooperative to buy goods cheaply and wholesale and to resell them among themselves. When men did form conferences, the women often organized auxiliary conferences, pledging themselves to raise a certain number of hogs or chickens and to keep enough chickens to produce a set number of dozens of eggs each year.

In addition to the Tuskegee Conferences and their offspring, the students and teachers at Tuskegee engaged in several local extension projects. For example, J. H. Palmer led the faculty and students in trying to influence the home life of all blacks living within a twenty-mile radius of Tuskegee. With one or more of Tuskegee's teachers, Palmer also visited a different church each Sunday to give a talk stressing "the need of a wholesome physical life as a basis for real moral improvement." Other teachers and students established a library and a young men's temperance society in Tuskegee and cared for an old black lady who lived alone. Tuskegee's Humane Society set up and cared for a watering trough in the town.[39] While other schools conducted similar extension activities, Tuskegee's larger income gave its extension work the widest spread and variety of any in the state.

But even a service institution needed money, and Washington was quite successful in raising money for his school. When Washington came to Tuskegee in 1881, the only money available was the Legislature's annual grant of $2,000. In 1883, after an impassioned plea by W. F. Foster, the Speaker of the Alabama House of Representatives, the Legislature increased the annual appropriation to $3,000 and Tuskegee first received grants from the Slater and Peabody Funds. Alabama did not increase this $3,000 by 1901, although the Legislature did establish an Agricultural Research and Experiment Station with an annual appropriation of $1,500 at Tuskegee in 1896. By 1900, the original Slater Fund grant of $1,000 had risen to $11,000 and the Peabody Fund grant (allocated by Alabama) rose from $500 in 1883 to $1,500 in 1900.[40]

From the very first most of the funds for Tuskegee came in response to direct solicitation by Washington and his staff and trustees. In the first two years at Tuskegee, Washington and Olivia Davidson raised $10,000; in the third year alone they raised $11,000. In 1884 Washington spoke to the National Education Association. This speech had much the same impact on educators as did Washington's speech in 1895 on the country as a whole. After the NEA speech, Washington found friends of education in the North quite receptive to appeals for aid and by 1886 he was able to raise $20,000, "a figure which continued to rise annually."[41]

Washington's fund-raising trips caused him to be absent from Tuskegee for extended periods. To provide Tuskegee with a surer income and to enable Washington to spend more time at Tuskegee, several graduates began an endowment fund in memory of Olivia Davidson in December, 1890. Tuskegee used the money in this fund to build Davidson Hall.

Friends of Tuskegee began work in 1898 on a permanent endowment fund with a meeting of philanthropists in Madison Square Garden in New York City. Most of the prominent philanthropists in the United States attended this meeting. Although former President Cleveland was unable to attend, he sent a letter praising Washington "and the movement he was fostering." This meeting alone netted the endowment fund $100,000. By 1900, the endowment fund amounted to $165,662.49. The interest for that year was $1,227.40.[42]

In 1889 the U.S. Congress evidenced Tuskegee's national reputation by granting the school 25,000 acres of mineral land to be sold to develop its educational program. In 1900, the estimated value of this land was $125,000. Also in 1899, friends of Washington and Tuskegee sent him to Europe for a tour and to relax.

In 1900 Tuskegee owned 2,488 acres of land, 700 acres of which were under cultivation. Tuskegee also owned six hundred head of livestock—horses, mules, cows, hogs, and sheep—and fifty vehicles—buggies, surreys, wagons, and carts "built by the students in the school's wheelwrighting shop." There were forty-six buildings on the grounds. The value of the plant with the equipment was $350,000. Since its beginning Tuskegee had spent $850,000. The cash income in 1900 including beneficiary funds was $197,630.69.[43]

Tuskegee taught twenty-eight industries in 1900. The average number attending was 1,083 out of a total enrollment of 1,231. The students came from twenty-seven states and territories and from Africa, Porto Rico, Cuba, Jamaica, and Barbados. There were 103 teachers and staff members. By 1900 Tuskegee had graduated 342 from its Normal Department. Of these, 114 were then teaching, although "many of them work at their trades in connection with their teaching."[44] Tuskegee had indeed come a long way since its beginning in 1881 when Washington gathered thirty students in a borrowed, leaky, rundown church and shanty.

6

PLURALISM OF BLACK PUBLIC NORMAL SCHOOLS

Three men—W. B. Paterson, W. H. Councill, and Booker T. Washington—directed the state-supported, normal school and secondary education for blacks in nineteenth century Alabama.[1]

The basic pattern of the education was pluralism. No one person, school, educational philosophy, or style of leadership was dominant. Since he was white, Paterson probably had less personal influence in the black community throughout Alabama (apart from those connected in some way with his schools) than did Councill and Washington.[2]

Washington and Councill agreed on many important subjects in addition to the need for industrial education for blacks.[3] Councill and Washington were essentially ambiguous in urging higher industrial training for blacks so that they would not be displaced by native whites or immigrants in the labor market and, at the same time, urging blacks to stay on farms in the South and to avoid the cities. They accepted the agrarian myth that the farm was inherently superior to the city. Both were outspoken nativists in their opposition to immigrants, whom they saw as a threat to the black laborer.

Washington and Councill forsook elective or appointive politics for work in education. They dedicated themselves and their schools to serving and to trying to uplift their race and tried to pass this concept of service on to their students. Both men disliked labor unions, favored businessmen, and tried to teach their students an appreciation of the essential dignity of all labor. They agreed that religion would not solve the race problem. Both tried to ameliorate the condition of the black clergy by starting Bible Training Schools on their campuses. In the case of Charles Octavius Boothe, they even hired the same man to teach these schools at different times.

Although both realized the necessity of cooperating with Southern white men if their schools were to prosper, they saw that race difficulties were primarily the white man's problem. Their schools were similar in the industrial training that they offered; but both men spoke out for higher academic training for blacks. The two schools' rigid schedules, which kept the students busy from 5:30 a.m. until 9:30 p.m. were similar although Tuskegee's was more detailed. In addition to academic and industrial training, both schools offered training in nursing, music, religion, and practice teaching.

But there were also important differences between the two men and their schools. Although Washington received his education at a school begun by the American Missionary Association, he felt that "the schools planted in the South by the Northern white people have remained . . . in a certain sense alien institutions. They have not considered in planning their courses of instruction, the actual needs either of the Negro or of the South."[4] Even private lessons from Southern white men for several years, however, did nothing to dampen Councill's appreciation of the contributions of Northern educational missionaries to the blacks. Councill once rhapsodized that he wished he could

> get angels from heaven, turn them into workmen, then I would select the highest place in the South, and there I would erect a monument, lifting its shaft above the stars in the clear blue of heaven, in honor of those thirty-five hundred teachers, who came down from the North and gave lives to further lift up the Negro and give beauty, strength and honor to our beloved South-land.[5]

Councill and Washington also differed on the educational theory actually embodied in their schools. Councill's school reflected his more literary approach even when he stressed industrial training (1883–1893). The classical allusions and poetry in Councill's speeches had a different effect on his students than did Washington's everyday stories on his students. Councill believed that, in addition to people trained in the industries and agriculture, blacks also needed "strong intellectual giants in the pulpit, at the bar, in the school room, in medicine—as scientists, linguists, artists, inventors—in order that [blacks] may be accorded a creditable standing in the society of races."[6] Councill's inclusion of Latin in his curriculum as an aid to those students who intended to do further study gave a substance to his support of higher education for blacks that cannot be found in Washington's curriculum.

While both men offered their students jobs to help them work their way through school, Washington viewed such manual labor as a major benefit of the school, whereas Councill came to view such work as a regrettable detraction from a student's studies. In Councill's reports to the State Superintendent of Education in 1898–1899 and in 1899–1900, Councill noted favorably the parents' increased support of students which gave them "more time for study and application, thus bringing about a greater degree of proficiency both in the literary and industrial courses." Such statements, along with Councill's reporting in 1899–1900 that his school drew its students "from the better element of the Negro population"[7] illustrated his leaning more toward an elitist view of education than did Washington, who constantly strove to keep in touch with the common black man, especially the average black farmer.

In politics Councill was a Democrat, Washington a Republican. This was not just a matter of courage; if anything it took more courage for a man who aspired to leadership in the black community to be anything but a Republican. Washington played down any active participation of blacks in actual elections (although he always voted, even after Alabama's 1901 disfranchising constitution). Councill believed that as long as blacks had the vote they would be involved in politics, whether they wished to be or not. After the mid-1880's, however, Councill saw that the political situation was so hopeless for blacks that he ceased even advocating that blacks vote Democratic and became politically silent. Councill's withdrawal from politics after he had incurred a good deal of censure by urging blacks to vote with the Democrats as a means of preserving their ballot, was a graphic commentary on just how limited Washington's options were in politics. Open political involvement in Alabama for Washington, a black Republican, was never a viable alternative to the course he took.

Whereas Councill was an ordained A.M.E. minister and a member of several lodges, Washington was never active in either church or fraternal groups. When discussing religion, Councill either honored the spirit of Christianity or condemned the prejudice in organized white religion. Washington, having a more materialistic orientation, attacked the other-worldliness of pietistic religion and constantly stressed the difficulty of making a good Christian out of a hungry man. Washington was more concerned with combatting pietistic elements in the black church which downgraded the need for social action. Councill spoke more about the failure of white churches to live up to their professed ideals.

While both Councill and Washington were known as outstanding public speakers, the content as well as the style of their speeches were quite different. Washington's speeches were simple, direct, and utilized everyday stories and images to illustrate points. Only a few of Councill's speeches have survived, perhaps only his most literary. In these speeches, Councill appealed much more to the intellect than did Washington. Councill drew his imagery from the classics and mythology and often constructed complex metaphors in making a point, practices which Washington usually avoided. Councill's speeches, especially *The Young Negro of 1864*, contained more flowery language and many more quotations of poetry than Washington ever used. This 1904 speech, especially, showed Councill to be a deeper thinker, with a much better classical education than Washington had.

In discussing black crime and lynching, Councill and Washington agreed (as did Paterson of Montgomery) that education was one of the best ways of eliminating crime. Washington, however, stressed more the evils of lynching, often at some peril to himself. It was no accident that Tuskegee produced some of the earliest and most accurate statistics on lynching after the Civil War. Councill, at the Race Conference in Nashville in 1897, condemned the crime that caused lynching as well as lynching, but he blamed evil whites for causing black criminals. In true accommodationist style Councill deified the Southern white women, posited an idyllic era of race relations under slavery, and hoped for a speedy return to a time of love between the races.[8]

Such statements by Councill (and he made many) are an important part of Horace Mann Bond's, August Meier's, and Louis R. Harlan's treating Councill as much more an accommodationist than Washington. Bond stated this view of Councill most succinctly. Councill helps us understand Washington because Councill's "career exhibits in aggravated degree all of the opportunistic characteristics which some critics have ascribed to the more prominent man."[9] Such a direct comparison ignores the different situations the men faced. The backgrounds, times, and connections of these two men had tremendous influence on their modes of dealing with whites. Also, the fact that Councill went first both necessitated a more conciliatory role for him and paved the way for Washington. Councill's example revealed possible traps such as state control which Washington could see and try to avoid. So Bond's, Meier's, and Harlan's one to one comparison of Councill and Washington is hardly just to Councill. Assessments of the two men that argue that Councill "out Bookered Booker," mistake the direction of accommodation for the degree. Washington turned to Northern businessmen just as Councill turned to Southern politicians. Both men "sold out" for white money (the only kind available in sufficient amounts for their purposes at the time). Councill's "crime" was choosing the wrong customer, not in going further than Washington in selling himself.

There was also a strain of condemnation and judgment of whites in Councill's later writings. In the speech in which he praised Uncle Tom, Councill also said that white mobs and crimes especially their cold-blooded murders are "no excuse for our committing crime. Two crimes cannot make one virtue."

Councill made other jabs at the white man. In a speech in 1904, he discussed black criminality. He first pointed out that few black criminals had any education. He next condemned the "bad men" who judge an entire race by the actions of a few of its members. Then he claimed that most black crime was really caused by whites!

> The negro brute, . . . is not the product of the negro. . . . We make no laws, we construe no laws, and we execute no laws. No board of aldermen, no judge or jury, would establish saloons on the recommendation of negroes. This negro brute is a product of the white man's gambling hells, low dives, and saloons, where he is dehumanized, brutalized and licensed to go through the land, a demented brute, to commit outrage upon fair women.[10]

But the best evidence that Councill was not solely a "Sambo" was an article he wrote for *Forum* in 1899. Councill wrote "The Future of the Negro" during his most pessimistic period of cooperation with Bishop Henry McNeal Turner in a back-to-Africa movement.

Councill noted that the "race problem" was really the question of whether or not whites would ever be willing to grant equality to blacks, not just in the United States, but throughout the world. He rejected arguments that education, more property, Christianity, or excluding blacks from politics would solve the problem. The first two proposed solutions would actually make the situation worse as wealthy, educated blacks increasingly entered competition with whites. Men always bent their religion to suit their prejudices and blacks would always be a political issue whether they voted or not.

Like his contemporaries, Brooks and Henry Adams, Councill rejected the easy optimism of thinkers from Herbert Spencer to Booker T. Washington, who believed in inevitable progress through education and economics. Accepting Social Darwinism's concept of the struggle for survival of races, Councill noted that blacks could not take power from American whites and that the blacks' former allies were gone. Paternalistic, Southern, upperclass slaveowners were dying or losing power to race-baiting popular demagogues. Northern politicians in 1899 were "no more like Sumner or Lincoln or Phillips or Garrison than the mummy of Rameses II is like the real old king himself."

But Councill's despair was proximate, not ultimate. While he believed that blacks could never win in the struggle with whites in the United States, Councill wrote that blacks could begin to realize their full potentialities and contribute to world civilization by working among themselves, as had the Jews, who had "suffered most, but have helped the world most." Councill had faith, like the Jewish faith in a Messiah and a Promised Land, that eventually the "New Negro" would lead America's blacks to their fulfillment in Africa. Until then black leaders should do all they could and suffer all they must to create an outstanding black culture. Like the Protestant Reformers—Luther, Zwingli, Melanchthon, and Calvin—who laid the foundations of the later New England culture, black leaders could begin preparing the black culture that would ultimately produce the "New Negro."[11]

Washington's buoyant optimism about the possibility of blacks' raising themselves through agriculture, education, and business (and, perhaps, freshly brushed teeth), stood in sharp contrast to Councill's short-term despair. Judging from the Tuskegee curriculum, blacks needed only elementary academic training, a craft, and a sense of mission to succeed and win acceptance from the white power structure, as Washington had. Consequently Tuskegee offered just such an industrial program, although Alabama had established Tuskegee as a normal school and it trained many of Alabama's black teachers, preachers, and other leaders.

As Tuskegee's president, Washington had to make concessions to the white power structure of Alabama. His primary concern, however, was always with Northern businessmen and foundations, not with Southern politicians. Washington distrusted the Alabama legislature and secured legislation making

Tuskegee's Board of Trustees independent and self-perpetuating as soon as he could (1893).

Washington was extremely skilled at wearing masks and operating behind the scenes.[12] Despite these secret maneuverings, Washington did not dominate public, black, higher education in nineteenth century Alabama. At no time did Tuskegee's share of the normal school fund exceed Montgomery's share or (excepting 1883–1885) Normal's share.[13]

In two tests of strength with the heads of the other two black normal schools, Washington lost both in the Alabama legislature. In 1887 he was unable to prevent the legislature from locating the Marion Normal School in Montgomery (where it would compete with Tuskegee for students) despite extensive secret and public maneuvering. Then in 1891 Washington tried to get the blacks' share of the Second Morrill Land-Grant Bill and lost to Councill.[14]

Although Washington served for several terms as President of the Alabama State Teachers Association, both his predecessors and his immediate successors stressed higher education over industrial education. The 1899 STA convention decided to reprint only one address, the one dealing best with higher education.[15]

If Washington did not dominate black education in Alabama, why did his arrival in 1881 coincide so closely with the development of industrial education in the state? The frequent appearance of "Slater Fund" in the first mention of black schools' beginning their industrial programs strongly indicated that Atticus G. Haygood's administration of the Slater Fund (1883–1890) was primarily responsible for the rise of industrial education in Alabama.

Many of the schools' reports indicate that the industrial work would not have been possible without the Slater Fund. A possible corollary of this statement would be that the industrial work would not have been *necessary* except for the Slater Fund. As badly as most of these schools needed money just to scrape by, they certainly welcomed aid from any honorable source. The interest in industrial education in most black Alabama schools (excepting Tuskegee, its offshoots, and the AMA schools) seems to indicate a pragmatic search for funds, not a commitment to the primacy or even the desirability of industrial education *per se*.[16]

Washington, thus, was more a symbol of than the cause of the development of industrial education in black schools. Washington was also basically a white symbol, especially after 1895. His power among blacks derived from his ability to control or influence white philanthropists and politicians at the national level. Even then, black educators who favored academic, liberal education over industrial training were sometimes willing to stand by their beliefs even at the price of losing money from Washington and his philanthropic supporters such as the Slater Fund.

PART II Seeking a Way Out: Private Schools

7

NONDENOMINATIONAL SCHOOLS

Since Alabama's private black schools and colleges were not under the control of local white school boards or the state legislature, their leaders had more room to maneuver seeking ways out of the web of subordination than did the public schools. Like the public schools, the private schools followed a variety of educational programs. Most of the nondenominational schools were primary schools that emphasized industrial training. Most of the schools established by white denominations stressed liberal, academic, or theological training. The major exception in this group, Barber Seminary, was a primary industrial mission school for girls. All of the schools established by black denominations emphasized liberal, higher education for their pupils.

The American Missionary Association's schools were a special group. While they offered industrial work from the first, they also were firmly committed to higher education for blacks. The AMA school, Talladega College, was the only black school in Alabama that had a traditional collegiate program (as distinct from a normal course) by 1901. The AMA schools, therefore, offered Alabama's blacks the fullest opportunity to develop the intellectual, elite leaders denied blacks by the public school system. These AMA schools daily denied the dominance of Booker T. Washington and industrial training over black education in Alabama. They also reinforced the determination of the other black and white denominations' educational leaders that black education would *not* be different from the education available to Alabama's whites.

Only one group of black schools in nineteenth century Alabama chose industrial training over liberal, academic education. These were the private, primary, nondenominational black schools. Many of these were short-lived, most were small, and almost none preserved their records or even the story of their development. Among the better known of these schools were the Langridge Academy and the Montgomery Industrial School in Montgomery;[1] the Industrial Missionary Association School, the Calhoun School, the Mt. Meigs Colored Institute, the People's Village School, and the Snow Hill School in Alabama's rural Black Belt.

If it was aptly named, the Langridge Academy was the only one of these schools that stressed academic over industrial work, but insufficient records have survived to show its curriculum. This school began when two missionary sisters, Misses Clarinda and Ann Wilkins, and their brother, John, from Patties Run, Ohio, came to Montgomery soon after the Civil War and established a school. These missionaries taught in an apartment they rented from Mr. and Mrs. Henry Campbell on Bell Street.

They named the school after Dr. Langridge, a white Englishman, who visited the school frequently and gave talks to the students. Probably because of an increase in enrollment, the school moved to a building on the south side of Dexter Avenue.[2] The church that became the Dexter Avenue Baptist Church met in the same building and black Baptists such as C. O. Boothe and Holland Thompson taught in the school along with Dr. Langridge and Miss Nutting (white).

When the church moved to its present location, Langridge and Clarinda Wilkins (who had married) moved the school along with the church and taught the school in this location until 1885. When the church tore down that building to build a new one, Dr. and Mrs. Langridge organized interested local citizens into the Langridge Academy Association and moved the school across town to the building that later housed the Daisy Lawrence School [1961].[3] From 1898 to 1900, Stephen W. Hewlett (black) was the Principal of Langridge Academy, and Misses Mary J. Byrd (black) and Emma Langridge (white) taught there. In 1901 Misses Byrd and Langridge still taught the Langridge School.[4]

In 1886 two white ladies, Misses Alice L. White and H. Margaret Beard, came to Montgomery and began the Montgomery Industrial School for Negro Girls. Alabama incorporated this school under an independent board of trustees. From the first, tuition and contributions from Northerners supported the school. The founders wished to produce black teachers who would show their pupils how

> to be true gentle-women in manners and thoughts, to be faithful mothers and homemakers, . . . to be earnest Christians . . . [and] to train them to earn a livelihood, to make them capable and efficient in some one industry, that would be of service to themselves, their families, and the community in which they lived.

This school quickly filled and remained full.

The main building of the school contained a hall, three recitation rooms, a kindergarten, a library, a sewing room, and a kitchen. Misses White and

Beard taught kindergarten, primary, and grammar grades. The curriculum included music, Bible study, and the industries—cooking, sewing, housework, simple nursing, and raffia work. Girls four years old could enter the kindergarten. Most pupils lived in Montgomery County, although a few each year came from other parts of Alabama or other states.[5] From at least 1886 to 1894, the teachers distributed a newspaper, *The Gleaner*, which told of their work and appealed for aid.[6] On April 20, 1894, a fire destroyed the school,[7] but the teachers were soon able to obtain another building and to continue their work. By 1897 another teacher joined the faculty, which remained three in number through 1901.[8]

Another black, primary, nondenominational, industrial school—the Industrial Missionary Association School at Beloit—grew out of an evangelistic effort to reach blacks through a land-settlement program. Reverend Charles B. Curtis, a white Congregational minister, established the Industrial Missionary Association in October, 1888. The IMA sought to carry its version of true religion to the rural plantations of the Black Belt in Alabama where the IMA believed that ignorance and superstition prevailed even in the churches. The IMA decided to try to reach these people by first ministering to their physical needs. The IMA bought up lands which it planned to rent and then to sell to local blacks at fair prices to help them escape the "iniquitous tenant system." While the blacks rented the lands, the IMA workers planned to teach them the latest methods of agriculture and simple industrial skills, always stressing the importance of self-help. Having met some of the blacks' most pressing physical needs, the IMA sought to "infuse new courage and hope and the spirit of self-help and independence, and at the same time get their attention, win their confidence, and prepare their hearts for the reception of a pure, scriptural gospel."[9]

After successfully trying his plan on a small scale, Curtis appealed to several missionary associations, but they felt they could only continue their current work in the towns and villages. Finally, in October, 1888, Curtis gathered a group of missionaries and businessmen of ten denominations in a meeting in Selma, Alabama, and organized the nondenominational IMA. Alabama soon recognized the IMA by incorporating it.

By the late 1890's, the IMA had succeeded in getting the endorsements of the Alabama Congregational Association (black), the Alabama State Teachers Association, W. B. Paterson (President of Alabama State College in Montgomery), Josiah Strong, and the presidents and some professors of Yale and Beloit Colleges. The IMA's Prudential Committee was almost entirely from Ohio, largely from Oberlin. For a while the IMA issued a bimonthly magazine, *The Plantation Missionary*, from its northern office in Oberlin. Near the end of the nineteenth century, the IMA claimed that its assets consisted of four thousand acres, a sawmill, a gristmill, a cotton gin, a blacksmith shop, a carpenter shop, a store post office, railroad stations at Beloit and Crawford, Alabama, three day schools, two night schools, and property worth $40,000.

It claimed that one hundred families lived on this land. If this report was accurate, the IMA declined disastrously by 1912–1913, when its income was only $4,067 and the estimated worth of the school plant was $4,000.[10]

Education was not very important to the IMA although it did sponsor a school. The promotional literature mentioned only that a school and a church would be established on each plantation that was large enough to support them. From one small building in 1888, the IMA's school plant by 1912 had grown only to three frame buildings on two acres of land. In 1912–1913, the school had 157 students and 6 teachers, all blacks except Curtis. The school went only to the sixth grade and offered industrial work only in sewing.[11]

Unlike the founders of the IMA, the leaders of the Calhoun Colored School in Calhoun were primarily concerned with educating and helping the people, not with saving their souls or making even a minimal profit. Calhoun grew out of a speech and a severe racial incident. In 1888 Booker T. Washington spoke at Hampton Institute on the desperate need of education for blacks on the rural plantations in Alabama's Black Belt and referred to a letter he had received from a black preacher in Calhoun asking for someone to teach there. After the speech, two white teachers at Hampton, Misses Charlotte R. Thorn and Mabel W. Dillingham, spoke to Washington about going to Calhoun. For some reason, Washington tried to discourage them, but they kept thinking about the problem and planning.

Some time later, a severe racial conflict broke out near Calhoun and forty blacks lost their lives. For two weeks after this tragedy, Calhoun blacks held religious services and appealed to Northerners for aid. Misses Thorn and Dillingham could not resist this appeal. In 1893 they established the Calhoun Colored School, supported entirely by contributions. Mr. J. Bell, a leading white man in Calhoun, gave ten acres of land for the school, even though he knew that Northern ladies would be conducting it. He also sold them another ten acres for $25 per acre.[12]

Lowndes County blacks desperately needed aid in education. Although blacks made up eighty-five percent of the county's population, the county officials distributed the educational fund in a thirteen to one per capita ratio in favor of the white children. Many blacks lived in run-down, unsanitary cabins; few owned land. The tenant system there was unusually repressive.

These conditions caused Misses Thorn and Dillingham (the latter survived only two years of the work in Alabama)[13] to divide their work into four areas. The school proper was much like Hampton. It offered boarding accommodations to a few pupils and elementary school work along with agricultural and industrial training. The boys learned carpentry, blacksmithing, and shoe repairing—the girls, domestic arts. Boys and girls studied agriculture. The teachers also traveled around to several nearby cabins to teach other students. The teachers were active in promoting community activities and extension work such as parents' meetings, farmers' conferences and fairs, and homemaking clubs. The teachers infused a strong moral tone, although not so blatantly religious as that of the IMA, into all their community uplift work.[14]

Miss Thorn was deeply troubled by the plantation system's negative influence on the education of black children. It kept them out of school until all the crops had been gathered in the fall. Even in the winter, some of the children had to stay out of school "to do the bidding of the plantation landlords." In early February, the children had to leave school again to begin preparing the land for the spring planting. Miss Thorn finally concluded that, the "only way for me to have a school for Negroes is to put them on land of their own, so they can be free to send their children to school."

While Miss Thorn worked closely with the black farmers, the initiative for such a land scheme came, as had the idea for the school itself, from the local blacks. In several farmers' conferences in 1895, the local black farmers came to see the necessity of owning their land if they were to grow any crops other than the cotton forced on them by white landlords. At the September conference, the farmers organized a land company and pledged $10 toward a fund to buy land. The high cost of the advances of food and supplies limited the success of the company in the early years, but by 1908, sixty farmers had paid off their mortgages and received deeds for 3,037 acres. The company continued to prosper until 1920 when it declined rapidly.[15]

While several factors contributed to the relative success of Calhoun and failure of the IMA, the two most outstanding factors were initiative and attitude. The IMA began when several white Northerners came South to begin a program of plantation settlement to save souls. Calhoun School began when Misses Thorn and Dillingham responded to a plea from Alabama blacks for a school. They were sincerely interested in the material well-being of the community. Although they did try to improve morals, they did not use their activities to win acceptance by the people so they could convert them, as the IMA sought to do. The people desperately needed a school and Misses Thorn and Dillingham established one for them. The land company then grew out of the school's activities, at the initiative of local blacks. While Misses Thorn's and Dillingham's ties with Northern philanthropy through Hampton cannot be ignored as an excellent source of funds, the success of Calhoun primarily resulted from Misses Thorn's and Dillingham's treating the local people with concern and respect, and responding to their needs as the local blacks saw them.

In addition to these private, nondenominational, primary, industrial schools led by whites, there were three such schools which black teachers established and conducted in Alabama. The teachers of these schools were graduates of Hampton or Tuskegee. They reproduced the programs of their alma maters on a smaller scale.

The founder of the People's Village School in Mt. Meigs, Miss Georgia Washington, was born a slave in Virginia. After Emancipation she cared for her former owner's children to get food and lodging. While working with these children, she decided to get an education. Her mother taught her what she knew, the alphabet, and some words from the Bible. Miss Washington then studied with a local white lady. After moving to the country to save money, she begged her mother to allow her to attend a country school taught by a Hampton graduate. In October, 1876, her mother allowed her to enter the school where she learned to write.

Against her mother's wishes, Miss Washington entered Hampton Institute in 1877 and graduated in 1882. For the next ten years she worked with the Indian girls in the Winona Lodge at Hampton, much as Booker T. Washington had done with the Indian boys earlier. In 1892 she went with Misses Mabel Dillingham and Charlotte Thorne to open their school at Calhoun. Throughout the year Miss Washington looked for a school of her own.[16]

Prior to 1893, whites had taught the public school at Mt. Meigs. After visiting a Tuskegee Conference, some of the leading blacks at Mt. Meigs decided to try to establish a school with a longer term and a better teacher. They wanted to choose their own teachers in a "school independent of the public." At the suggestion of Booker T. Washington, these men wrote Miss Washington and offered her $30 a month for eight months to come and establish a school in Mt. Meigs.

She arrived during cotton picking time so "no one met her at the station [and] no boarding place was ready" for her. She was able to stay for a month with the local pastor, Reverend Silas Jones. In October, 1893, she rented a cabin, ten by twelve feet, and opened her school. During the first month only four small boys enrolled, but the school then grew so rapidly that it had to move from the cabin into the black church. Miss Washington lived by herself in another small cabin, a quarter of a mile from the school. She cooked and kept house for herself, but her $4 a month rent included her laundry. She spent her free day, Saturday, teaching sewing classes and writing Northerners for aid for the school. On Sunday, she held a meeting for the mothers of the community.

During the school's second month, its patrons met and planned to buy three acres of land and to build a schoolhouse. As soon as they had partly paid for the land and had bought lumber, a local carpenter, aided by the men in the community, built a schoolhouse and made seats for it. They finished the eighteen-by-thirty-six-foot schoolhouse "with ceiled walls and ten windows with sash" on February 12, 1894 and Miss Washington and her seventy-five pupils moved into it. One hundred students from thirty-five families enrolled during the first year. The monthly tuition was 50 cents for the primary, 60 cents for the intermediate, and 75 cents for the advanced grade. Despite this low tuition, so many of the families were so poor that only one-third of the children were able to attend the first year in the new building.[17]

Industrial training began at the school when a barrel from the North arrived containing needles, thread, patch work, and sewing material. Miss Washington then invited some of the older girls to come to her house each Saturday afternoon for classes in sewing. The class met on clear days under an oak tree, with the girls sitting on chairs they had borrowed from nearby cabins. The class began with simple stitches and progressed to more complicated work. In later years, the girls in the advanced classes made the uniforms they wore to church on Sunday. The girls also learned cooking, laundering, and house cleaning during 1893.

Three additional teachers had joined Miss Washington by the school year, 1894–1895. So many students came that they soon had to begin using the fifty-year-old Antioch Baptist Church, "with its creaking walls and broken windows." The church provided poor teaching conditions. Each of the four teachers used a corner of the church for a recitation room. They made the center into a study hall. A real babble arose when all the classes recited at the same time. Over two hundred pupils attended, 1894–1895. At the end of the second term, the teachers and their pupils moved into a new, two-story schoolhouse. This fifty-three-by-fifty-two-foot building contained three recitation rooms on the first floor, an assembly hall (also used as a chapel), and sewing room on the second floor; a front and back porch, with a hall running through the center. The school soon added other buildings—an eight-room teacher's home; a five-room cottage for the kitchen, dining room, laundry room, and pantry; and a small, one-room cottage for teaching the younger students.[18]

The farm, which the school used for training its students and for revenue, was ten feet behind the schoolhouse. The farm and the sewing room were the only industrial features of the People's Village School. Miss Washington stressed the need for training students' minds as well as their hands. This emphasis on academic education led to a conflict between Miss Washington and Miss Cornelia Bowen of the nearby Mt. Meigs Colored Institute, who was almost totally committed to industrial training.[19] As a result of this conflict, in 1896, Booker T. Washington wrote to Miss Washington saying that, although he was a trustee for both schools, he felt that his first duty was to Miss Bowen. People were confusing the two schools, so he wanted Miss Washington to change the name of her school.[20]

Despite this difficulty, the People's Village School grew steadily. The faculty increased from one in 1893, to four in 1894, then to six by 1902–1903. The average annual teacher's salary increased from $90 in 1893–1894 to $120 in 1901–1902. The school's enrollment and average attendance grew from 75 and 65 in 1893–1894 to 200 and 178 in 1897–1898. The total enrollment dropped sharply for the next two years, but by 1901–1902, the totals were back up to 250 and 237.[21]

Throughout this time Miss Washington was content to teach only elementary subjects. She did not try to prepare young men and women to be teachers, "but to give them a start and a taste for better things." She was willing to leave further training up to one of the black normal schools. She served as principal from 1893 until 1941, when her failing health forced her to turn the position over to a former graduate, Oscar I. Pinkerton.[22]

The school which Booker T. Washington favored over the People's Village

School in 1896 was the Mt. Meigs School in Waugh, Alabama. Both the school and its teacher, Miss Cornelia Bowen, were "children" of Tuskegee Institute. Miss Bowen's mother was a slave on the plantation of Colonel William Bowen. Miss Bowen was born on this plantation in a cottage that later became the first building at Tuskegee Institute to be used as a girls' industrial building after Tuskegee bought the plantation and its buildings. Her mother had learned to read when she belonged to a lady in Baltimore, so she helped her daughter get an education. Miss Bowen studied with a white lady in Tuskegee before attending Tuskegee's black school. Miss Bowen, her classmates, and their teacher, left their school on "Zion Hill" and enrolled at Washington's school when he opened it in 1881. She became a member of Tuskegee's first graduating class in 1885. An honor student, upon graduating, she received a first grade diploma and one of the three Peabody Medals, which went to the best students each year. She also studied in New York and at Queen Margaret's College in Glasgow, Scotland.

In 1888 Mr. E. N. Pierce of Plainville, Connecticut, decided to provide a school for the plantation he owned near Mt. Meigs. When Pierce asked Washington to recommend a teacher, he chose Miss Bowen, principal of the "Children's House" at Tuskegee. She accepted the job and moved to Mt. Meigs in 1888. She worked to help improve the lives of the older people as well as to teach the children. She began Bible Classes and a variety of meetings and conferences in the community's old, run-down church. She stressed the importance of health, family, and property ownership. She made the school into a real community center where the women could learn cooking, sewing, housekeeping, how to rear their children, and work more cooperatively with their husbands and neighbors. Miss Bowen tried to convince the women to stop dipping snuff, smoking, and chewing tobacco. She also worked with the men and boys, urging them to try to own land and to build up their homes, families, and churches.

In addition to her community work, Miss Bowen, with the aid of contributions from the North channeled through Washington, developed her school for the children. She bought forty acres and erected school buildings. In addition to grammar and arithmetic, she stressed industrial training in gardening, farming, poultry-raising, the care of livestock, and bee-culture.[23]

In 1893 Alabama incorporated the school as Mt. Meigs Colored Institute. The school also built an industrial building in 1893. By 1895 the faculty consisted of Misses Cornelia and Katie Bowen, Miss Webster, and J. H. Michael, Superintendent of Industries. In 1895 Miss Webster resigned because of a salary disagreement with the Bowen sisters.[24]

Mt. Meigs was a little Tuskegee. Its funds came through a board of trustees, composed primarily of Northern men. The office of the treasurer, Noah C. Rogers, was in New York City. The Secretary of Tuskegee, Robert Charles Bedford, a white Congregational minister, was also the Secretary of Mt. Meigs. He did most of his fund raising for these two schools. Booker T. Washington served on the school's board of trustees and worked for the school.[25] Although Mt. Meigs offered some elementary teaching, its main emphasis was on industrial training and community services.

While Misses Washington and Bowen established their schools close together, near Tuskegee, William James Edwards opened the Snow Hill Institute in Wilcox County to serve the western part of Alabama's Black Belt. While little has been written about him, if the obstacles one overcomes to succeed were criteria for greatness, Edwards and Snow Hill might supplant Washington and Tuskegee.

Edwards was born at Snow Hill on September 12, 1869. On September 9, 1870, his mother died, leaving his father with three small children. Edwards' father then persuaded his mother to leave her job as a cook in Selma to come and care for the children.[26]

Soon after Edwards' grandmother arrived, his father left to find work and the children did not see him for several years. The Edwards family raised cotton and corn on three acres of land, but they were poorer than some of the other blacks. One of Edwards' earliest humiliations was having to take a piece of bread to school for his lunch and being mocked by the other children. But Edwards stayed in school because he was determined to be able to read the Bible to his grandmother. He succeeded just before she died in June, 1880.

Soon after the grandmother's death, Edwards' father came and took the children to live with him in Selma where he was working. He showed little concern for the children. What little money Edwards was able to earn, his father took from him.

Shortly after moving to Selma, Edwards became very sick from "scrofula . . . [which] affected the bone of his left arm . . . near the elbow joint, and the heel bone of his left foot." As a result Edwards could walk only "with much difficulty and pain." When Edwards' aunt, Mrs. Marina Rivers, heard that he was sick and not being cared for, she came and took him back to Snow Hill. Her neighbors gave him only three months to live, but she was determined to care for him.

Too sick to work, Edwards tended chickens and spent his spare time reading the Bible and studying an arithmetic book in an old, deserted cabin. Edwards felt guilty about living off his aunt's meagre income so he refused to eat a full meal and slept on some old blankets in a corner of the cabin instead of forcing himself into bed with his aunt's grandson.

When Edwards' illness did not improve, his aunt begged enough money from neighbors to take him first to a local doctor, then to Dr. George W. Keyser in Richmond, Alabama, eight or ten miles away. Seeing that Mrs. Rivers was paying him all she could earn or beg, Keyser agreed to treat Edwards and sometimes gave him medicine. Beginning in 1884, Keyser operated on Edwards several times "to remove the dead bone . . . from his arm and heel," and visited him for several months until Edwards recovered.

While recovering from his operations, Edwards lived with Lucy George

("Aunt Lucy"), a former slave on the same plantation as Mrs. Rivers. "Aunt Lucy" then lived on the doctor's plantation. Edwards' aunt visited him and brought him rations once a week after his operation. For the first three months after the operation he could not walk, so he had to crawl around the cabin to get food or to go outside when "Aunt Lucy" was gone during cotton picking season. In December, 1884, Edwards could walk with a stick, so he returned to Snow Hill to make some toy wagons for Christmas money. In 1885 he was well enough to work on the plot of ground his aunt rented.

Since Edwards and his aunt had to work for others to pay for plowing and rent, they had little time to work for themselves. Most of the year, therefore, they had little to eat. Some days they had only water plus what little milk Edwards could beg and cornmeal his aunt could borrow on the promise to work for it the next day. They ate better when wild fruits were ripe, but they had enough to eat only during cotton picking time. Edwards then worked all day and most nights, sleeping on his cotton sack when he could work no longer.

Despite this hard life, Edwards always found some time to read. Unable to afford oil, he used light-wood pine to read by until late at night. He dreamed of an education, but knew he could never afford the seven to eight dollars a month for the schools at Talladega, Normal, and Montgomery.

At the close of a revival in Snow Hill in August, 1887, the speaker told of a school at Tuskegee, where one could work one's way through school. Edwards determined to go to Tuskegee.

When he learned that his brother, Washington, was making "good money" working on a bridge gang at Hazen, fifty miles from Snow Hill, Edwards walked to see his brother and asked for aid in getting an education. His brother rudely rebuffed him, however, and Edwards returned disconsolately to Snow Hill.

Edwards then told his aunt of his plan to go to Tuskegee. She agreed to help him rent and work a small plot of ground, the only aid she could give. That year, Edwards, his aunt, her daughter, and grandson rented and worked small farms. When they gave out of provisions in midsummer, Edwards' cousin and her son mortgaged their crops for food. When Edwards refused to mortgage his crop, they refused to share their food. He then lived on bread, water, what milk he could beg, and the pot liquor of his cousin. During cotton picking time, Edwards earned enough to replenish his savings, pay Dr. Keyser, and start for Tuskegee. Although everyone but his aunt had discouraged him, when they saw his determination, many gave him a nickel or a dime to see him off.

Edwards worked hard up to the moment he left for Tuskegee. The night before he left, a neighbor offered to pay him a dollar to haul a cord of wood to the railroad trainyard by six o'clock the next morning. Edwards agreed and arrived at the neighbor's house at two o'clock the next morning, hitched the team, hauled the wood, and returned by five o'clock to get his dollar before leaving for Tuskegee.

Edwards arrived at Tuskegee on January 1, 1889. The school first placed him with a very rough group of boys from Pensacola, Florida, who made life so unpleasant that he decided to return home. When he went to Washington to say good-bye, however, Washington changed his room and asked him to stay. Edwards found the new group "very congenial" and stayed. Edwards had never used a knife and fork, a nightshirt, or a toothbrush; but he avoided embarrassment by always watching others before he tried these new devices.

On his entrance examination Edwards placed in the second year of the normal school in every subject but grammar. He was so poor in this area, a subject he had never encountered, that he had to begin in the A-Preparatory Class.

After unsuccessfully trying the tin shop and the printing shop, Edwards went to work on the farm, where he remained while at Tuskegee. He worked with the poultry, dairy, landscape gardening, horticulture, general farm, and truck farm. Although the brick-yard caused Edwards considerable pain because of his old sickness, he even worked there to get an education. Edwards stayed out of night school by doing extra work, regulating the campus clocks, building fires in the girls' buildings, and servicing the electric bells. He earned no money for these tasks, but the school gave him room and board, and he received clothes from barrels sent from the North. While some complained about the food, Edwards was pleased to have three meals a day and a bed.

Washington's Sunday evening talks impressed Edwards more than anything else at Tuskegee. Edwards felt a personal challenge when Washington urged the students to return home and share their education. Washington directly inspired Edwards in two classes during his senior year. Edwards graduated second out of a class of twenty on May 17, 1893. He borrowed $15 from R. O. Simpson, the owner of the plantation where Edwards grew up, to buy himself his first new suit for graduation.

When Edwards returned to Snow Hill on May 19, 1893, he found his aunt still living in the same one-room log cabin with her daughter and grandson. He worked for neighbors for his meals. After viewing conditions in Wilcox County, he worked his way through several adjoining counties to see what the people needed most and how he could help supply it.

From this trip Edwards concluded that whites denied many opportunities to blacks, but that blacks "abused many privileges." He discovered that the Black Belt west of Montgomery had 85,499 potential pupils out of a black population of 200,000. These blacks could not use any public or private libraries or reading-rooms. This area, "strictly speaking," had "no public schools and only one private one." Edwards believed that most of these blacks "were ignorant and superstitious [and] . . . that the teachers and preachers for the most part, were of the same condition." He believed that these blacks needed an industrial school to correct their

> erroneous ideas . . . of education; . . . to make education practical rather than theoretical; . . . train men and women to be good workers, good leaders, good husbands, good wives, and finally train them to be fit citizens of the State and proper subjects for the Kingdom of God.

To achieve these goals, Edwards started the Snow Hill Normal and Industrial Institute in 1894 in "an old dilapidated one-room log cabin." He began teaching three students with no state appropriation or promise of support from any church or society.[27]

Just as the school began, it experienced a severe crisis because of denominationalism. The local African Methodist Episcopal church to which Edwards belonged tried to make him turn his school into an A.M.E. school. When he refused, the local minister persuaded a district meeting of the church to establish a district high school in Snow Hill. The church then offered Edwards the principalship of the school and threatened to "crush . . . [him] out of existence" if he refused. He did refuse, however, because he had a "foundation," a gift from R. O. Simpson, and the support of Booker T. Washington. Edwards' school also had a better location. It was at least a mile and a half from any white family, whereas the church school was "located in the heart of the villadge [*sic*] and surrounded by members of the white race, which prevents an outlet of any kind." Instead of fighting the church, Edwards continued "working for the people and not a certain class," and Snow Hill prospered. By the fall of 1894, he had almost completed his schoolhouse, which contained a thirty-six-by-twenty-six-foot chapel and two, twenty-by-fifteen-foot recitation rooms. He had also begun collecting a library.[28]

From the first, Edwards stressed agricultural and industrial training. Many parents objected that they had always worked and they "did not mean to send . . . [their children] to school to learn to work." Some forbade their children to work, others withdrew their children. A few "illiterate preachers and incompetent teachers, who had not had any particular training for their profession" led this opposition to industrial training. Edwards persisted in stressing industrial training (especially agriculture since so many of the people were farmers), and added new industries whenever he could. Gradually the people came to accept industrial education. Edwards felt that the acceptance came as the people realized its value. Another possibility was that the people had no alternative if they wished their children to study under a trained teacher.

The older blacks primarily supported Edwards and industrial education. Evidently many of those who had been slaves felt that children needed manual training, while the younger blacks born since the Civil War wanted something better for their children. These older men and their wives helped Edwards raise money by giving suppers, fairs, and entertainments. They also worked at the school, especially building the schoolhouse, without pay.

When Edwards finished the first year at Snow Hill, he saw that he needed assistants, but there was no room for them in the one-room school. Edwards offered to work in a nearby sawmill, taking his wages in lumber, if the school's patrons would feed him. They agreed, and he worked in the sawmill from May through August, 1894. Edwards and the school's patrons then used the lumber he got for this work to build two additional rooms. In October, Edwards opened Snow Hill with 3 teachers and 150 pupils. The two new teachers, Misses Ophelia Clopton and Rosa Bradford, had graduated with Edwards from Tuskegee in 1893. They worked at Snow Hill for four years and the school "never had two teachers who did more work for the *old* people in the community and who were loved more by them."[29]

In 1895 Mr. Barnes and Mr. Rivers joined the faculty at Snow Hill. Barnes, another 1893 graduate of Tuskegee, stayed until 1918, except for two years he spent in Boston. Rivers completed Tuskegee's agriculture course but not its academic course. He had charge of the Snow Hill farm "off and on" from 1895 to 1918. In 1896 Julius Webster, another of Edwards' classmates, joined the faculty as a carpenter.

Ransom O. Simpson, who owned most of the land around the school, exemplified Southern paternalism in his aid to Edwards and the school. While Edwards was sick as a child, Simpson would often toss him a coin when he saw him lying beside the road. Simpson also loaned Edwards the money for his commencement suit at Tuskegee. Simpson was interested in having an industrial school on his plantation, so he gave Snow Hill seven, then thirty-three, then sixty acres. He later sold the school half his plantation, "making in all nearly two thousand acres."

After Edwards established Snow Hill, he bought and paid for a home as an object lesson to his neighbors. Edwards also established several community organizations—the Negro Farmers' Conference, the Workers' Conference, and the Black-Belt Improvement Society, to improve the living conditions of the people near the school. The Black-Belt Improvement Society strove for the moral, mental, spiritual, and financial uplift of its members. The Society sought to eliminate the credit system by urging its members to raise all their food supplies and to pay cash for what they bought. It also tried to persuade the members to buy cooperatively those goods which they could not raise. The Society urged strict economy, and attacked wasting money or time. It condemned "those evils such as intemperance, gambling, and social impurity." It stressed the importance of owning and improving one's home. The Society collected ten cents per month from each member "to aid . . . [its members] in sickness and in death." To realize these goals the Society established committees on government, education, business, housekeeping, labor, and farming which met monthly to discuss topics pertaining to the welfare and uplift of the people.

From the first Edwards was determined that Snow Hill should be nondenominational. While most of the church schools in the South did not exclude students of other denominations, Edwards felt that they did exert "undue influence . . . upon the pupils to make them become members of the church that supports the school." Edwards wanted his pupils to be able to belong to the church of their choice, so he sought to keep Snow Hill free from all "isms . . . thoroughly religious in its spirit, but entirely undenominational." Since this approach shut Edwards off from most support in the South, he had to go North to seek funds.

Edwards first went North in 1897, but he had little success. In 1898 Booker T. Washington invited him to accompany the Tuskegee Quartet when it went North that summer. While Edwards could not take up a collection for Snow Hill at these concerts, the trip did allow him to meet many philanthropists, especially in Massachusetts. On this trip Edwards met Miss Susan D. Messinger and William S. Messinger in Roxbury, Massachusetts and their cousin, Mr. Reed, and Mrs. J. S. Howe of Brookline, Massachusetts. All of these people became long-time supporters of Snow Hill.

On the Isles of Shoals, Edwards spoke after the concert, since Washington had left the group, and received as large a contribution as did Tuskegee. This aroused the jealousy of the director of the quartet so he forbade Edwards from traveling with them farther. Washington, however, intervened personally and restored Edwards to the tour. After this, Edwards toured the North alone, but his contacts and letters of endorsement gave him entrees to many philanthropists.[30]

By 1897 Snow Hill was incorporated and a board of trustees owned the school's property, which was worth $2,000. Snow Hill then owned forty acres of land, twenty of which it cultivated. It also owned two small buildings, a horse and wagon, a few tools, and a one-thousand-volume library. During the last term, 4 teachers taught 185 students for 7 months. When funds were sufficient, Edwards received $20 a month; the other teachers, $25 a month. When funds ran short, Edwards got only $10, "sometimes $5, sometimes $1.50, and occasionally hope."[31]

Edwards remained the principal of Snow Hill Normal and Industrial Institute[32] from 1894 until 1924.[33] Snow Hill was the most successful of the offshoots of Tuskegee in Alabama, both in its achievements and in the hardships which its founder had to overcome. Indeed, in some ways Edwards was more successful in his school than Washington was in his. Washington limited the effectiveness of his school by trying both to train leaders and to raise up the people near the school. Especially in academic areas, Washington's insistence that all the programs of Tuskegee Institute must be simple enough for any visitor to understand precluded serious scholarship by teachers or pupils. Snow Hill, however, was not a state normal school. Edwards sought to improve the lives and living conditions of the people near his school. Although some of Snow Hill's graduates did go on to found industrial schools of their own,[34] Edwards was not primarily concerned with producing leaders. In his thirty years at Snow Hill, Edwards did achieve a large part of his goal, using a small school to help blacks in the western part of Alabama's Black Belt to have better lives.

8

WHITE DENOMINATIONS' SCHOOLS

While most of the nondenominational schools were elementary, industrial schools, the white denominations' schools were more varied in scope and in curricula. These schools tended to fall into two groups. Most of the schools established before 1890 stressed normal, or secondary and liberal arts, or theological education. Most of the schools established between 1890 and 1901 emphasized primary and industrial training.

The Methodist Episcopal Church (North) organized the Freedmen's Aid Society (FAS) in 1866 to coordinate its relief and educational work with freedmen in the South. The FAS decided to organize its schools like New England schools, following the classical, liberal arts curriculum. The main FAS school in Alabama was in Huntsville.[1]

The FAS took charge of this school in 1866 when the Pittsburgh Aid Society withdrew one year after it began the school. The teacher-student ratio was so bad for the first few years at Huntsville that the teachers had to divide the students into sections and hear them separately, "giving but a short time to each division." When the FAS began supporting the school it had no building, so the classes met in rude churches. The teachers usually worked from eight to five with only an hour off for lunch. They would then return for night sessions which often lasted until eleven o'clock. This pressure caused a rapid turnover of teachers and broke the health of many of them.[2]

In 1866 the FAS bought a lot and began constructing a two-story brick building to accommodate up to 250 pupils. The school opened there in 1869. The Freedmen's Bureau aided the FAS in building the schoolhouse and in buying furniture. Huntsville blacks furnished a bookcase, many of the desks and tables, some funds for buying an organ, and several books to begin the library. By 1869 the physical plant was worth $7,000 and was free of debt. Misses M. Hindman and Lakin served for several years as the first principals of the school.[3]

The name of the Huntsville school varied. In 1871 it was the Rust Institute; in 1872, the Rust Normal Institute; 1873–1876, the Rust Biblical and Normal Institute; 1876–1888, the Rust Normal Institute; after 1888, the Central Alabama Academy. Until 1888, the name of the school honored Dr. R. S. Rust, Secretary of the FAS. The new name reflected the Central (black) Alabama Methodist Episcopal Conference's adopting Rust as the conference's school in 1880, and the FAS's decision to establish a Rust University in Holly Springs, Mississippi.[4]

By 1872, Rust had about one hundred students in four divisions. The first division read history; the second and third, the National Fourth Reader; and the fourth, the National Third Reader. There were also several grades in grammar, geography, and arithmetic. Rust offered one class in algebra and one in geometry. Most of the students worked their way through school as they prepared to become teachers or preachers. For prospective preachers, Rust offered "such an education . . . as their age, means and circumstances will allow." The teachers' course followed "that of the best normal-schools in the North, and the best advantages for those preparing to teach [were] afforded." Although most of the students were in the primary, English branches of study, by 1875 Rust had one class reading Caesar, and another studying Ray's Higher Algebra.[5]

In 1879 the FAS planned to close Rust. D. S. Brandon (a local black), Rust's Acting President, wrote to the FAS imploring it not to close the school. Exaggerating at a few points, he wrote

> . . . here we receive instruction in the higher branches, which are not taught in the public schools of the State. . . . The best teachers in this county and North Alabama come from its rooms—nearly every teacher in this and many other counties in the State is indebted directly or indirectly to Rust Institute for what education he possesses. It furnished the first colored teachers for our public-schools in North Alabama, and continues to turn out the best.[6]

Brandon also noted that two of the leading blacks in Huntsville, Charles V. Hendley and H. C. Binford, studied at Rust.[7]

Brandon also stressed the close relation in Huntsville between Rust and the local church. Many of those in Huntsville who were most interested in education and who were the best Sunday School teachers were members of the church and the school. Brandon closed by explaining why many of the pupils were sometimes poor students. They attended the school under great disadvantages.

> They are servants in white families—have to rise at five o'clock, work hard until nine, and get to school at half past nine—some as late as ten o'clock. They leave school at one and work until nine o'clock at night, when they are too tired to

> study, hardly having time to look at their books except while in the schoolroom. . . . Many come several miles from the country to school every day, while others from a distance rent rooms in private families and do their own cooking and washing.[8]

While factors other than Brandon's plea must have affected their decision, the FAS did decide to continue the work at Rust. The FAS also considered closing Rust in 1883, but local blacks led by Charles V. Hendley, editor of the Huntsville *Gazette* and a former Rust student, launched a successful campaign to keep the school in Huntsville.[9]

For several years, the leaders of Rust reported to the FAS that Rust's main need was a boarding department to allow the school to combat the tendency of the environment of most students to pull them down. In 1877 Mrs. Raines wrote asking for $5,000 to buy and outfit "an eligible property, consisting of a medium sized brick house with ten acres of excellent ground," near the school.

Mrs. Raines explained that boarding accommodations were crucial to the task of the school. Children in educated families continually learned through home influences, but the children who attended Rust from poor, uneducated families "hear nothing there which even so much as keeps in mind what they have learned during school-days." The influence of such homes was "backward and but too often downward." If the school had a boarding department, the teachers could supervise the pupils until "they are ready to enter upon their life-work with, at least, a reasonable hope of success." A boarding department would increase the school's influence "fourfold, as is proven by the results of the work in every place where such homes exist."[10]

Ironically, Rust did not open such a home until immediately after Mrs. Raines left. By September 19, 1885, Rust had enough money to buy and begin to repair the old Ware homestead across from the school to use as a boarding department. By October 17, 1885, the boarding department was ready and Rust offered to board students for $6 a month, ($7 a month by November).[11]

During the 1880's, Rust received aid from other sources than the FAS. At its annual meeting on December 9, 1880, the Central (black) Alabama Methodist Episcopal Conference adopted Rust as the conference school and provided "for the erection of an additional building, a financial agent being appointed in each Presiding Elder's District, to raise money for the purpose." In February, 1887, the Mayor of Huntsville gave bricks for the new building and the city council instructed the Mayor to furnish the Rust School with coal. The students at Rust also periodically raised funds for the school by giving benefit concerts and Principal A. W. McKinney made trips seeking funds for the school.[12]

Although Rust stressed academic subjects, it did offer some industrial training. In 1887, Rust began planning an industrial department. By 1888, Central Alabama Academy (Rust's new name) had two teachers conducting industrial work for forty-eight pupils; forty of whom studied sewing; eight, carpentry. A $300 grant from the Slater Fund made this industrial work possible. In the same year, Central employed 3 teachers to instruct 148 pupils in academic work. By 1888, 103 of Central's pupils were in the Normal Department, 39 in the Preparatory Department, 6 in the Primary Department, and 5 in a Biblical Class.[13]

The Industrial Department did not flourish at Central. In 1891, only twenty-five students were in carpentry, domestic economy, and bookkeeping. None of the four faculty members listed industrial work as one of their fields. By contrast, in 1891, the college preparatory course enrolled 4; the normal course, 43; the English course, 164; the theological course, 4; and music, 26. In 1891, 213 students enrolled at Central. An advertisement for the school in 1892 listed its English, normal, college preparatory, and academic courses but did not mention industrial training.[14]

The costliness of good industrial training in an urban school might have discouraged Central's leaders. Except in farming and the most basic "industries," the requisite teachers, equipment, and shops for industrial work ended up costing the school even more than academic training. By the time a student became sufficiently proficient in skilled crafts to benefit the school, it was time for him to graduate. Technological advances made this cost difference even greater.

In 1891 the blacks of Huntsville offered to give Central several acres of land if the FAS would locate the school there permanently and build the needed buildings. Either the offer was refused, or it was only temporarily successful. In 1904 the FAS moved Central to Mason City, near Birmingham, where there was a "larger number from which to draw students."[15]

Central differed from both the AMA and the Tuskegee type schools in three basic ways. Central was never really involved in the local community. It held few or no conferences, excepting teachers' institutes, and it had no organized program of extension and community work. While the teachers and students of the school were involved in the local church, Central (unlike Talladega and Tuskegee) had no organized program of using its theological or biblical students for evangelization of the countryside. Central did hope that its graduates would begin churches or improve the ones they served, but the school, itself, was not really evangelical. This was somewhat surprising for a denominational school. This policy was directly opposite to the Southern Presbyterian Church's school's concentration solely on training ministers before 1893. Central also started late and soon discontinued its industrial work.

Despite these unique characteristics, Central clearly belonged with the AMA in its insistence on the necessity of higher, liberal education for blacks, especially black leaders. Here the philosophy of the school and the ideas and actions of its graduates coincided in Charles V. Hendley and H. C. Binford's long struggle against the idea of "black education" or different education for blacks, which was implicit in Washington's philosophy and explicit in his program at Tuskegee Institute.

The next black school which a white denomination established in Alabama was Geneva Academy (Knox Academy after 1885). The Central Board of Missions of the Reformed Presbyterian Church began Geneva in Selma in 1874. Rev. George Milton Elliott, the pastor of Selma's Reformed Presbyterian Church and the second President of the State Teachers' Association, was principal of the school from 1876 until he resigned in 1886. Elliott was born in Virginia, June 4, 1849 and received his early education in Ohio. In 1873 he graduated from Geneva College. After studying theology at Allegheny, he received his license from the Pittsburgh Presbytery, August 21, 1877. He became the pastor of the Presbyterian Church in Selma on December 14, 1877. In March, 1886, he began editing the *Guiding Star*, "a weekly and monthly paper, devoted to the moral and religious welfare of the Negro race." After leaving Knox, Elliott served as a missionary in several places in the South.

A noted linguist, Elliott spoke and wrote seven languages, although he preferred Hebrew and German. When he taught the Bible "he often wrote for his students the Hebrew translation of the English biblical version under discussion." Elliott's interest in languages led him to give his students at least the language part of a liberal education. His background also indicated that he probably emphasized traditional, liberal arts education at Knox.[16]

Of all the other white denominations, only the Southern Presbyterians established and maintained a black school for any appreciable period in nineteenth century Alabama. Tuscaloosa Presbyterians led this work with blacks. The First Presbyterian Church in Tuscaloosa established a black Sunday School in its lecture room before the Civil War. This Sunday School continued until the black Presbyterians formed the Salem Presbyterian Church in 1880. This limited interracial cooperation in education paved the way for the establishment of Stillman Institute in Tuscaloosa in 1876.

Motivated either by a concern for blacks or a desire for segregation, the General Assembly of the Presbyterian Church (South) in 1874 urged all its churches to help local blacks prepare for the ministry and to help organize black churches, presbyteries, and synods. The General Assembly established the Colored Evangelistic Fund to help with this work. In 1875 the General Assembly appropriated five percent of its Sustentation Fund for work with blacks.

Rev. Charles Allen Stillman, pastor of the First Presbyterian Church in Tuscaloosa, led the Assembly in taking this action. He introduced an overture asking the Assembly to appoint a committee to consider establishing a school to train black preachers and "to digest a plan for . . . such a school, and report to the next Assembly." The Assembly established this committee and appointed Stillman one of its members.

In 1876 the committee recommended that the Assembly establish a school to train black preachers. The Assembly's Standing Committee on Education considered the report and recommended that the Assembly establish such a school at Tuscaloosa under Stillman.

Stillman then had a long record of concern for working with blacks. Born March 14, 1819, Stillman grew up in the Second Presbyterian Church in Charleston, South Carolina. This church and its pastor, Dr. Thomas Smyth, had long records of work with blacks. After graduating from Oglethorpe University at Midway, Georgia, and Columbia Theological Seminary in Columbia, South Carolina, Stillman returned to the Charleston Presbytery. He supplied the pulpit of his home church for six months before going to the Presbyterian Church in Eutaw, Alabama (1844–1853).[17]

Stillman next pastored a church at Gainesville, Alabama (1853–1870). Since Gainesville was on the edge of the Black Belt, he worked to involve his congregation in plantation work with blacks. In 1870 he became pastor of the First Presbyterian Church of Tuscaloosa, Alabama, where he remained until his death on January 23, 1895. His coming to Tuscaloosa gave new impetus to the work that Dr. and Mrs. Reuben Searcy and others had been doing in the church's black Sunday School. Church members like the Searcys strongly supported Stillman's plans for establishing a school for blacks in 1875.

In addition to working with his congregation, Stillman sought to remind all Presbyterians of their responsibility to blacks. By writing his fellow ministers, working with laymen, and appealing to church courts, Stillman "stirred the minds of the Church at large to a remarkable degree." Slowly he persuaded presbyteries and synods to overture the Assembly in support of a black school. His campaign reached its climax in 1876 when the General Assembly approved the school in Tuscaloosa.[18]

From 1876 to 1893, Stillman laid the foundation for the future development of the school. Most Presbyterians were primarily interested in converting blacks and they saw the school as a means of training preachers to attain this end. Even so, the support for the school was minimal. On five percent of the Home Mission Committee's receipts for Sustentation, Stillman had to find a location and a "suitable house," hire a "willing and competent teacher," recruit students, organize and administer the school. The presbyteries or the students paid their personal expenses.

In 1876 Stillman rented a "small brick house" at 2727 Eighth Street, where he opened the school in October. For a teacher, Stillman turned to a boyhood friend, Rev. Andrew Flinn Dickson (A.B., M.A., Yale University, B.D., Yale Divinity School), a Presbyterian pastor in Chester, South Carolina. While Dickson did most of the teaching as professor of theology and allied subjects for $1,500 per year, Stillman handled the administration.

Stillman and Dickson developed the curriculum, a two-year course in reading, writing, arithmetic, and "elementary instruction in Biblical and theological subjects." The students' lack of preparation soon forced Dickson to extend the course to three years. He had "initiated a well planned piece of work" by January, 1879, when he died suddenly.

In the fall of 1879, Rev. D. C. Rankin of Tarboro, North Carolina became professor for $1,000 per year. He worked out a plan allowing the students to support themselves partially and nearly doubled the enrollment.[19] When Rankin resigned in 1883 to edit *The Missionary Magazine*, Rev. D. D. Sanderson, pastor in Eutaw, commuted to Tuscaloosa for four years to teach. In 1886 Rev. J. G. Praigg, M.A., came to the school from his pastorate of the Carrollton churches. Praigg had studied law as well as studying for the ministry. When he died his widow donated most of his personal library to the school. Rev. J. R. Howerton became professor of theology in 1887. He was a "successful instructor" despite his youth (M.A., Southwestern Presbyterian University at twenty-one, graduate of Columbia Seminary at twenty-four).

Rev. R. B. McAlpine joined the faculty in 1889 to help develop an academic department. After Rev. A. L. Phillips became Secretary of the Executive Committee of Colored Work in 1891, he and McAlpine worked closely together to improve Stillman's academic program. Both men's resignation in 1898 was a severe blow to the school.

Throughout the nineteenth century, the lack of funds and the insufficient preparation of the students hindered and annoyed the teachers. In his first annual report, Dickson wrote that he could not do "satisfactory work under the present circumstances." Some entering students could "barely stumble through the simpler verses of the Bible." Few knew anything about writing, arithmetic, or grammar. Many came "provisionally; certain of only a few months, or at most two years; whereas, two full years spent upon academic studies would be but scanty preparation for their proper theological course." The annual reports continued to complain about poorly prepared students until Stillman began an academic department in 1893.

The teachers and the General Assembly urged the presbyteries to be more careful in selecting candidates, "both as to character and as to mental ability." The educational opportunities for blacks were so limited, however, that the presbyteries continued to select candidates by their consecration. As a result, the faculty reported in 1885 that they sometimes had "to recommend the withdrawal of students of Good Christian character, but incapable of pursuing the course of study with any encouraging degree of success." The situation had improved by 1887, when the faculty reported that most of the students were "of much more than average capacity, and some of them have extraordinary mental power. As a result they have made encouraging progress. . . ."

By 1880–1881, the teachers established a regular routine for the school. Each Monday the teacher conducted practical exercises, "pulpit readings of the Scripture, declamation, and reading of original essays on religious topics." On Saturday, the teacher supervised the students in textual analysis and interpretation of the Scriptures. The students began each day with one hour in a Bible class, where the students learned to use the Bible "by . . . find[ing] and read[ing] in class all the parallel passages." The class also taught students how to use "all other available helps" in learning a Bible lesson. In this way, students with limited educational backgrounds could become fairly proficient in using the English Bible. The students spent one morning each week studying the International Bible Lesson so they could teach in the Sunday Schools, where most of them worked.

After a few years, Stillman moved into a rented house at 1406 Greensboro Avenue. Finally, in 1881, the school was able to buy a lot and build a house at 1008 Twenty-First Avenue. Stillman remained at this location for sixteen years. It opened in its new building, which contained one small and two large rooms, on January 1, 1882. By the time the General Assembly met in 1882, Stillman had entirely paid for the school plant, which was worth $1,888.35.

Stillman's students boarded in private homes until 1885. In 1885–1886, to secure more careful supervision of the students, the teachers arranged with Nathan Luffborough, "a highly respected colored man and a member of Salem Presbyterian Church, to board the entire student body." This arrangement proved satisfactory and remained in effect for many years.

Although McAlpine tried to stress academic training at Stillman after 1889, the real push to develop academic subjects came under the direction of Rev. A. L. Phillips and Rev. D. Clay Lilly, between 1893 and 1903. The 1891 General Assembly had made work with blacks independent by taking it from the Executive Committee of Home Missions and giving it to the Committee of Colored Evangelization. Phillips was the first secretary of the latter committee. Under Phillips, the committee organized a Board of Directors "to plan for an academic department to meet the needs of better preparation on the part of students." When the Assembly accepted Stillman's resignation in 1893, it appointed Phillips as his successor, uniting the offices of Superintendent of the Institute and Secretary of Colored Evangelization.

Phillips took charge of the school in July, 1893, and began "an aggressive policy for the work along several lines." He launched a campaign throughout the denomination to arouse greater interest in and support for the work with blacks. He began looking for a rural location for the school. With McAlpine, he reorganized the academic and theological departments. By studying the graded, public elementary and high schools, Phillips saw the need for a three-year preparatory course of study before the students began work in theology. Phillips and McAlpine then reorganized the curriculum to provide such a course of study beginning October 4, 1893.

In 1894 the faculty's report to the Executive Committee of Colored Evangelization described the establishment of the new curriculum and its results:

> we received from you instructions to open an academic department . . . "strictly preparatory to the theological department." . . . So by a careful study of the relative importance of studies, the amount of work the students could do, and their capacities, we arranged our courses of study and scheme of recitations . . . we added to the curriculum higher English Grammar, Universal History, History of the United States, Geography, Introductory Logic, Introductory Natural Science, Elementary Psychology, and Vocal music. We projected a course of academic study covering three years.

Presbyterian interest in African Missions led to the establishment of a missionary department at Stillman for graduates of the regular course in the fall of 1893 under Phillips. Evidently J. B. Lindsay (1893) and H. P. Hawkins (1887) were the only students to enroll in this program. They studied medicine and French. A "hasty marriage" kept Lindsay from actually becoming a missionary, but Hawkins did serve for several years in the Luebo Mission in the Congo.

Although the missionary department was not very successful, the academic department improved in the 1890's. Phillips taught the academic department when he first opened it in 1893. In 1894 he turned the work over to Rev. S. Phillips Verner, who had just returned from mission work in the Congo. Verner conducted the work intermittently until 1903.

In 1897 Phillips summed up the achievements and problems of the academic department. Many of the school's problems during its early years arose when it tried to teach theology to students who had, at best, only elementary training. The rationale for this practice was the idea that a man who had "very little secular learning" could still "expound the plan of salvation." Phillips felt that this theory made first-rate education impossible.

Separating the course of study into academic and theological departments had solved some of the problems, but much still needed to be done. The academic department needed to be divided into primary, intermediate, and advanced courses. Students should be allowed to pass through these stages only after being carefully examined.

Phillips believed that only students in advanced courses should receive aid. He wished to open the school to anyone who was willing to pay to attend, instead of limiting admission to "candidates of approved character." He did not believe that such a policy would interfere with the purpose of the Institute, "the training of colored men to preach the Gospel to colored people."

Finally, Phillips wished more stress on the practical aspects of theological training. He did not want to make instruction in Systematic Theology and allied studies less thorough, but he did feel that students should be "more thoroughly drilled in methods of conducting Sabbath schools, missionary societies, church courts, and young peoples' societies."

The Institute moved to a new location during Phillips' administration. Stillman had always wanted to move the Institute to a farm to give industrial training and to allow the school to become partially self-sustaining, but he did not live to see the fulfillment of his dream. During the Panic of 1893, the Executive Committee bought a house by paying back taxes, but had to give it up when the former owner paid the taxes. In 1893 the Assembly gave the Executive Committee the authority to move the Institute to Birmingham, but many Presbyterians wished it to be in a rural setting.

In 1897–1898, Phillips finally succeeded in finding a location for the school, immediately adjoining the corporate limits of Tuscaloosa. He had begun advertising for a location through the church papers as early as 1894. He wanted the school to be on a farm to permit more self-support by the students. People in Birmingham and in Tuscaloosa offered to give land to get the school. The Pioneer Mining and Manufacturing Company of Thomas, near Birmingham, offered the school a site three miles from Birmingham. People in Tuscaloosa offered $745, and urged the committee to buy the old Cochrane homestead, which was for sale at a reasonable price. The committee finally decided on Tuscaloosa. They bought a house and twenty acres of land for $5,000. The new building was a two-story house, "well built and fairly well adapted to [the school's] purposes," although it did need some repairs. The house was located "on a high hill, commanding a fine view of the city and of the river valley in the rear. It [was] in the midst of a beautiful grove of fine oak and other trees." The land bought along with the house was then being cultivated and could "be easily brought up to a high state of productiveness."[20]

After doing so much for Stillman Institute, Phillips resigned as superintendent of the school and as Secretary of Colored Evangelism in 1898. His retirement was "a real calamity forced by the lack of funds." The Assembly chose D. Clay Lilly, pastor of the First Presbyterian Church in Tuscaloosa, to replace Phillips as Secretary of Colored Evangelism and Rev. O. B. Wilson to take Phillips' place as Superintendent of the Institute. Upon finishing his ministerial training at Union Theological Seminary in 1889, Wilson resolved that he would "not go to any place which already has anything like an adequate supply of ministers." After being ordained, Wilson volunteered to be a missionary to the Congo, but the Foreign Mission Committee rejected him because of his health. Wilson then worked for the Home Mission Board in Arkansas, where he ministered to blacks as well as to his white congregation. He came to Stillman to teach in 1894. There he seemed to feel that he was where God wished him.

Phillips' ideas about expanding and developing the academic department continued to bear fruit during Wilson's administration. In 1899 the General Assembly opened the academic department to any male who wished to enter and to female students under fourteen years of age,[21] and required each student to "earn his board by laboring on the farm, and [to] bear all his other expenses." By 1899 the move to the farm enabled Wilson to report "both a curtailment of the expenses of the institution and also the cultivation of a spirit of independence and self-help on the part of the students."

In 1899 Wilson hired Rev. Daniel D. Little to teach a summer school at the Institute. Little taught all the regular branches of the school to about twenty-five students, whose ages ranged from twelve to thirty years.[22] Wilson also began a night school for the summer students to allow them to work during the days to pay for their training. These summer classes ceased for several years after Wilson's sudden death in 1900. Finally, Wilson began Preachers' Conferences after the close of the winter session. Although Wilson was superintendent for only two years, he laid the groundwork for much of the later development of Stillman Institute (especially after the reactionary administration of J. G. Snedecor, 1903–1916).

Wilson died in a freak accident on April 16, 1900. He was talking to D. Clay Lilly on the telephone during a storm. Suddenly, Lilly heard the phone go dead. A bolt of lightning had struck a wire, killing Wilson instantly.

Lilly was then Pastor of the First Presbyterian Church in Tuscaloosa and Secretary of Colored Evangelization. Deeply shaken by the circumstances surrounding Wilson's death, Lilly resigned his pastorate and moved his family to Stillman's campus to become its superintendent. He also taught the theological department. Rev. S. Phillips Verner taught the academic courses.

Lilly thought very highly of Phillips, so he continued most of Phillips' policies, especially the stress on academic training. Like Phillips, Lilly felt the pressure of a lack of funds. When Lilly resigned in 1903, J. G. Snedecor became superintendent and reasserted the school's original primary emphasis on theological training. Not until the 1920's did Stillman again turn to an emphasis on academic subjects.[23]

The student body of Stillman Institute was never very large. The school's leaders lacked the funds to teach very many, and they felt that the purpose of the institution did not require a large student body. During its first year, the Institute enrolled only six students. Only two were Presbyterians, and neither was from Alabama.[24] The Institute's enrollment gradually increased until 1884–1885, when it leveled off. From 1896 to 1898, the General Assembly "'under stress of financial stringency' closed the academic department and limited the entrants to 'ten men who should be selected from the old students according to their records of scholarship, conduct, and general promise.'" Then, with a few exceptions, the enrollment increased to around fifty students for the first two decades of the twentieth century.

The debate over the kind of education to be offered at Stillman always centered on theological versus academic education. These Southern, white Presbyterians never showed much interest in providing industrial training *per se* at Stillman. In his first report to the General Assembly, Stillman described his desire to develop "some practical plan for the self-support of the students, and some means of connecting manual labor with study as a means of partial support, and for the promotion of health and industrious habits." All succeeding reports continued to stress the need for a farm or industrial work primarily as a means of relieving the financial problems of the school. They mentioned other benefits that might accrue from such training as a second thought. Thus, Alabama's white Presbyterians who supported black education in the nineteenth century never showed that they felt that blacks should have industrial education.[25]

After the initial surge of establishing black schools, 1866–1876, white denominations waited until the 1890's to begin other black schools. The schools begun in the 1890's were basically primary schools which included some industrial work or focused on evangelism or "character training."

The Episcopal Church's St. Mark's Normal and Industrial School in Birmingham began as a local girls' school in 1891. In 1892 Richard A. Wilmer and a group of Birmingham blacks took their plans for expanding this school to Deacon James A. Vanhoose, a white Episcopal deacon, banker, merchant, and mayor of Birmingham. For some time, Vanhoose had shown an interest in working with "under-privileged and neglected Negro youth." He believed that his church should work with all people. A history of work of the American Church Institute for Negroes commented that "he had the courage to found a Mission and School . . . to train and educate the Negro youth of this community."[26] This statement that it took "courage" for a white man to establish a black school in Birmingham in the 1890's was a graphic illustration of the racial attitudes of the city's society and churches.

Vanhoose liked Wilmer's plan to expand the school so he talked it over with the Bishop and they decided to support Wilmer. The new school first met on the second floor of the Jackson building between Eighteenth and Nineteenth Streets. Vanhoose contributed twelve chairs, an organ, six lamps, and $1 to the school.

From 1894 to 1899, St. Mark's offered only elementary work. In 1899 a black man, Rev. Charles W. Brooks, became principal and led in reorganizing the school under a board of trustees consisting of two clergymen and three laymen elected by the Diocesan Convention. St. Mark's also moved from its cramped quarters into a brick building in 1899. By the spring of 1900, St. Mark's began a four-year high school course. This prompted the Birmingham public schools to begin a high school for blacks. Thus, St. Mark's indirectly affected black education in Birmingham beyond just the students it directly trained.

St. Mark's always stressed self-help and character training. As a result of the former, blacks provided almost one-third of its funds. Because of the latter, no St. Mark's graduate was ever convicted of any crime.[27]

Both the Disciples of Christ and the Seventh Day Adventists established black schools in Alabama around 1895. Representatives of the General Conference of the Seventh Day Adventists came to Huntsville in 1895 and selected a site for a school they planned to establish for blacks. In 1896 they opened the denomination's only institution of higher learning for blacks, the Oakwood Industrial School (Oakwood College) near Huntsville. Some of the Huntsville black children went to Oakwood's grammar and high school, but most of its pupils came from outside Alabama.[28]

The Board of Negro Education and Evangelization of the Disciples of Christ supported and aided Robert Brooks in establishing the Lum Graded School (later the Alabama Christian Institute) at Lum. After studying at the Southern Christian Institute, Brooks took the Alabama Teachers' Examination and received the highest certificate available. He then returned to his home at Lum. With the aid of the blacks in the local Christian Church, he opened a school in "a miserable shanty." In 1895 Lum enrolled 111 pupils.[29]

The Board of Missions for Freedmen of the Presbyterian Church in the United States of America (North) did support at least two black schools in Alabama before 1901,[30] the Emmanuel-Miller Memorial School in Birmingham and the Barber Memorial Seminary in Anniston. The BMF established the Emmanuel School in connection with the Emmanuel Church (a new church in the Kingston Presbytery) in Birmingham in 1894. During the first year, the school's principal, Rev. E. M. Clark, enrolled seventy-five pupils and the school raised $5.20 for its support, probably through tuition. In 1896 the school became the Miller Memorial School and Miss Willie J. Clark joined Reverend Clark in teaching 103 pupils. Miller Memorial's reported enrollment varied greatly over the next few years; 1894, 75; 1895, 115; 1896, 103; 1897, 266; 1898, 100; 1899, 152; 1900, 156; 1901, 82. In 1899 Miss Alice Harney joined the Clarks on the school's faculty. In 1900 only Miss Clark and H. P. Thurman taught at the school. In 1901 the school got totally new teachers, Rev. L. B. Bascomb and E. J. Ravennah. The BMF Reports never described the level (primary or secondary) or the type (industrial or academic) of education offered at this school. Since it was an urban, small, short-lived school, it probably offered only primary, academic training and became a public, primary school when the BMF withdrew its support.[31]

In its report in 1896, the BMF announced that Mrs. Phineas M. Barber of Philadelphia, Pennsylvania, had given a "munificent" gift to the board in memory of her husband. Mrs. Barber wished the money to go to establish a girls' boarding school to promote "character, industry, economy, and education," which she believed were "the four primary uplifting powers for the individual and the race."[32] The board had already begun a building in Anniston, which it completed in November, 1896. The school opened on November 17, 1896. Rev. and Mrs. George B. Crawford and five ladies taught the fifty-four girls who enrolled during Barber's first year.

The main school building was four stories high, had a basement, and could accommodate from two to three hundred pupils. The school was located on sixty acres of ground. Mrs. Barber paid $50,000 for the school building, a church, a parsonage, a training house, and several out-buildings.[33] No other black school in Alabama began with such an expensive plant.

Barber had only been open for six months when a fire totally destroyed the main building. Fortunately no one was injured, although the fire occurred at night. The building was fully insured, so little additional money was needed for rebuilding. Since the fire occurred so near the end of the term, the school lost comparatively little class time while the rebuilding took place. Rev. George A. Marr, Mrs. Barber's brother, directed the construction of the new building, which was finished January 1, 1898.

Barber finished its interrupted work under the Crawfords, five ladies, and one man. Fifty-seven students enrolled in 1898. In 1899 Rev. and Mrs. S. M. Davis replaced the Crawfords and remained through 1901. The Davises and five other teachers supervised seventy girls in 1899. Industrial work for the girls also began by 1899, when the school taught its students kitchen gardening, cooking, and "thorough housekeeping." Three more teachers joined the faculty in 1900 to teach 110 girls. The parents of twenty-two of the students supported them fully. Seventy students got some aid. The school gave full scholarships to eighteen students.

The Industrial Missionary Association school and Barber were the most blatantly evangelistic schools for blacks in Alabama. Barber's founders wrote, "Our work is first Evangelistic and afterward humanitarian." But Barber did offer academic and industrial work by 1900. By 1901, the school had a faculty of 11 and an enrollment of 158. Barber's self-support increased from $653.93 in 1898, the year of the fire, to $2,219.31 in 1901.[34]

Barber was never very concerned about the intellectual development of its pupils. Throughout its existence it stressed more "the moral life and untarnished reputation than the intellectual development." Barber was an evangelistic finishing school. Although the school taught that "Christianity sanctifies for its use 'the heart, the head, the hand,'" Barber's main concern was with the girls' hearts.

> By precept and example, Barber taught that no profession of faith or church relation is credible which does not produce a moral life and an untarnished reputation; that Christianity molds everyday life; that spiritual development into Christlikeness is the crown of all attainments. . . .[35]

Barber, therefore, had much less impact on the community in which it was located than did most black schools in the state. With its emphasis on individualistic Christianity and personal morality, its lack of concern for community development and serious academic training, Barber justified many of the attacks made on Northern sponsored schools in the South.[36]

While the Roman Catholic Church did not establish any permanent school of any size in Alabama for blacks before 1901, it did have a real, indirect influence on black education in Alabama. When the AMA and the denominational boards appealed for money for black schools in the South, they constantly stressed the need to keep blacks out of the Roman Catholic Church. The mission boards magnified the work the Roman Catholics were doing among blacks and appealed to their members to contribute generously to turn back the tide of Romanism. The frequency with which this nativistic theme appeared in the reports of the mission boards indicated that appealing to Protestants' anti-Roman Catholic feelings must have been an effective means of raising mission funds in most churches in the nineteenth century. Although the "threat" was negligible in Alabama, Alabama black schools still benefited from this tactic of the mission boards.

This chapter has shown that the basic pattern of white denominations' black schools in nineteenth century Alabama was academic education (Rust), preparatory academic education (Geneva), and academic and theological training (Stillman). Although St. Mark's name included "Industrial," there was no evidence that it developed an industrial program by 1901. Evidently the BMF began supporting those Wilcox County schools with "Industrial" in their titles only after 1901. Even the one school that did emphasize industrial training, Barber, primarily stressed evangelism and religious instruction. Clearly, then, Northern and Southern white denominations did not perceive industrial training as the proper kind of education for blacks, nor did Booker T. Washington exercise any significant influence on these schools even after his famous speech and national prominence in 1895.

9

BLACK DENOMINATIONS' SCHOOLS

Most black denominations could not afford to establish large schools during the first two decades after the Civil War. Several associations, conferences, and local churches did establish small, usually poorly equipped and short-lived schools. Since most black schools met in churches during their early years due to the lack of schoolhouses, local congregations sometimes pressured the public school teacher to teach that church's doctrines to the students. If the teacher bowed to this pressure, the other local church or churches frequently sought to establish their own schools. If the teacher resisted, the denomination that first complained sometimes established a school to compete with the public school.[1]

Although white denominations dispersed their money in the same way, the situation was more serious in the black community, which had less money and which received increasingly less money from white educational officials. This denominational devisiveness caused most of the leaders of the Alabama black normal schools to try to keep their schools strictly nondenominational. Several primary and normal school leaders also studiously avoided denominational involvement to appeal more successfully to Northern philanthropists.

The influence of black denominations, however, was not entirely negative. Several black denominations did work strenuously to establish schools and colleges in Alabama. Because of their close ties with the white Methodist Episcopal Church, which had begun a black school during Reconstruction, the blacks in the Central Alabama Conference of the Methodist Episcopal Church decided to support Rust Normal Institute in 1880 instead of beginning their own school. Similarly, the black Congregationalists joined with their white brothers in supporting the nominally nondenominational AMA schools.

The other leading black denominations in Alabama climaxed long struggles for educated leaders by establishing schools of their own.

The Colored Methodist Episcopal and the African Methodist Episcopal Zion denominations were unable to begin lasting state schools in Alabama until 1898. These denominations' schools, therefore, had little impact on Alabama blacks in the nineteenth century.

In 1898 the North Alabama and Alabama Conferences of the C.M.E. Church joined to found the Miles Memorial College in Birmingham. Although the two conferences had bitterly debated the location of the school for some time, Miles' corresponding secretary wrote that he had never seen such unanimity in church matters as that displayed during Miles' founding. Even so, two more years passed before Miles actually opened in 1900. In 1901 the school's only teacher, Miss Mattie Welch, "conducted her work in a pavilion on the grounds where the school was to be located." A Thomasville school (1898) and a Booker City school (1902) merged with Miles by the time it received its charter in 1908.[2] C.M.E. educational work, therefore, really began during the twentieth century in Alabama.

The A.M.E.Z. Church did not begin a lasting school in Alabama until 1898, but it began its educational work by organizing a denominational literary society in 1867. In 1890–1891, Bishop Calvin Petty, with the help of the West Alabama Conference, established Jones University in Tuscaloosa about a mile from the courthouse. By 1892, the school had a small brick building and a large frame building containing eight recitation rooms and a chapel which seated two hundred pupils. In 1891–1892, Jones had 7 teachers and 175 pupils. Unfortunately, Jones failed after two years. The A.M.E.Z. Church also tried unsuccessfully to establish Zion Institute in Mobile. The A.M.E.Z. Church finally succeeded when it established the Lomax-Hannon High and Industrial School in Greenville in 1898.[3] Like the C.M.E. Church, the A.M.E.Z. Church really began its educational work in the twentieth century, but the A.M.E.Z. Church was the only major black denomination to establish an industrial school in nineteenth century Alabama.

The A.M.E. Church was the most successful black Methodist body in Alabama in education. A.M.E. leaders showed an interest in education for several years before they established a school in 1888.[4] Beginning at least as early as 1878, the Alabama A.M.E. Conference asked a leading educator to preach an educational sermon at its annual meeting.[5] In this and later meetings, the A.M.E.'s Commissioner of Education, J. C. Embry, spoke in the interest of education. The Alabama District's Bishop, Jabez Pitt Campbell, encouraged education by ruling that anyone wishing to attend the annual conferences

> must attend Sunday School and must be able to spell, read, write and know something of history and geography as well as the discipline and the Bible. All exhorters and local preachers are required to study or their licenses will not be renewed.

The 1878 conference also scheduled a Ministerial and Educational Sunday School Convention to meet in Troy in June, 1879. This convention heard papers on history, "The Colored Man in History"; race, "Race Pride"; morality, "How Can We Best Check the Downward Tendency of Our Young Men, and Inspire Them With Nobler Aspirations"; the ministry, "What Kind of Ministers Does This Age Demand?"; church activities, "Missionary Societies"; doctrine, "Baptism"; education, "Importance of Reading"; and the danger of Roman Catholicism, "Have We Much to Fear from Catholicism?"

The A.M.E. pastors felt strongly that they should have educated leaders. When Bishop Alexander Washington Wayman appointed Jesse Frazier as Presiding Elder of the Florence District at the annual meeting in 1881, Rev. M. E. Bryant rose to protest. Bryant noted Frazier's "inability . . . from an intellectual standpoint," and threatened to resign. Wayman relented, appointed Frazier to a church, and appointed someone else Presiding Elder.

By 1882, the Alabama A.M.E. Conference had appointed I. N. Fitzpatrick as the Conference Commissioner of Education. In 1882, he reported that he had raised $1,673 toward establishing an A.M.E. school, the Garfield Memorial University, in Montgomery. The plans for this school, however, never "materialized save on paper."

When Daniel Alexander Payne became Bishop of the District which included Alabama in 1884, he "instituted the writing and reading of essays in [the] Conference Literary and Historical Association" and gave prizes for the best essays.

By 1889, the A.M.E. Board of Education realized that the Garfield Memorial University would never get started. Instead of doing more planning, they decided to establish a school and to present that year's annual conference with a *fait accompli*. On November 4, 1889, the Board of Education, led by members of Brown Chapel in Selma, established Payne Institute in Selma, Alabama. They began the school there because the Congregationalists, Presbyterians, and Baptists already had schools there; they felt that A.M.E. young people needed a church school; and they believed that establishing such a school would "be one of the greatest means for indoctrinating the faith and principles delivered to us by the fathers." With this justification, these men "carried the Payne School to Greensboro [the site of the conference] and handed it to the North Alabama Conference with the machinery in perfect running order, and scholars matriculating daily."

The Conference's Committee on Education recommended that the principal be retained, the teachers paid, a Quarto-Centennial Day be proclaimed "for a special collection to be raised in all our churches for the school," and that a library be established by each delegate to the conference pledging to send one volume or set of volumes to the principal of the school. Faced with the school already in existence, on the recommendation of the conference's General Board of Education and Committee on Education, the North Alabama Conference adopted the school and asked the Alabama Conference of the A.M.E. Church to join them in sponsoring the school. The Alabama Conference accepted this invitation at its next meeting.

W. B. Johnson was the first Principal of Payne Institute. After Payne had been open a month, it had increased its enrollment from 88 to 149 pupils. Payne received a new organ ($150), a bell ($5), and "school records" during its first month from citizens of Selma who wished to have the school in their town. Although Payne was $1,341 in debt by the time the first conference met, it slowly repaid the debt and prospered.[6]

From 2 teachers and 88 pupils when it opened on November 4, 1889, Payne had grown to 3 teachers and 280 pupils by 1890. After Johnson, Professor W. S. Dugged became the school's principal in 1890. Professor J. S. Moten, A.M., LL.B., was in charge of the school for several years prior to 1896.[7] By 1896, Payne offered College, Normal, and Academic courses of study. There was no evidence that the school ever offered industrial training.[8]

The black Baptists, by far the largest black denomination in Alabama, had to begin very close to the bottom in developing an educated ministry.[9] Because Alabama forbade black education after 1832, when the Civil War ended in 1865, only one man, Rev. Moses B. Avery, "could with any degree of honesty, claim to be an educated Baptist negro preacher." Slavery also hindered the development of black churches and preachers since the slaves had to attend their masters' churches. There were at least four black preachers in Alabama before the Civil War, but Avery was the only one who was educated while still a slave.[10]

Black Baptists lost little time after Emancipation in showing an interest in education and a desire to improve themselves. At the organizational meeting of the Colored Missionary Baptist Convention of Alabama in Montgomery in 1868, the delegates[11] unanimously adopted a resolution,

> That in view of our profession as ministers of the Gospel of Jesus Christ, and the legitimate claims of the people upon us for correct Gospel knowledge and instruction, we will devote all the time we can spare from our other labors connected with the ministry to reading the Scriptures and such standard works of divinity and ecclesiastical history as we are able to obtain, and, by every means within our reach to improve ourselves; and we will encourage our ordained and local ministers to do the same, thereby elevating the standard of ministerial education, piety and usefulness.[12]

To support this resolution and to encourage education, the black Baptists established a Standing Committee on Education at their next convention in 1869.[13] In 1870 the convention advised its churches "to build schoolhouses and churches in their own means, declining all union proffered by others, unless considered absolutely necessary." The convention also urged the churches to be sure that they got a clear title to the land on which they built their schools and churches. The Education Committee recommended that the 1870 convention establish an Educational Board to "take charge of and conduct the [convention's] educational work." The committee felt that the Educational Board should be joined to the Mission Board to save money.

The 1870 convention also expressed its dissatisfaction with those mission bodies which were

> professing to work for us, and to do for us what we feel we can better do for ourselves. We have not been recognized and fellowshipped with by any of the white Baptist societies laboring among and professedly for us; and although hundreds of thousands of dollars have been collected for this work, its influence and the policy of its almoners have been and are against us as a body, rather than adapted to our peculiar wants. . . . Faithfulness to the original donors requires us to say to them, Please find for us another agent, or give not at all for we do not receive your gifts. If you would help us, do it directly through channels of our own creation, and such as we endorse as faithful to us.[14]

In 1872 the convention chose Rev. W. H. McAlpine to preach an educational sermon.[15] Each year thereafter, one of the leading educators in the convention preached an educational sermon.

It was only fitting that the man who preached the convention's first educational sermon introduced the resolution in 1873 which eventually led to the establishment of a black Baptist college in Alabama. McAlpine moved that the convention establish a Theological School for young men and asked all Baptists to contribute one dollar a year for the school.[16]

Before adopting this resolution, the convention appointed a committee to visit the white Baptist convention, also in session in Tuscaloosa, to ask their aid and advice in the matter. The white Baptists received the committee cordially, carefully considered the resolution, but decided that "the best and most practical thing to be done" was to seek the support of the American Baptist Home Mission Society in using the seminary in Atlanta, Georgia instead of establishing a new school. The white Baptists pledged "their council and aid in that direction."[17]

The black Baptists thanked the whites and "received" the report.[18] Discouraged by this advice, the blacks defeated McAlpine's resolution. The next day, however, they reconsidered the motion and passed it.[19] Thus, black Alabama Baptists began working for their school in spite of the advice of their white brethren. Such a course of action in 1873 required courage as well as faith. The 1873 convention also adopted a resolution of the Committee on Missionaries making "each member of this Convention . . . a missionary . . . to collect the dollar asked for in [McAlpine's] resolution."[20]

In 1874 the convention adopted McAlpine's motion to elect a Board of Managers to find a location for the seminary, and to report the cost of the necessary land and building. To maintain interest in the school, Holland Thompson moved that the 1873 educational resolution be printed each year in the convention's minutes. At the board's first meeting, it decided to establish the school in a central location, and to request each church in the convention to establish a "treasury" and to try to get $1 from each of its members.

To urge prospective pastors to get an education and, indirectly, to encourage the establishment of the Baptist school, C. O. Boothe, in 1874, moved "that no person shall be licensed to preach the gospel who cannot read," and that "this Convention shall do all in its power to aid young men who desire to preach the gospel in learning to read."[21]

The 1875 Committee on Education stressed the need for educational preparations, as well as piety, on the part of ministers since "an educated ministry is one of the greatest needs of our people as a race, and the only interpreter of the truth as it is in Jesus." The committee requested their "ministers of all ages and sections to pray fervently and study perseveringly." Booth reemphasized this point in his educational sermon in 1875. While all men contained God's image as "a seed ordained to development," the seed could develop only by feeding upon truth. Boothe then went further than many Baptists in his day, "As truth may be found in nature as well as revelation, in matter as well as in mind, *Christians should be informed on all sciences.*"

Until Alabama black Baptists had a school of their own, McAlpine and the Education Committee sought to guide the pastors' study. In 1875 McAlpine proposed that the convention endorse the following books as being especially helpful to ministers: *Dag's Manual of Theology*, *Pastor's Manual*, *Pastor's Hand Book*, and *Church Manual*. He persuaded the convention to ask the American and Southern Baptist Publication Societies to sell these books to the black Baptists as cheaply as possible. The Education Committee also proposed a list of seminaries for prospective ministers: Wayland Seminary, Washington, D.C.; Calvin Institute, Richmond, Virginia; Baptist Institute, Nashville, Tennessee; Baptist College, Atlanta, Georgia; and Leland University, New Orleans, Louisiana. In addition to recommending these schools, the 1875 Executive Board selected three promising students and awarded them $50 each to attend the Baptist Institute in Nashville, Tennessee.[22]

While pursuing these interim measures, the black Baptists did not neglect their work for a seminary for Alabama. The 1875 convention authorized C. O. Boothe to act as an agent of the convention in raising money for the school, and elected W. H. McAlpine to act as the convention's missionary and agent for the school at a salary of $500 above expenses. From June 1 to November 24, 1875, McAlpine traveled 1,923 miles, visited 52 churches, and collected $385.19.[23] McAlpine and Boothe were also to help find a location for the school and "to call to the attention of the white brethren of the North our needs regarding educational facilities in Alabama."[24]

The 1875 convention adopted a constitution for their proposed school. The Board of Managers was to become the Board of Trustees of the Theological Seminary of the Colored Baptists of Alabama. The fifteen-member board, composed of members of the convention, would be elected in three groups of five: for one, two, and three-year terms.[25] The board was to erect and manage a school for educating colored ministers, but the school was to be open to anyone "regardless of race or sect," who complied "with its laws and requisitions [*sic*]." A bonded treasurer, elected by the board, would handle all the school's finances. Although the board was bound by the will of the Convention, the board was the school's legal agent and could make an honest settlement of all its financial contracts.[26]

In 1875 the convention first received delegates from other Baptist bodies asking their cooperation in beginning a school. N. G. Scurlock from the Southern and Southwestern Convention asked their aid, "in order that we may be the better able to defend ourselves against 'popery.'"[27] Elder R. Ramsey from the General Missionary Association of Mississippi reported that his convention had secured the cooperation of some Mississippi whites in establishing a school fund, and asked the Alabama convention to cooperate.[28] The convention took no action on either of these proposals.

By 1876, the white Baptists had decided that the blacks were serious about beginning a school, so the whites decided to support instead of oppose them. The 1876 Alabama Baptist State convention unanimously resolved that it had "heard with great gratification of the earnest desire of our colored brethren for an educated ministry and of their laudable efforts to establish a Theological School in this State." The white convention then expressed their "strong and abiding interest" in the black Baptists' "welfare, both temporal and spiritual, and our willingness to aid them not only in this, but in every undertaking which may conduce to their good and the glory of our common Lord."[29]

The 1876 convention considered working with the Georgia Baptists. When the Georgia Baptists asked the American Baptist Home Mission Society in New York for aid in beginning a school, the society had replied that it was too involved with its school in Nashville, Tennessee, to establish a school just for Georgia. If, however, the Georgia and Alabama Baptists would combine and raise $25,000, the society would contribute $50,000 toward establishing a school for the two states. The Georgia delegates wanted to locate the school in Atlanta.

After careful consideration and heated debate, the Alabama convention was unable to give a definite reply to this proposal. They did appoint a committee to write the society "laying before them the plans and purpose of this Convention." They also appointed delegates to see if the Georgia Convention was "willing to allow Alabama an equal chance at the selection of a location, and . . . whether they will propose a plan by which the location can be fixed by vote."[30]

In 1877 the Georgia Baptist Convention replied that their delegates were only to convey the proposition to the Alabama convention and that they would not negotiate on the school's location. Georgia noted that the idea of a Georgia-Alabama school originated with the ABHMS, so "it would not be in good taste, even if we thought it expedient for us to make any other proposal to you than the one laid before us." The Alabama Convention saw through this devious, adamant stand. The convention ordered the communication printed in the minutes and agreed "that all communication with the Georgia Convention, relating to the school question was closed."

The convention then appointed a committee to write the ABHMS thanking them for their proposition; telling them that Georgia and Alabama could not agree, but that the Alabama Convention intended to build a school in Alabama, "and asking them whether they can make the State of Alabama a proposition of similar nature."[31] The ABHMS did not give a large grant to Alabama, but it did serve as a channel for funds for teachers as early as 1879.[32] In 1880 the Society adopted the school and granted it $2,000 for salaries. This grant varied, but the Society continued to aid Selma for the next fifty years.[33]

Since the ABHMS was Selma's largest single support during the nineteenth century, its philosophy of education influenced the instructors in the school. Henry L. Morehouse, the Society's secretary, summed up the Society's ideas about education in 1883.

> A few principles may be regarded as established. We are to educate the Freedmen as *men*. Any education that fails to recognize their full, absolute, equal humanity, is fatally lacking. They are to be educated, not as colored men, not as ex-slaves, but as *men*. In the opinion of your Committee, allusions (in addressing them) to their former condition should be very sparing. If it is affirmed that Jehovah often reminded the Hebrews of their former servitude, yet your Committee would suggest an inquiry as to whether such reminders would have come very gracefully from the Egyptians.[34]

While still negotiating with the Georgia Baptists, the Alabama convention, in 1876, authorized their Executive Board "to begin a theological class, at Marion, as soon as 10 or more students can be obtained." The convention chose Marion as the site for the class since the students could pursue their academic work in Marion normal school while they studied in the Baptist theological class.[35] This economical plan of church-state cooperation did not work out, however, and the proposed Baptist class at Marion never opened.

C. O. Boothe's correspondence with Northerners, as requested by the 1875 convention, had a revolutionary impact on the subsequent history of black Baptists, beginning in 1876. While the 1876 convention accomplished many things, it was the arrival of Rev. Harrison Woodsmall that caused black Baptists to call it "The Eventful Session." Woodsmall had come to Alabama from the Indiana Baptist State Convention to hold Bible Institutes for black Baptists.[36] The convention endorsed any institutes that Woodsmall might hold in Alabama for ministers, deacons, Sunday-School superintendents, and teachers and urged all the "good people of Alabama" to support him. The convention also authorized and requested Woodsmall to seek such aid from Alabama whites in conducting these institutes as "he and our brethren attending the Institutes, may deem to be necessary." The convention then cooperated with Woodsmall in setting up institutes for the coming year in Selma,

Uniontown, Marion, Demopolis, Eufaula, Lowndesboro, Greenville, and Union Springs.[37] Although most white Baptists of Alabama were opposed to the idea of a black seminary, many of them supported (and some taught in) these institutes.[38]

Woodsmall's main contribution to Alabama black Baptists was guiding and assisting them in establishing their school and serving as its first president. C. O. Boothe later recalled Woodsmall's central role in establishing the school.

> We vacillated till Brother Woodsmall appeared, so far at least as our school project was concerned. As the queen bee draws together her wandering swarm and fixes them in settled habitation and orderly toil, so did this saintly man do for the colored Baptists of Alabama. And his spirit is still [1895] with us.[39]

Woodsmall was born in Owen County, Indiana on June 9, 1841. He entered Indiana State University in 1857, but dropped out in 1861 to fight in the Civil War. After being wounded at Antietam, he received a furlough to go home where he was converted and became a Baptist. He studied law in the army and enrolled in the law school at Ann Arbor, Michigan after the war. He then practiced law in Indiana for about six years, working in Sunday Schools, temperance organizations, and politics in his spare time.

After moving to St. Paul, Minnesota to practice law, Woodsmall attended the Minnesota Baptist State Convention. This meeting so moved him that he gave up law and returned to Indiana to do voluntary work with blacks. In 1872 he entered the Southern Baptist Theological Seminary in Greenville, South Carolina. In 1873 he accepted an appointment from the Sunday-School Board of the Georgia Baptist State Convention to work with blacks. He continued this work the following year as an agent of the American Baptist Publication Society. He then became an evangelist for the American Baptist Home Mission Society and began ministers' institutes in Georgia, Alabama, Tennessee, and Kentucky until late in 1877. In January, 1878, he became the first President of the Alabama Baptist Normal and Theological School (Selma), 1878–1881.[40]

In 1877 the black Baptists decided to open their school. The Board of Trustees decided to offer literary and theological courses and to admit girls. They set aside the $1,008.44 that had been collected and the uncollected pledges to buy property for the school, and suggested that future collections support the current expenses of the school. Although the board suggested that the school be in Montgomery, the convention chose Selma. The convention then appointed W. J. Stevens and W. H. McAlpine to canvass the state for funds. Woodsmall agreed to teach beginning on January 1, 1878, for $600.[41] On the cover of the convention's minutes for 1877, the Board warned the churches "if you fail to take up the December and January collections, the school will go down, and you will be disgraced."

Selma opened as scheduled in January, 1878. When the Board met in December, 1877, they had not been able to buy or rent a building for the school.

By January 1, 1878, however, they had persuaded the St. Phillip Street Baptist Church in Selma to allow the school to meet in the church. The church donated oil for light and fuel. The board hired W. R. Pettiford to teach for $20 a month and the privilege of taking theology from Woodsmall.[42] The first term, taught by Rev. and Mrs. Woodsmall and Pettiford, lasted for five months. The average attendance was forty: eight theological students, the rest, literary.[43] For the rest of the century, normal students greatly outnumbered those in theology.

Immediately after Selma closed in May, 1878, the Board of Trustees decided to buy the old Selma Fair Grounds for $3,000. A large, four-room house, an amphitheater, and several sheds were on this thirty-six-acre plot of ground.[44] The board paid $1,000 down and agreed to pay the rest in two $1,000 payments. To raise money, the convention sent out McAlpine, Boothe, and Stevens. They usually combined their fund raising with work from either the convention or from one of the mission or publication societies as a missionary, agent, or colporteur.[45]

Woodsmall traveled and his wife wrote friends in the North for aid during the summer. They were quite successful for leaders of a beginning institution. A man in Connecticut agreed to support Professor M. W. Alston as a teacher in the school. The Baptist ladies of Indiana agreed to pay the salaries of Misses Emma Jordan of Indianapolis and Emma Heustis of Lawrenceburg. Woodsmall got $400 in books from Sheldon & Co. in New York City and persuaded the Indiana Colored Baptist Convention to appoint men in Boston, Brooklyn, Philadelphia, and Indianapolis to act as agents to collect and forward money to Selma.[46]

While these men were out raising funds, the students and friends of Selma spent the summer preparing the building and grounds for the school. Selma opened in its newly repaired building at the Fair Grounds in the fall of 1878 with 5 teachers and 112 pupils—a dramatic increase over the 2 teachers and 4 students when it first opened the preceding January.[47]

In 1879 Woodsmall organized the Baptist Missionary Society of Selma. In cooperation with the American and Foreign Bible Society of New York and Captain Morgan of Connecticut, the Selma Society sent out four ministerial students as missionaries: W. R. Pettiford, D. T. Gully, J. C. Curry, and M. W. Alston. These students visited fifteen counties in central, western and southwestern Alabama, preaching, visiting, reading the Bible, and selling and distributing "nearly one thousand Bibles and other books." They collected more than $300 for Selma. The Selma Society continued sending out these missionaries each summer to enable them to get practical ministerial training and to earn money to pay their way through school, to raise money for the school, and to evangelize and distribute religious literature and materials to Alabama blacks.

With money raised by these students and funds contributed by several churches in response to an appeal for aid, Selma built its first new building, a boarding hall costing $700 during 1879. By November, the school had paid all but $200 for the boarding hall.

During 1879, Woodsmall persuaded the ABHMS to select and support two teachers for Selma, Professor E. H. Rishel of Illinois and Mrs. L. N. Stone.[48] By 1880, Woodsmall succeeded in getting the ABHMS to adopt Selma and to pledge $2,000 for teachers' salaries. In May, 1881, Woodsmall and W. H. McAlpine, Selma's Financial Secretary, visited the annual meeting of the ABHMS and persuaded the Society to raise Selma's grant for teachers' salaries from $2,000 to $3,000. This additional income enabled Woodsmall to devote his full time to teaching theology and to turn the presidency of the school over to McAlpine.[49]

W. H. McAlpine, Selma's second President (1881–1883), was born a slave in Buckingham County, Virginia in June, 1847. In 1850 a slave trader brought McAlpine, his mother, and his brother to Alabama and sold them to Rev. Robert McAlpine of Coosa County. When this Presbyterian minister died in 1855, McAlpine became the property of his previous owner's son, Dr. John McAlpine of Talladega. McAlpine did not see his mother again until 1874. The doctor's wife had her children tutored at home since the public schools did not meet her standards. Since McAlpine was the children's nurse, he also benefited from this training in reading, grammar, geography, and arithmetic.

In 1864 McAlpine became a Christian and J. J. D. Renfroe, D.D., baptized him into the Talladega Baptist Church (white). Renfroe also instructed him in theology, ordained him, and installed him as pastor of the Mt. Canaan Baptist Church in Talladega in 1871. McAlpine remained there until 1875, when he resigned "in order to give his whole time to his school project."[50] While a pastor in and near Talladega, McAlpine organized three Colored Missionary Baptist Associations.

After emancipation, McAlpine worked briefly as a carpenter and taught school at Mardisville, near Talladega. In the winter of 1866, McAlpine entered Talladega College, where he remained until 1873. He worked before and after school to pay for his education. After he finished the high school at Talladega, the school offered him a scholarship if he would become a Congregationalist. He refused, wishing to remain a Baptist. He did, however, accept an appointment to serve as the state canvasser for the AMA while he was at Talladega.

At Talladega, McAlpine attended all the meetings of the Colored Missionary Baptist Convention, beginning in 1868. McAlpine left Talladega in 1873, "having been aroused to undertake the establishment of a similar institution for his own denomination."[51] This ambition led McAlpine to introduce the resolution to begin a school at the 1873 convention. He also led much of the fund-raising and traveled throughout the state seeking to interest people in the school. On these trips he "established societies all over the state as feeders to the school." According to his daughter, McAlpine asked Woodsmall to become Selma's first president "because the people seemed to believe in a white person more so than a Negro."[52]

During 1881, McAlpine's first year as president of Selma University, Professors Woodsmall and Rishel built homes on the campus. The school ceiled the boys' boarding hall and hired Richard Hudson of Uniontown to take charge of the hall and "to open up some labor advantages to the young men." This was the first mention of industrial work for students and nothing more was said about it.

Selma also rented a girls' boarding hall, less than one-half mile away, for $300 a year. The president and his family supervised the girls' hall and did not allow any boys to board there. The enrollment of students from twenty countries in 1880–1881 was: Theological Department, 30; Preparatory and Normal Department, 124.[53]

In 1882 Selma's officers carefully described its purpose, "to supply our churches with an educated ministry . . . to train missionaries for Africa . . . and to train workers for the Sunday-school and other departments of christian work." This course of study focused primarily on the Bible.

In a speech to the 1882 convention, Woodsmall, the theological instructor, stressed the importance and sufficiency of a good English education. He realized that many could benefit from "the higher branches, including Hebrew and Greek." If a student had only "a good English education, I desire to say as plainly as I can that with such an education men may become good strong preachers."

In addition to teaching the basic English courses and the Bible, Selma gave special attention to training preachers to prepare and deliver sermons and to read the Bible and hymns. Woodsmall and Miss Hammond urged the students "not to read sermons, but rather . . . to stand up and open their mouths and speak." Woodsmall taught his students to write out their sermons carefully, but then to

> leave the manuscript at home. . . . Of all the preachers in the world colored preachers are the last men who ought to think of reading sermons. . . . You have the emotional nature, warmth and vigor of imagination, and other qualities that real orators always possess, and that also needs the inspiration of an audience to arouse. You also have voices suited to sway men, when not hampered, as in reading.

Woodsmall also sought to teach his ministerial pupils to pray, to be good organizers and leaders, to "win souls to Christ, and to be true, strong, Christian men."

Selma also offered a normal course for teachers, which included training in spelling, reading, writing, arithmetic, geography, grammar and composition, history, vocal and instrumental music, and the theory and practice of teaching. Since the school stressed Christian education, the Bible was a primary text in the normal and theological courses.

In 1882 Selma received $3,350 from the ABHMS toward paying the salaries of five teachers. The black Baptist convention supplemented one teacher's salary, paid his wife $176, and paid a $500 salary to McAlpine, the president. Selma also built another building, twenty-five by forty-eight feet, to house the school's printing press and theological classroom. The school bought a printing press to print the denomination's paper, *The Baptist Pioneer*, and its other literature. The press enabled Selma to give the students training in printing and to raise money by doing job printing.[54]

In 1883 Woodsmall,[55] McAlpine, and Miss Hammonds all resigned. When Woodsmall left, Selma had to pay him for the house he had built on the campus; but, by adding a dining room and other rooms, the school could use the building for the girls' boarding hall and save $300 a year rent. Selma also bought several fruit trees for income and to provide industrial training for the students. The board of trustees set forth an ambitious plan for an industrial department. This did not, however, show a commitment to industrial training, but, rather, the school's need for money. "If we had the Industrial Department of our school now in operation, we could get some of the State [Slater?] Fund to help the School."[56]

In 1883 Selma reinstated its primary department (dropped in 1879) because many Baptists preferred to send their children to a regular Baptist school rather "than to send them to the poor schools in the country where they are so much exposed in winter in open houses, and where they have such poor school-room advantages." The trustees required this department to be self-supporting.[57]

The board of trustees hired Edward MacKnight Brawley, A.M., D.D., to replace Woodsmall (theology) and McAlpine (president)[58] in 1883. Brawley, Selma's third president (1883–1886), was born to free parents in Charleston, South Carolina on March 18, 1851. In 1861 his parents sent him to grammar and high school in Philadelphia, Pennsylvania. After the Civil War, he became an apprentice shoemaker in Charleston.

After briefly attending Howard University during 1870, he transferred in 1871 to the college at Lewisburg, Pennsylvania (now Bucknell). With the aid of friends, he worked his way through college "by giving voice lessons and by preaching during vacations." He received his B.A. in 1875 and his M.A. in 1878. After joining the local Baptist church, he received his license to preach in his second year at Lewisburg. During college, he studied theology, so a council of the school's professors ordained him the day after his graduation. In 1885 the State University of Louisville, Kentucky awarded him the D.D. degree.

From 1875 to 1883, Brawley served as the American Baptist Publication Society's State Missionary in South Carolina. Although many conservative blacks initially opposed him, by 1876 Brawley had succeeded in persuading the leaders of the associations and Sunday Schools to meet in Sumter to form the Colored Baptist Educational, Missionary, and Sunday School Convention.

As the convention's corresponding secretary and financial agent, Brawley helped guide its work until he came to Alabama.[59]

While Brawley was at Selma (1883–1886), he stressed the importance of higher education more than had his predecessors. In 1885, he addressed the convention.

> When you went to Montgomery and asked for a charter for a Normal and Theological school, despite the difference of political opinion, they gave us a University charter, and said, go and attain the very highest education that can be had. The charter was highly received and the advice given highly appreciated. And it is the aim of the Institute to furnish the State with men of classical education. I have no patience with a man who says that the low course will do; you have not the mental capacity to grasp the high education. For we have the brain, tact and thrift to acquire the classics. We can not afford to stop with the good English education, but we must go on and attain the highest that can be had.

Perhaps through Brawley's influence, this 1885 convention for the first time urged the pastors to use their influence to get the best possible teachers in their public schools, "to do all in their power to do and encourage general education," and to try to extend the public schools in their communities by two or three months.[60]

Brawley's emphasis on quality higher education had positive results. In 1884 Selma graduated its first class of students. This class of eleven included Rev. R. T. Pollard (a future President of Selma), his wife (later President of the Baptist Women's State Convention, teacher at Selma, missionary, and Jeanes teacher), and R. B. Hudson (later President of the State Teachers Association). Brawley also led in getting a new charter for the school in 1885, changing its name from the Alabama Baptist Normal and Theological School (1881) to Selma University.[61]

Unfortunately, some Baptist leaders did not approve of this new emphasis. "The founders of the work were not sufficiently willing to confer with each other." Also, either Brawley or his trustees were not very good business managers, or the disagreement over the kind of education led to a decrease in contributions. A disagreement over the location of the school also arose. During Brawley's administration the debt of the school rose from $2,000 to over $6,000.[62]

In 1886 Brawley resigned and Rev. Charles L. Purce became Selma University's President (1886–1893). Purce studied at Richmond Institute under Dr. Corey and was the "principal assistant" at Selma before becoming president.[63]

In the 1886 convention, dissatisfaction with the location of the school came to a head. Many felt that other cities were more healthful, more convenient, closer to a large population which could better support the school, and less likely to have the school property depreciate. As a result the convention appointed a committee—composed of an equal number of members (3) from Selma, Montgomery, and Birmingham (three cities desiring the school)—to conduct a campaign to determine the location of the school. The location would be determined by a "silver ticket," that is, each city would raise as much money as it could for the school. The school would then be located in the city which cast the most votes (each dollar raised counted as one vote). Many people, including the editor of the *Baptist Leader*, favored Marion as the site for the school, but it was not represented on the committee.

"The contest was heated, and here and there rather ugly." As a result, the 1887 convention was a "stormy time, and no small amount of bitter feeling [was stirred up]." When the convention counted the "ballots," Selma won easily, 873 to 83 for Montgomery. The proponents of Montgomery, McAlpine and others, did not give up, and moved that the competition be extended for another year, but the presiding officer ruled the motion out of order. W. B. Paterson, President of the State Normal School at Montgomery, "seeking to bring about reconciliation made some very pointed remarks."[64]

President Purce announced in 1887 that his "chief aim was to keep within the income." He spent most of his administration trying to reduce the school's debt. During 1887–1888, the trustees were able to reduce Selma's debt from "between seven and eight thousand dollars" to $2,600. They did this by settling many claims "in one way or another" and by selling six acres of the school's land.[65]

Although the economy measures forced on Purce by the debt kept him from enlarging Selma as he wished to do, he still had a successful presidency. In 1890 Selma reached its peak total annual enrollment in the nineteenth century, 515 students, and also graduated its first classical, college class by awarding four A.B.'s. It also awarded one B.S. (for completing the scientific course) degree, one B.D. (for completing the full, theological course, including Greek and Hebrew) degree, eleven normal degrees, and twelve high grammar certificates. Two of the college graduates went directly to medical school.[66]

Black Baptists added to Selma's physical plant under Purce, despite the debt. The Women's Baptist State Convention began raising money to build a girls' dormitory in 1888 under the leadership of Miss Susie Stone, for whom the hall was later named. The ABHMS pledged $2,000 for this building in 1888. With these funds, the convention laid Stone Hall's cornerstone in 1889 and completed the building's central part in 1890. The building cost $8,000. The ABHMS gave $2,600 of this amount; the black Baptist men and women of Alabama raised the rest. Despite the pleas of the president and board of trustees, the convention did not raise enough money to finish the building until 1898.

Purce was more successful on completing smaller projects—a model schoolhouse, a two-room washhouse, a better water system, and (with the aid of the students) two new stories on Stone Hall's south wing. Even more satisfying was the 1891 convention's treasurer's report that "for the first time since you owned this school property . . . there are no mortgages, Builders'

Lien or any other kind of lien on your school grounds and school property at Selma."[67]

Purce was interested in providing some training for those who could not attend Selma. In 1889 he proposed a three-year home study course for ministers. Purce proposed to give examinations for each year's work at the State Convention and to award those who passed a certificate. Anyone who completed the entire course could exchange his certificates for a diploma "with the seals of the Convention and Selma University attached."[68] Woodsmall had proposed a similar, but less comprehensive, course of study to be administered by Brawley. Both schemes evidently failed, for there was no further mention of either after they were introduced.

At the 1892 convention, "there were signs of a rising stormcloud, which, it was feared, foretold approaching evil; and perhaps a clogging of our educational and missionary operations would then soon come." Serious disagreements within the denomination, especially in regard to the university, led in 1893, to the resignation of Purce as Selma's President, and, as a result, the resignations of McAlpine and Pettiford from Selma's Board of Trustees. "A division of the denomination was threatened in consequence of the presidential changes."[69]

A rising feeling among many Baptists that Selma was neglecting its duty to train preachers was at the root of the controversy. This feeling began to be manifest in increasing criticism of the school after 1890. In 1892 Purce used his report to the convention to try to stem this tide of discontent. He stressed that the school had always emphasized its work with preachers as well as with teachers; but he also stressed that preachers needed sound literary as well as theological training. Institutes and ministers' classes, where preachers could learn the basic doctrines of the Bible and church polity, were certainly needed, but they were not sufficient. In addition to such training,

> if you really want to make *men* of our preachers, . . . carry them through a good elementary English course, if no more, then put them into a good English Bible course, then when they get away from their teacher, they can study and think independently of the teacher. . . . They will be men that cannot easily be turned down. If you find young men apt to study Greek and Hebrew, put such into the full theological course with Greek and Hebrew. . . . It is much better for a young man if he has only four or five years to spend in school, to spend those years in taking a library [literary?] course than to attempt to take a theological course aside from the literary studies, for the literary work is *necessary* for a foundation.

Purce vigorously denied that he opposed theological work. His concern was that the people should have the real substance instead of being led off by a shadow. "Give the preachers an education, give them a foundation—Let us have an educated ministry—*Mere Bible knowledge will not do.*" Citing the example of Newton Theological Seminary near Boston, Purce urged the convention not to be discouraged by a small enrollment in the Theological Department.

Purce listed convention leaders like McAlpine, Boothe, Pettiford, Dinkins, Pollard, and stressed that they could never have made their contributions without a literary education.

> No, they would be like a good many brethren to-day in the State who have been taught the doctrines of the Bible and Church Polity, committed a few hymns; and yet they cannot read or write. Even many who can read and write cannot interpret what they read. Now, let us give the instruction that will do that. We must recognize fundamental principles in any system of education. Our preachers as well as our people must have more education. They must understand how to read with the understanding as well as by the letter. In fact, they must have the three R's. '*Reading, Riting, Rithmetic.*'

Purce closed by stressing that he was not "opposed to Theological instruction."[70] Purce's remarks must have fanned instead of quenched the flames of discord, for the opposition to his policies soon forced him,[71] along with McAlpine and Pettiford (two of the school's founders and strongest supporters) to resign their positions as president and members of the board of trustees, respectively.[72]

The 1893 convention showed the intensity of feeling about this subject when it passed a resolution saying that Selma's charter did "not embody fully and clearly the original intention of the institution." The convention then instructed

> the Board of Incorporators and the Board of Trustees . . . to take such legal and other steps jointly and severally as may be necessary to secure from the Legislature of the State of Alabama at its next session a new charter for Selma University, which shall place the Institution in the organic relation to this Convention intended by its founders, and which shall also make full and definite provisions for the proper administration of all the internal and other affairs of the University.[73]

In 1895 the legislature granted this request and issued Selma a new charter, changing Selma University to the Alabama Baptist Colored University.[74] The new constitution provided that the board of trustees had to be nominated and elected during the annual conventions.[75]

It was strange that black Baptists should turn from academic studies to theology so emphatically at this time, the early 1890's. Even the white Presbyterians began their trend toward academic studies in 1893. In a speech in Nashville, Tennessee in 1890, Booker T. Washington had attacked the Alabama black Baptists by saying that they were "numerous, but not fifteen are qualified mentally or morally to preach the gospel." The Baptists passed a resolution denouncing this charge,[76] but the statement evidently did not spur the Baptists to improve their academic training. Nor did the 1891 Alabama law which permitted flagrant discrimination in distributing the school fund lead the Baptists to emphasize education. It was also strange that the black Baptists would repudiate Purce, who had reduced the school's debt, built up the enrollment, served longer than any other president, and greatly improved the school's physical plant.

The graduation of the first college class in 1890 might have stirred up latent anti-intellectualism among black Baptists. The tightening noose of segregation and discrimination might have choked some of the blacks' aspirations and hopes causing them to seek release through a more pietistic religion.

When Purce resigned in 1893, the board of trustees selected Charles Spencer Dinkins as his successor. Dinkins, Selma's fifth president (1893–1901), was born September 15, 1856, near Canton, Mississippi. He never knew his father. His mother died when he was thirteen. In 1865 his mother bought him a blue back speller and taught him the alphabet, which he claimed he learned in one night. Mr. and Miss Highgate and Hon. J. J. Spellman also taught Dinkins while he was a child. Dinkins later said that he "saw something of the horrors of slavery, which I can never forget."

Rev. Jordan Williams converted Dinkins in 1867 and baptized him into the Mount Zion Church in Canton in 1868. Williams saw Dinkins' aptitude for study and persuaded the church to send Dinkins to school. On January 28, 1870, Dinkins left for Nashville, Tennessee, to enroll in the classical course at Roger Williams University. He taught each summer to help pay his way through school. In 1877 he graduated as valedictorian of his class. In 1878 he returned to take a postgraduate course and joined the faculty. In late 1878 he left Nashville to enroll in Newton Theological Seminary, near Boston, Massachusetts. He graduated in 1881.[77]

Rev. C. O. Boothe, who worked with Dinkins, felt that he had one fault, an "*exceeding tenderness of conscience*, whereby one may be so entirely possessed by present views of law and duty as to forget that new light and other views may modify appearances."[78]

In his first speech to the black Baptist convention as Selma's president, Dinkins said he was "seeking to do more in the theological department than ever." Selma had only had a part-time theological instructor for the past few years, but Dinkins wanted at least two full-time men in the theological department.

Even E. M. Brawley, a long-time advocate of higher education, told the 1894 convention that he esteemed "mental culture, [but] the man who has only a smattering of Bible knowledge is not fit to shove the work on."

During Dinkins' first year as president, 1893–1894, Selma's nine teachers taught 184 students. Of these students, forty-four were preparing to teach; nineteen, to preach. Only six students graduated that year. Excluding the model school, Selma received $3,683.33 during 1893–1894.[79]

Dinkins' report to the 1895 convention made it clear that Booker T. Washington's speech that fall did not represent Selma's educational philosophy. Selma would continue to stress "mental and religious training," but it would "devote some time to manual training as our means, time and facilities will allow." Dinkins emphasized that he would not "detract from the mental for manual training, *knowing that at this time we are more in need of the former than of the latter.*" Since Selma "was founded for and dedicated to the cause of religious and mental development, other things must be subsidiary to that." Selma did give industrial training to 82 of its 226 pupils that year, but it never made industrial training its basic emphasis as did Tuskegee.[80]

During Dinkins' presidency of Selma (1893–1901), several serious problems arose. A continuous controversy over the denomination's paper came to a head in 1896 when Rev. J. H. Eason, editor of the *Baptist Leader*, refused to publish Selma's *Student Voice*. During a heated debate in the 1897 convention, Dinkins offered to drop his paper if Eason would publish school matters in his. Eason agreed and as these two men "shook hands amid the great applause of the audience," the controversy ended.[81]

Although Dinkins wanted to strengthen Selma's Theological Department, he could get few pastors to support it financially. Instead of the two instructors Dinkins desired, the department had no instructor one year and only a part-time instructor, C. O. Boothe, the other years. In each president's report Dinkins sought unsuccessfully to stir the pastors to fulfill their responsibility to the department.[82]

Around 1890, the convention began trying to develop a comprehensive plan for academies to prepare students for Selma. In 1889, the convention endorsed the Marion Baptist Academy (taught by Dinkins, 1889–1891) as a preparatory school for Selma University.[83] In 1896 the convention memorialized the legislature to exempt from taxation Selma University; the North Alabama Baptist Academy, Courtland; the Normal and Industrial School, Anniston; and the Eufaula and Marion Baptist Academies. By 1898, there were also Baptist academies in Demopolis, Mt. Pilgrim, and Opelika. The Anniston Baptist Academy, conducted by Rev. A. A. Battle had a school plant worth $7,000. These academies were the schools of their respective associations. Each school sent a representative to the 1898 convention seeking recognition and support.

W. R. Pettiford spoke against this splintering of funds for education among the associations to the detriment of the school at Selma. Rev. R. T. Pollard, a Selma graduate who was to become its president in 1902, urged a comprehensive plan for establishing three or four academies in various parts of the state. These schools would cooperate with Selma, sending their graduates there for higher training. The convention finally decided to request the principals of all the Baptist academies to meet with President Dinkins during the ensuing year. The meeting was inconclusive, for in 1899 Dinkins issued a plea for unity and cooperation as a part of his presidential report.[84] The Baptists were too individualistic, and the local principals too ambitious, for a carefully planned educational system to work. The academies continued to grow, to spread, and to compete with Selma University for students and for funds.[85]

In the late 1890's, a movement developed in Alabama to split black Baptists into two conventions. Many black Baptists felt that the regular convention slighted country churches and did not sufficiently cooperate with the National Baptist Convention.[86] This controversy was not directly related to Selma University, but these black Baptists' opposition to the convention diverted funds which would have gone to Selma.

Despite these organizational problems, Selma made several important strides forward in the closing years of the nineteenth century. In 1895, for the first time, the convention contributed more to Selma than did the ABHMS ($1,723.23, and $1,500.00, respectively), in spite of the depression then limiting incomes throughout the United States.[87] In 1897, at Dinkins' earnest request, the board of trustees began paying teachers for twelve months. This larger income enabled teachers to devote their full time to teaching during the school term. They then worked during the summer raising money for Selma. This new plan freed Dinkins from his duties as Selma's financial agent, improved the teaching, and resulted in a larger income for the school.

On May 13, 1898, Selma celebrated the removal of its "long-standing and burdensome debt" with a speech by W. H. McAlpine. Dinkins then led the school in 1898–1899 in raising the record amount of $7,535.68. In 1899 Selma finally finished the north and south wings of Susie Stone Hall, begun in 1889. Dinkins next launched a fund-raising campaign for a new chapel. Selma had raised $2,500 when Dinkins died in the middle of September, 1901.[88]

From 2 teachers and 4 students meeting in the St. Phillips Street Baptist Church in 1878, Selma had grown to 12 teachers and 279 students in 1899. In 1899, as in previous years, most of the students in the higher courses were preparing to teach—seventy-nine—as compared to thirty-three preparing to preach. Selma had only fifty-eight students in its industrial department.[89] By 1901, Selma had graduated 176 students from its normal, theological, and college classes. The 1901 graduating class, sixteen normal and one college, was one of the largest in the school's history.[90]

While the leaders of Alabama's largest black denomination, the Colored Missionary Baptist Convention of Alabama, differed frequently and often bitterly on a wide range of subjects, none of their leaders ever overlooked the importance of a solid, English education. Even Woodsmall and Dinkins, who primarily emphasized theological training, insisted on a thorough literary course for ministers. Neither the "Atlanta Compromise" speech by the nominal Baptist, Booker T. Washington, nor its subsequent publicity caused the black Baptists to alter their course. Through Selma University, black Baptists in Alabama showed that they understood the importance and necessity of having liberally educated leaders in their schools and churches. That the black Baptists only imperfectly realized their ideal should not obscure the tenacity and perseverence with which they clung to it.

10

THE AMERICAN MISSIONARY ASSOCIATION'S BLACK SCHOOLS IN ALABAMA

Black secondary and normal schools in Alabama, whether public or private, showed a great variety in their origins, location, leadership, and development. Despite this diversity, none of Alabama's black secondary schools or colleges followed Booker T. Washington's lead in sacrificing academic and theological education for industrial-vocational training as the means of escaping from the web of subordination. The American Missionary Association (AMA) went one step further in undermining Washington's educational theory and racial strategy by providing both industrial and rigorous normal, theological, college preparatory, and liberal, college education in its schools in Alabama.

The AMA, the most influential Northern missionary organization in Alabama, began its work among freedmen in the South when Rev. Lewis C. Lockwood arrived at Fort Monroe, Virginia on September 3, 1861. Lockwood came to the South because of his "missionary impulse to save the soul of the black people. . . . That a school was begun was largely accidental." The local blacks, led by Mrs. Mary Peake, a free black, began a school on September 17, 1861. The AMA, seeing the blacks' desire and need for education, decided to support this school and began establishing other black schools throughout the South soon after the Union armies captured various sections. Indeed, "for a long time even the evangelical mission of the Association was lost in the universal zeal favoring the elevation of the freedmen through education."[1]

During the Civil War, the AMA received support from the Wesleyan Methodists and the Free Will Baptists. Immediately after the war, at least twelve other denominations expressed support for the AMA. The National Council of Congregational Churches provided the main support when it adopted a resolution in 1865 pledging $250,000 to the AMA. Since the Congregational

Church provided most of the AMA's money and Congregational ministers were its most active members, other denominations began establishing their own missionary boards in the late 1860 s.[2] Although the AMA became increasingly identified with Congregationalists, it continued to proclaim that it was nonsectarian. This stance did much to secure the cooperation of the Freedmen's Bureau.

The AMA worked closely with the Freedmen's Bureau throughout its existence. George Whipple, Senior Corresponding Secretary of the AMA, carefully cultivated the friendship of General Oliver Otis Howard, Head of the Freedmen's Bureau. As a result, the Bureau and the AMA carried on regular and frequent correspondence, especially about their personnel, which sometimes overlapped.[3]

In 1866, George Whipple took over the leadership of the AMA after the resignation of Lewis Tappan, Secretary since 1846. Whipple's administration, 1866–1876, spanned "the most important decade in the history of the Association." In addition to its home office in New York, in February, 1866, the AMA established offices in Boston, Cincinnati, and Chicago to collect funds from their respective areas. Erastus Milo Cravath, head of the Cincinnati office, was in charge of directing the work in most of Alabama.[4]

During Whipple's administration, the AMA often went into debt if necessary to secure "promising school properties in the South." These debts were actually good, long-term investments since land was very cheap in the South after the Civil War and the Freedmen's Bureau agreed to match AMA funds for buying school property and then to build schools on the property. The Bureau often rented these buildings from the AMA to provide it with additional funds for its work with freedmen. This practice, although legal since the AMA partially owned the land, led to many charges of corruption.

Several factors in the 1870's combined to force the AMA to retrench on its school program. The end of the Freedmen's Bureau cut off rent and other funds. The 1871 Chicago fire severely limited funds from the Northwest and the Panic of 1873 cut contributions.

The retrenchment forced by these factors had one beneficial effect on the AMA's educational program. Faced with growing debts and diminishing income in the 1870's, the AMA reexamined its entire educational philosophy and decided that the most efficient and economical way of educating the freedmen was to abandon most of the common schools (taught primarily by Northern whites) and to develop normal schools to train black teachers. These debts of the early 1870's also had a deleterious effect on the AMA's program by causing it to become more conservative to try to avoid going into debt in the 1880's.[5] Unlike most denominational aid societies, the AMA saw its role as that of a pioneer. Whenever a local school board agreed to assume responsibility for a black common school, the AMA turned the school over to the local board. This policy did not apply to normal and higher schools because the facilities for such schools were so poorly developed in the South.

Local blacks usually strenuously opposed these transfers. They foresaw a great loss to their children if local whites controlled the school. Many blacks preferred "the sympathizing and generally superior instruction of the mission school to the lax officialism and neglect of the public authorities." They pled with the AMA to continue to furnish primary schools because "otherwise their children will get poor teaching in unsanitary buildings—often on immoral streets."[6] As a result, blacks usually raised a "great protest" whenever a transfer took place. The last AMA commencement was always "funereal." Many blacks believed that the departure of the AMA meant the end of the possibility of quality education for their children.

One AMA secretary wrote that his "most painful experiences have been connected with such occasions." He believed that "the way the mission school operated" made the difference between AMA schools and the typical public schools which replaced them. The AMA began schools "as an act of love" and continued them

> on the basis of the actual human oneness of the workers with their pupils and the parents. In the process, the latter came to believe that there were white people who would treat them as equals. This was a priceless heritage. The public school authorities were accepting responsibility as a duty, almost as a necessary evil. It was the difference between a wanted and an unwanted baby.

Despite all the anguish giving up the schools caused black parents and its workers, the AMA (partly from economic necessity) continued this policy of turning black common schools over to local, white, Southern school boards in an attempt to secure free education for all children.[7]

The dynamic, pioneering days of the AMA ended when Whipple died in 1876, "for Michael Strieby proved too hesitant a leader to push boldly into new fields with consistency." Under Strieby the AMA liquidated its debts and guaranteed its fiscal stability by obtaining a million dollar gift from Daniel Hand, but Strieby's organization stood "in marked contrast to the dynamic crusading Association of the days of Tappan and Whipple."[8] Thus the shift from Whipple to Strieby in 1876 had much the same meaning for the AMA as the national election of 1876 and the Compromise of 1877 had for the nation—the beginning of accommodation with the South. Under Whipple the AMA carried forward the spirit of its abolitionist founders by working primarily with freedmen. Under Strieby it became briefly involved with an African Mission and in work with Indians, Chinese, and Southern whites.[9]

Equally important in shifting the AMA's orientation was Strieby's detestation of controversy which caused him to lead the Association "far toward accommodating itself to the sentiment of the South, thus diverting the original intention of the founders of the Association." After 1876 its policies "gradually changed in favor of a stand more in keeping with both the attitudes of the South and the desire for peace and prosperity of the dominant orthodox groups of the North." The Association's racial policy was still far more advanced than that of contemporary American society, but the AMA had retreated considerably from its outspoken championing of black rights in the 1860's. Several radicals remained active, but "when the mild lip service given to the doctrine of egalitarianism" in the 1880's is compared to "the aggressive crusade in favor of biracial education which characterized the attitude of the Association just after the war, the term 'compromise' takes on meaning."[10]

This compromise or accommodation with the South went through two phases under Strieby. Changing leadership, financial crisis, and national conditions caused the AMA to hesitate "at dead center" from 1877 through the early 1880's. While paying off the old debts the leaders decided to follow conservative policies to avoid future debts. When the AMA began to expand its operations in the South in the late 1880's, it moved slowly along the line of least resistance by implicitly accepting *de facto* segregation. It even appealed for funds to make its schools as good as white schools. But it never embraced the caste system by making its schools racially exclusive as a matter of policy nor did it accept the South's plan of "black education," i.e., vocational and inferior training.

Despite all these compromises, many AMA workers continued to espouse the organization's original, radical humanitarian ideals. Community pressures kept white children (except the children of white faculty members) out of the schools, but the Association's basic policy statements always emphasized that race was not a factor in admission. The AMA seldom aggressively demanded integration after 1880, but "it did quietly witness against caste in America, in matters of basic policy and general interest."[11] Living among the people they taught, the missionaries and their families (at work, play, or worship) gave daily witness to their belief in the basic equality and essential human dignity of blacks. These teachers spurned the Southern shibboleth of "the evils of social equality."

The AMA did not attack economic class distinctions directly, but it consistently opposed the special privilege of caste which

> excludes people from common rights and privileges . . . degrades people on the ground of race or color . . . denies equal rights, civil, political, and religious. It is seen at its worst forms when it has the consent of Christian gatherings, and when it appears in religious bodies. . . . Those who wear his name . . . decline his spirit when they proclaim the fatherhood of God and refuse the brotherhood of man. In his name the Association has always protested—and, please God, always will protest—against imposing on a race the weight of an impassable caste, so that an established ruling class shall direct a permanent serving class, or that Christians of one race shall deny fellowship to that [*sic*] of another.[12]

Despite all their failings and compromises, the AMA's schools continued to oppose caste and to witness to the essential equality and humanity of blacks by offering the same range of educational opportunities available in white schools. Even after Reconstruction the AMA continued to support one purely primary school, Trinity School in Athens. The Association showed its agreement with Booker T. Washington that primary-industrial schools were sometimes appropriate by partially supporting two such schools: Cotton Valley School at Fort Davis, and Kowaliga Academic and Industrial Institute at Kowaliga. It also offered some industrial training along with normal classes at three schools: Burrell School in Selma, Lincoln School in Marion, and Emerson Institute in Mobile.

Indeed, industrial education in Afro-American schools did not originate with Booker T. Washington at Tuskegee, J. L. M. Curry of the Peabody Fund, Atticus G. Haygood of the Slater Fund,[13] or even with Samuel C. Armstrong at Hampton. An army chaplain had established industrial education as a program for slaves who fled to Union lines during the Civil War. One of the earliest programs of black industrial education, if not the first, began in 1867 at the AMA's Talladega College in Talladega.

But Talladega and the AMA in general (excepting Hampton Institute, which dissociated itself from the Association in 1885) realized that blacks needed rigorous academic education as well as industrial training. In 1887 Talladega's President, Henry Swift DeForest, explained that the

> "higher range of studies" was necessary . . . "to supplant self-conceit with self-reliance." He noted that ignorant people were inflated by the mere rudiments of knowledge, but "broad scholarship gives modesty." The Negro should have as good an education as his capabilities entitled him to, and experience had shown that he could learn anything a white man could.[14]

This conviction led DeForest and George Whitfield Andrews to establish classical, theological, and full collegiate education at Talladega, along with industrial training. Under the leadership of DeForest and Andrews, Talladega College supplied for Alabama's AMA schools what all other black, public and private schools in the state lacked, the top or capstone of the educational system—the liberal arts college.[15] By offering collegiate education along with industrial training Talladega showed that the true issue in black education in Alabama was not academic versus industrial education, but whether or not any rigorous, college level, liberal arts education should be offered by black colleges. Since this was exactly the kind of education Alabama offered its presumed future leaders, its white university students, Washington's most severe failure at Tuskegee was his refusal to take the responsibility for providing the future black leaders with the same kind of education and training for leadership. Thus, the very comprehensive organization of the AMA's schools in Alabama—primary, industrial, normal, and collegiate—along with the example of inter-racial brotherhood supplied by white men and women living and working among blacks and the equalitarian teachings of the schools, all testified to the Association's rejection of caste and provided another strategy for escaping the web of subordination.

11

PRIMARY, INDUSTRIAL, AND NORMAL SCHOOLS

The base of the AMA's black educational system in Alabama after Reconstruction was the primary school, Trinity School, in Athens.[1] Although Trinity (the Association's only school in Alabama with a theological name) opened in May, 1865, under the auspices of the Western Freedmen's Aid Commission, most of the school's development came under the AMA. Trinity's first teachers were the wife of the chaplain of a Wisconsin regiment then stationed in Athens, a soldier of the regiment, and Miss Mary Frances Wells, an army nurse and graduate of Mount Holyoke College.[2]

Trinity began in a little old brick church, which Union troops had used as a barracks. The Union troops still in Athens protected the three teachers as they instructed their three hundred pupils, who were "hungry and thirsty, half-naked, but 'so happy'" to get an education. Five hundred black pupils attended Trinity's first three terms. They were "all so eager to learn" that the teachers often worked "from eight in the morning till six or seven in the evening." Then, after a quick meal, they taught another class later in the evening. After establishing a Sunday school, the teachers organized a church and a missionary society.[3]

Soon the school moved from the church to an old hotel, a "gaunt old house with wide-open cracks, through which pea-shooters and pop-guns were often introduced to the great discomfort of both teachers and pupils." There Miss Wells and her two assistants taught day and night classes. Miss Wells was a "frail, alert little woman." Her pupils included a "man in the linen ulster," seven brothers who came to school one at a time since they "had but one pair of presentable trousers between them," old ladies wearing homespun, and young girls in "cast-off finery." The students had real problems learning to read "with any odd leaf for a book and a candle end between two for a light." But pupils poured in, "day in, night out, and many of them learned to read [the Bible] and received enough [education] to be willing to go through fire and water, if only their children could get all which could be given them."

Finally, the old building became unsafe and could no longer be repaired. The AMA planned to close Trinity, but the people could not bear the thought. "It was freedom, life, heaven to them; few could ever hope to go away from home to study, the townspeople would never teach them, blackness of darkness would be upon them, the more dense for the ray of light they had enjoyed."[4]

Some whites of Athens, however, were "horrified at the prospect of having Negroes educated" and severely tested the courage and devotion of Miss Wells and her assistants. These whites indulged in "vulgar and sometimes brutal demonstrations of hostilities." On one occasion, the KKK "lined up around her school, fired volleys of shots and beans through her windows on either side of the chair in which she was sitting. After repeated threats, the school was burned over her head." The Association became concerned for her safety and urged Miss Wells to leave Athens, but the brave lady refused to do so. Instead, she and her assistants "prayed, and stayed and taught."[5]

By 1867 Trinity received aid only from the AMA and the Western Freedmen's Aid Commission. Miss Wells taught the highest class, Grade D (Fifth Reader, Grammar, Latin and Higher Branches). Miss M. C. Sturges taught Grade C (Fourth Reader, Geography, and Arithmetic). Miss S. Sturges, her sister, taught Grade B (Second and Third Reader and Arithmetic). Miss Adelle DuBois taught Grade A (Alphabet and First Reader). The students who were learning the alphabet when Miss Wells came to Athens in 1865 had advanced to the highest classes by February, 1867. Miss Wells felt that the pupils showed "a steady enthusiasm and a progress commensurate with the zeal." She believed her faculty to be "all faithful and efficient workers" who did "great good, not only in the School, but among the Freed people outside the School." All teachers also helped in the night school, which was "quite large."

Miss Wells wrote the AMA in 1867 seeking additional funds for a building. Although the blacks badly needed a church and a schoolhouse, they were too poor to build either. In that year the four ladies lived and conducted their school in "a dilapidated Hotel," which the Freedmen's Bureau had temporarily lent them. After mentioning these quarters, Miss Wells remarked, "we have our treasure here in 'an earthen vessel' most emphatically."[6]

When fire destroyed Trinity's building, the black students "of all ages and grades had nowhere else to go." The $5,000 needed for a new school seemed prohibitive. With the AMA making up the difference, the blacks of Athens "shared their meagre living, underwrote $2,000 and promised their labor." By buying a building with ample adjacent grounds, the Association provided for a long life for Trinity after 1869. In 1881 Trinity added Trinity Hall at a cost of $10,000, one-fifth of which the students and former students paid in working to build the new brick building. The students, under the direction of Miss Wells, established a brickyard and made many of the bricks that went into Trinity Hall.[7]

In 1872 Miss Wells organized a model school at Trinity to help train teachers. By October, 1890 Trinity could offer boarding facilities for the students. Graduates and students of Trinity had attended Fisk University or had become teachers, preachers, doctors, or merchants by 1891.[8]

Miss Wells left Trinity School in 1892 bearing "with her the gratitude of hundreds who owe their elevation and Christian life to her personal instruction and character." In 1893 Miss Katherine S. Dalton of Fremont, Ohio, became principal and reported the largest enrollment up to that time, 201, under six teachers. Miss Ada Louise Wilcox of Monroe, Michigan, became principal in 1896 and remained through 1901. Although the average attendance was around 150, the attendance in 1893 reached 201; in 1899, 230; and in 1900, 207. In 1901 Miss Wilcox had five assistants to help with 161 students.[9]

Even after the turn of the century, life was not easy for the students at Trinity. The school was so crowded that it had to use the parlor and hall for recitation rooms. Students did not come just for fun, nor because it was "a good place [to stay warm] in winter." They were determined to get an education, even if it meant making sacrifices. For example, two country boys slept "for months, rolled up in quilts on the floor with their feet in a box of sawdust to keep them warm." Others got up early every morning to wash and iron "until school time, and from the time school closes until late at night" to get "a few hours of instruction each day." In addition to doing "chores before and after school" other students would walk three or four miles a day to school, "if only 'paw' will give them the school hours."[10] These and other stories of sacrifices students made to attend all the black schools were eloquent testimonials to the deep and abiding desire many black students had for an education.

While the AMA had sponsored Trinity almost from its beginning, the Association began to support Cotton Valley School at Fort Davis and Kowaliga Academic and Industrial Institute at Kowaliga after these schools had been in operation for some time. Cotton Valley and Kowaliga were the most rural and vocational schools the AMA supported in nineteenth century Alabama.

Although the AMA never endorsed vocational training as the only or most important education that blacks needed, it showed that it agreed with Booker T. Washington that there was a place for vocational, primary schools by consenting to support a school which Washington was primarily responsible for establishing, Cotton Valley School at Fort Davis. When Washington appealed to Northern religious groups for aid in establishing a black school on a rural plantation in the Alabama Black Belt, the Women's Home Missionary Association (WHMA), especially the Massachusetts and Rhode Island branches, responded by establishing the Cotton Valley School in 1884.

The first teacher, Miss Lilla V. Davis, a graduate of the Boston High School, began the school in a black church and meeting house, "a wretched log building" with openings only for doors and windows. Miss Davis found families "removed from any contacts with the outside world." She began by teaching more by personal contact in the homes of her pupils than from books. When Miss Davis first arrived, she boarded with "Aunt Eliza Boyd," the "parent of a large share of the community," in a small log cabin. A curtain separated Miss Davis' section of the cabin from Mrs. Boyd and her nine boys.[11]

Cotton Valley School was the local blacks' first opportunity for an education. Although visitors found the local blacks to be "illiterate . . . [and] desperately poor and exploited," all commented on their eagerness to learn. One old lady told a visitor that she intended to hang around the teachers like Grant hung around Richmond because she had found that she was not too old to learn. The people were so poor that the WHMA at first made Cotton Valley an exception to its rule that all attending its schools had to pay some tuition. This proved to be a mistake, so the WHMA began charging ten cents a month after the first year, which they later raised to one dollar.[12]

Cotton Valley School prospered. By 1896 it moved from the old log church into a three-room schoolhouse on a few acres of land owned by the school. The students of nearby Fessenden Academy, under the direction of their manual arts teacher, Wesley E. Walthal, built the new schoolhouse and the teachers' cottage.[13]

The teachers' home became "the pride of the Valley as its only two-story building." But even this building was crowded when guests arrived. Gathering around the dining-room table required "evolutions of military precision," and, once seated, no one could leave until the others moved. One teacher, whose father had been a mechanic, built the sideboard in the house. She also showed some of the girls how to make their own clothes in one of the dilapidated shanties near the school.[14]

The WHMA found that it could no longer support Cotton Valley in 1889 and turned it over to the AMA. When Dr. Augustus Field Beard visited the school on an inspection tour during the following year, he found that many of the children of the black sharecroppers distrusted the white landowners. While visiting an arithmetic lesson, Beard saw the children learning how to determine the number of square yards of a carpet of a given width and length. He asked them why they were learning to measure carpets when none of their cabins had carpets. One young lad revealed a good deal about local conditions when he quickly replied, "It's so they can't cheat us when we buy their land."[15]

Miss Davis became Mrs. Courtney in 1896 and left the school. She had gotten along well with local whites as well as with her pupils and their parents. The whites had respected Miss Davis "to the highest degree, and [were] willing and glad to show any favors to her or her teachers." Although the school's building was up-to-date by 1896, it still needed settees, blackboards, maps, lights, and, especially, a piano. The only musical instrument the school had in 1896 was

> a baby organ, which is now so nearly worn out that many of the reeds instead of responding to the touch of the solicitous performer sit in silence, considering themselves too aged to jump up and down, and take part in such active service.[16]

Miss Corrie N. Johnson of Oberlin, Ohio, succeeded Miss Davis as principal. In 1899 Miss Carrie E. Alexander, B.A., of Louisville, Kentucky, replaced Miss Johnson. Both of the latter principals had two assistants. Although the enrollment declined from 160 in 1898 to 152 in 1899, by 1901 it had climbed to 267.[17]

Since its beginning, Cotton Valley had "a remarkable series of colored women as principals and teachers. They have had the genius for making much of little, a native faculty for business and an instinct for neatness and order." Their efficiency and earnestness made Cotton Valley a good school, even when it met in the little log church and nearby run-down cabins, which were later abandoned.[18]

The second rural, black school which the AMA began to support several years after its founding, Kowaliga Academic and Industrial Institute, started through the initiative, concern, and ambition of a local black man, J. A. Benson. In 1852 Benson was born into slavery three miles from the Elmore County plantation he was later to own. Soon after his birth, his master's estate was divided and Benson went to an heir in Talladega, where he worked until emancipation.[19] He returned to his birthplace in 1871 and purchased 160 acres on credit. He had saved $100 while working since emancipation. He used this money to live and to outfit himself for farming. His farm prospered and he continued buying land as rapidly as possible. The whites had poorly cared for the land and many of the farms went on the market.

Benson owned three thousand acres of land without encumbrance by 1898. On a stream, which ran for five miles through his plantation, he had a brickyard, a sawmill, a grist mill, a cotton gin, and compressing mill "combined in one and operated by the water of this stream." He leased his lands to about a dozen experienced farmers, who subcontracted with laborers to work the land on half shares. He sent teams regularly to Montgomery markets to buy the supplies for the forty families living on his lands. In addition to his lands, he had loaned $6,000 to his white neighbors, secured by mortgages on their farms.

Benson somehow picked up enough education to manage all these diverse enterprises successfully, but he was not satisfied with the educational opportunities available to the children in the families on his plantation. The only available school was one which students at one of the AMA's schools taught for three months of the year to put themselves through college.

When Benson's son, William E. Benson, returned from Fisk University, he and his father decided to do something for the education of the community. William persuaded Clinton J. Calloway, one of his classmates at Fisk, to come and help start a school. By the fall of 1895 William and Calloway had begun the Kowaliga Industrial School in the old schoolhouse, with William as treasurer and Calloway as principal. By November the school had added a sewing department and was planning a carpentry department as soon as they could get the tools. The elder Benson gave land for the school in addition to furnishing and hauling the lumber. The rest of the funds for the school came as contributions solicited by an advisory board in the North and a board of trustees in Kowaliga. The Kowaliga school appealed to the AMA several times. Finally, in 1898, Dr. A. F. Beard visited the school, saw the land and the two-story building with attic and basement in the process of construction, and decided to provide aid.[20] In 1901 Clinton J. Calloway, B.A., of Cleveland, Tennessee, was the principal of the school, which then had seven teachers and 225 pupils.[21]

Kowaliga's purpose was to give the local children an elementary education, not to train teachers. By 1916 the pupils studied academic subjects only through the grammar grades and also received manual, domestic, and agricultural training. Along with agriculture, the boys studied working with iron and wood. The girls learned cooking, sewing, millinery, and basketry. Although the school was nonsectarian and did not teach the Bible during day school, it did open each morning with devotional exercises. Teachers and students also often exchanged visits with ministers of the local churches.

Kowaliga offered several kinds of extension services. On the first Saturday afternoon in each month, the teachers invited the mothers of the community to come to the school for instruction in bread making, house cleaning, laundering, care of children, and other domestic subjects. The teachers also went out into the community to learn the needs of the families and to persuade the parents to send their children to the school. The school's boys' brass band also involved many in the community in the life of the school.[22]

In addition to its primary and industrial schools in Alabama, the AMA also operated three schools with normal departments—Burrell School in Selma, Lincoln School in Marion, and Emerson Institute in Mobile. The least successful of these schools, possibly because of competition from other denominations' schools in the same town, was Burrell School.

In November, 1866 one of the Association's pioneer missionaries in Alabama, Rev. John Silsby, opened Burrell School in a carpenter's shop in Selma. Before beginning school, Silsby had to install windows, partition off a corner, and make other minor repairs. When this shop proved too small, some classes met in a black church. The church's backless benches were uncomfortable for the students. In winter the cold wind whistling through the holes between the floor boards forced the teachers to stand on benches "to protect their feet from the cold." During its first term the school rented the top floor of one family's house for a classroom.

Silsby began classes in 1867 in an unfinished hotel. The three teachers held classes in a large room on the first floor, gathering their pupils around themselves as far from the others as possible during recitations. During 1867–1868, the AMA bought a lot and built a $7,000–8,000 schoolhouse on it. The Freedmen's Bureau gave some money for the building. The Association named the school after Jabez Burrell of Oberlin, Ohio, after he donated $10,000 to complete the work. The AMA dedicated the new two-story building in the fall of 1868.

Retaining the right to nominate teachers, the AMA turned Burrell over to the Selma School Board in August, 1869. In return for the use of the building, Selma agreed to pay the teachers. By 1868–1869 Burrell had eight elementary grades and a four-year high or normal school. The pupils began with the English primer and finished by studying Latin grammar.[23]

By 1872 Superintendent H. W. Carter of Tallmadge, Ohio, was in charge of 8 lady teachers and 500 pupils in Burrell's day school, 150 pupils in the Sabbath School, and 50 pupils in the Mission Sabbath School. The teachers organized a literary society in January, 1872, which many of the students of the higher grades joined. Carter optimistically reported that "prejudices are fast breaking down, and that a liberal spirit is rapidly extending. I am frequently assured by leading Southerners of their hearty sympathy and good wishes for our work."[24]

J. M. Cumings of Tabor, Iowa, Burrell's Principal in 1874, resigned after the first term. Rev. G. Stanley Pope, the pastor of the local Congregational Church, took his place. Since 1872, the number of teachers had decreased to 6, the pupils in the day school to 400, although the Sabbath School had grown to 415. Burrell first had a matron of the mission home in 1874. There must have been a severe drop in attendance in 1873, for Rev. Pope reported in 1874 that the attendance had "greatly increased over last year, although the times are much harder." Several of the students in the higher classes had requested the establishment of a normal class for the following year.[25]

The tone in the 1875 report of William C. Ward, Superintendent of Public Instruction of Selma, differed radically from the reports of the missionaries and revealed the local whites' attitude toward the school. Ward wrote that there was a simple explanation for the low attendance figures (relative to enrollment) in Burrell:

> The colored people, because of their ignorance, have little appreciation of the value of an education; and because of their poverty, and, in a large number of cases, because of their thriftlessness and a too great disposition to an idle life, make frequent changes of residence, and for the sake of precarious employments, often after enrollment, withdraw their children from school.[26]

Ward's statement that poverty frequently forced black children to drop out of school was true, but his charge that blacks did not desire an education only showed his ignorance of the black community and of the many sacrifices parents made to assure an education for their children.

By 1876 Edwin C. Silsby had become principal of Burrell, where he remained for several years before becoming Talladega College's Treasurer.

Burrell enrolled 428 pupils in the regular school and 450 pupils in the Sunday School in 1876.[27]

In the fall of 1885 the AMA stopped appointing Burrell's teachers, turned the school over to Selma, and began charging the School Board rent for the building. When Selma did not adequately support Burrell, in 1889, the AMA resumed support and control of the school. Selma had allowed the building to deteriorate so badly that the Association had to spend $558 to have it "thoroughly repaired" and to plant new trees and shrubs to restore the beauty of the campus. When the AMA began appointing Burrell's principals after 1889, it frequently was able to hire graduates of its other schools.[28]

Even the AMA's resumption of operation of Burrell, however, was not sufficient to stop its decline during the late 1880's. In 1891, under Principal Amos W. Farnham of Hannibal, New York, seven female teachers, and a special missionary, Burrell enrolled only 219 pupils. The number of students who remained in school through the last week in May was usually much smaller than the total enrollment. By the end of the school term in 1891, 119 remained; in 1892, 105; in 1893, 119; in 1894, 124; and in 1895, 175. For these years the higher grades (eight through ten) enrolled seven, eleven, five, ten, and seventeen, respectively.[29]

The closing exercises at Burrell, like those at most other AMA schools, consisted of speeches, exhibitions of things the students had made, tableaux, a drama by the students in the higher grades, and "the customary variation of recitations, dialogues, and songs." Burrell's exercises were in the Selma Congregational Church, which the students and teachers decorated for the occasion. The first mention of industrial training at Burrell occurred in the account of the 1894 commencement, which described exhibitions showing the school's work in carpentry for the boys, sewing for the girls, and drawing. The 1895 commencement featured exhibits of carpentry and blacksmithing, which the school added that year. In 1895 the girls modeled dresses they had made. In 1896 and 1897 three pupils graduated from the tenth grade, two boys and one girl each year.

An unusual feature of Burrell's 1897 commencement exercises was the baccalaureate sermon preached by a former opponent of black education, Dr. Cecil, the white pastor of the local Presbyterian church. Although there were at least twenty meetings as part of the closing exercises of Selma's five black schools, the people of Selma enjoyed these events and a large crowd usually attended all the ceremonies. Burrell contributed the money it made from these entertainments to the AMA.[30]

Burrell briefly recovered from 1894 to 1898 under the leadership of Rev. A. T. Burnell, Ph.D. of Denver, Colorado and his wife, Mary. In 1894 Burrell enrolled 231 pupils with a faculty (in addition to the Burnells) of five women and one man. By 1898 the enrollment had grown to 323, although the faculty remained the same size.[31] That year Burnell left Burrell to go to Emerson Institute, the AMA school in Mobile, and Burrell declined sharply. There was no report of the school in the Association's *1899 Annual Report*. When fire destroyed Burrell's building soon after the turn of the century, the AMA decided to rebuild the school in Florence, Alabama since Selma then had one public and three other black denominational schools.[32]

Although the AMA began operating Emerson Institute in Mobile in 1866, the same year it founded Burrell School, Emerson first opened in 1865. While Federal troops still occupied Mobile, the Freedmen's Bureau established a school for freedmen in the building that had housed a medical college. The Bureau's seizing this building and using it for a black school angered Mobile's whites and turned them against it from the first.

The Western Freedmen's Aid Commission sent Mr. Branch to teach the school in 1865–1866. The W.F.A.C. ran short of funds and Branch planned to leave Mobile in June, 1866, but he remained until December.[33]

The Freedmen's Bureau also sought aid from the AMA, which responded by sending four teachers for the 420 pupils. By 1866, the Association was in charge of the school under Professor W. J. Squire.[34]

When Mr. and Mrs. Ralph Emerson of Rockford, Illinois decided to establish a school for freedmen soon after the Civil War, they toured the South to select a site. They first chose New Orleans, but it "did not work out." They then turned to their second choice, Mobile, where they had visited relatives before the Civil War.[35]

After Emerson decided to concentrate on black education in Mobile, which he had already aided, he wrote and described his plans to his close friend, General O. O. Howard, who warmly approved. When the AMA in 1867 made a definite proposition to buy the property on which a permanent institution could be established, Emerson gladly furnished the money to buy the Blue College, an ante-bellum medical school valued at $60,000. It was a brick, four-story building which "fronted the most aristocratic street and was surrounded by four acres of garden." After a few minor changes, the building was ready to receive the six hundred children who enrolled.

The new school opened in January, 1868. The faculty consisted of George L. Putnam, principal; W. J. Squire, assistant; and eight Northern female teachers. Three of these ladies stayed at Mobile for several years, one for thirty years. The school planned to begin with a graded school headed by a normal department and later to develop into a full college with a preparatory department. Local blacks continued using the old name of the building, "The Blue College," but the AMA named it "Emerson College."

Unfortunately, Emerson College became involved in the politics of Reconstruction. The principal became Mobile's Superintendent of Negro Education, and began administering funds "of which he had lately been the beneficiary." Although many of the resulting charges of mal-administration and graft were politically motivated, the legislative investigation of the principal caused Emerson to suffer because of the "undeniable faults of some of its servants."

The AMA and the white citizens of Mobile disagreed too sharply to permit cooperative financing. First Mobile turned Emerson over to the Association; then the city took control in 1870–1871. Finally, in 1872 the AMA took control of Emerson and assumed the responsibility for its total support. In 1873 Emerson gave "a second considerable gift" for the school. Although Emerson had offered only common school work up to this time, the AMA decided to use Emerson's gift to establish "*a secondary school with emphasis on the training of teachers* [italics in original]." In line with this decision, the AMA dropped "college" and renamed the school the Emerson Normal Institute. Emerson's gift also enabled the AMA to add normal and academic departments and boarding facilities.[36]

Emerson's new principal, Edward P. Lord, A.M. of Olivet, Michigan, wrote graphically of the need for the school in 1874. He had found few common or private schools and "very few competent teachers" in Southern Mississippi, Alabama, and Western Florida. Lord's opinion of Mobile's blacks, however, was unusually paternalistic and not representative of the attitudes of most AMA workers in Alabama. He thought Mobile's blacks were "exceptionally intelligent and prosperous." While many young people already had some education, most of them used their training primarily "to make more money, or to get more political influence over the ignorant masses." To Lord this proved "with fearful distinctness that a 'little learning is a dangerous thing,' and that all efforts to educate them should be coupled with the most earnest and effective Christian influences." Lord was optimistic, however, about "the wonderful change in the feelings of the white people—the influential class—toward us as teachers of the colored people." Lord was impressed that rich white Southerners would "give up life-long prejudices, and . . . be willing to have a school for colored for a near neighbor."[37]

Lord either overestimated the good will of Mobile's wealthy whites or overlooked the viciousness of the city's lower classes; for, on April 16, 1876, someone set the school on fire. The fire was definitely "the work of an incendiary" since it began "in a hall under a stair-case with no stovepipe or chimney within forty feet of it, directly under a window opening upon a gallery reached by an outside stair-case." Lord had passed through the area "about dusk" that day, "finding nothing amiss." Then, about 11:30 that night, Lord suddenly awoke feeling uneasy. After checking the living area of the building, he went into the schoolrooms and smelled smoke. He grabbed a bucket of water and threw it upon the flames, but the fire was already too great for him to extinguish alone. After sending a student to summon the fire department, Lord awakened all those in the building and helped them to safety. The fire spread so quickly that in half an hour it was not safe to enter the building and, "in less than an hour the walls fell." Fire engines quickly arrived on the grounds, but without adequate water they only "waited calmly outside in the street and blew their whistles gallantly."

Emerson's neighboring white families did what they could to help in the emergency. Several men did all they could "to save goods from the burning building." All they were able to save, however, was some of the teachers' clothing, three hundred of the library's fifteen hundred books, "and some articles from the storeroom." These neighbors then "were very kind, offering their homes to the ladies, and in many ways sympathizing with them in their misfortune." Luckily, no one was harmed in the fire.

When the teachers came to the school the following morning, tears came to their eyes "when they saw before them only the six great pillars, standing like sentinels before the ruins, the grand old oaks withered and blackened." The scene was "one of desolation—Emerson Institute in mourning." As the teachers gathered they felt that they, the students, and friends of the school were "bound together by cords of sympathy stronger than ever before."

Lord called the teachers together and told them "all that had happened." Despite the tragedy the group began "songs of praise and thanksgiving, from hearts that felt that the hand of our Good Father had been outstretched in love to save the lives of all." Then came the tearful parting of the Emerson family of students and teachers who had lived in the building, for each person then had to "go to her own home or that of a friend."[38]

Emerson's faculty did not despair. After the day of mourning, two teachers reopened the school in Mobile's Congregational Church and finished the term there despite "many unfavorable circumstances." Even these difficulties did not keep Emerson from graduating its first normal class of three teachers that year.[39]

When the AMA's leaders in New York first heard about the Emerson fire, they considered issuing a special appeal for funds to rebuild, but then "they decided to await the gathering of additional funds so that they would not have to divert funds badly needed at other points." Finally, in 1877, the Association bought Holley's Gardens, an amusement park of three and one-half acres "covered with magnificent live oaks." This land had the advantages of being closer to the predominantly black section of Mobile and having outlets to four streets. An old plantation house "of some architectural distinction" standing in the middle of the land became the teachers' home. The AMA then built a new, brick classroom building fronting on Scott Street.[40]

In January, 1882 another fire destroyed Emerson's new main building. By this time the school was so large that the Congregational Church could not accommodate all the students, so classes met temporarily in nearby Baptist and Methodist churches. The AMA responded more quickly this time by building an "admirable brick building" by the summer of 1882 and dedicating it on October 2, 1882. Three hundred and six students began school in the fall of 1882 in this $8,500 building, which was "more commodious and convenient" than the earlier buildings.[41]

Emerson's fires caused it to lose little time, but they represented a "blow to [its] moral prestige" which became evident during the ensuing decade. From 1876 to 1887 fewer students attended Emerson than during any comparable period in the nineteenth century. Emerson had many principals (eight in ten years), but few graduates during this period. Still, one of the school's most famous alumni, Ferdinand A. Stewart, M.D., graduated during this "decade of disasters." Emerson's last principal during its darkest days was F. B. Wells from Rhinebeck, New York. In 1886 he supervised six Northern assistants including his wife who served as matron and special missionary.[42] Emerson's enrollment in 1886 was 320 including 23 normal students.

After 1887 Emerson "again showed substantial growth and steady usefulness. There were regular graduating classes and longer principalships, notably that of Rev. Charles M. [*sic*] Stevens." In 1887 Charles W. R. Stevens became principal over ten instructors. In 1887–1888 Emerson enrolled 355 students: normal, 16; grammar school, 29; intermediate school, 103; primary school, 204; music students not in other classes, 3.[43]

Emerson Institute first began offering industrial training in 1889 when the Association's Daniel Hand Fund provided the money for an industrial building. In this building female students studied sewing and cooking while the male students worked at manual training and wood working. Mr. Emerson also contributed to the development of industrial and musical training at the school in the 1890's. In 1896 he gave the money for a two-story frame building and equipment for female industries as a memorial to his son, Ralph Emerson, Jr. This building contained workrooms for the departments of domestic science and art, a large room for the chorus, and several small practice rooms for the music department. Later gifts from Emerson provided several pianos for the music department and expanded male industrial training. Throughout its existence Emerson received no state aid and the tuition "scarcely met the current expenses." So the school had to depend on Northern benevolence distributed through the AMA for all its money for repairs, improvements, and salaries.[44]

Emerson made some important contributions in educating Alabama's black leaders. Three graduated from the higher normal class in 1876 and two in 1880. The normal class, Grade B, graduated one in 1880, two in 1884, and nine in 1887. In addition to many good teachers and school principals, Emerson's graduates and former students included Dr. George Wilkerson, one of "the leading Negro physicians of the South";[45] Dr. F. A. Stewart (Fisk, M.A., Harvard, M.D.) of Nashville, Tennessee; Miss Lillie M. Thomas, Missionary to Luebo, Congo Free State; several "of the most brilliant and useful" young, black Congregational ministers (including Revs. J. H. Europe and S. Snell, college pastor at Talladega), and many postal workers in Mobile. Emerson's graduates began going into the post office in the late 1880's. For a short period all postal deliverymen in Mobile were black "and for quite a series of years all the male graduates of Emerson went into this service." As late as 1909 Mobile still had "the largest proportion of Negro employees [of any post office] in the United States."[46]

In 1901 Dr. A. T. Burnell, Emerson's principal since 1898, summarized his impressions of the school's students at the turn of the century. He noted that about ten percent of the students worked for the school to pay their tuition. Students worked before and after classes as janitors, cooks, nurses, and workers in the garden, woodshed, or house. If a student's home took in washing she would be "sometimes doing a family wash before school and ironing late into the night, to secure school privileges." In most of the students' homes "the mothers and grandmothers make strenuous efforts and undergo pinching sacrifices, that the oncoming generation may have advantages superior to their own."

Burnell noted that most young people everywhere were basically alike in seldom fulfilling "the full height of opportunity" available to them. Considering this tendency of all young people plus the fact that very few of Emerson's students were

> blessed with well-educated parents, the fact that our students show uneven progress and a certain lack of tenacity for holding out through the full normal course is not to be wondered at. Yet the average do average work, while a few do excellently, and the majority should be commended.[47]

The last AMA normal school to be established, Lincoln Normal School in Marion, certainly had the most unusual story of any of the Association's Alabama schools.[48] During the first two decades of its existence (1867–1887), Lincoln's development from an AMA school into the Alabama State Normal School and University for Negroes was relatively uncontroversial. Then, in 1887, an incendiary fire destroyed the school's main building. The arsonist must have represented widespread antipathy among whites for the school, for in February, 1887, the Alabama Legislature passed a severe law forbidding the use of the school's land for education. The law did, however, provide for a Negro Normal School and University anywhere in Alabama except in Marion.[49]

After the fire and the school law, the AMA decided not to reopen a school at Marion. On March 25, 1887, Marion's blacks held a mass meeting in the school's chapel, adopted a resolution to establish an independent school, and raised subscriptions for $300. Several local blacks then appealed to the AMA to resume sponsorship of a school at Marion. After careful consideration, the Association purchased the square, two-storied home of the former principal, William Burns Paterson, and sent teachers to begin a school in Marion. The response of Marion's blacks was so great that some classes had to meet in a barn, described by Alabama's Superintendent of Education, Solomon Palmer, as "not being fit quarters for a Kentucky horse." Despite these poor accommodations, Lincoln managed to train several teachers. The school at this time consisted of a boarding high school with a normal department.[50]

Principals of Lincoln before Miss May L. Phillips included Miss M. E. Wilcox of Benson, Minnesota (1893–1894), and Rev. William J. Larkin of Marion (1895–1896).[51] Industrial work began at Lincoln while Miss Wilcox was principal in 1894. At that time, the school taught sewing up to making clothes as well as mending to boys and girls.[52]

When Miss May L. Phillips of Cannonsburg, Pennsylvania left her work at Talladega College, "where she had shown much energy and administrative gifts of great ability," to come to be principal of Lincoln School in the fall of 1896, the school had only 150 pupils, who had to sit on benches and boxes. The school had few desks, blackboards, or books. Because of these poor accommodations, the AMA chose Lincoln School as one of the places to close when the Association had to retrench in the spring of 1897. Again Marion's blacks, led this time by Miss Phillips, rose up to save their school. The blacks met in the Congregational church and pledged $1,300 out of their very limited resources to continue the school. Many decided to live on only the barest necessities and to contribute all they could to the school. Parents of the students promised to feed the teachers if they would return for one more year. One small boy voiced the determination of the students when he said, "You teachers just come back and teach us, and we boys won't let you starve." The teachers trusted these pledges and returned in the fall to teach that year without salary.[53]

The students spent the summer working to redeem their pledges while the teachers canvassed for funds. In October, the students came to school with their pledge money. They had earned over $100 working in the cotton fields. Having redeemed their pledges, many had to return to the fields to earn money for clothes and tuition. Several students told pathetic stories of self-denial while earning their pledge money. Two boys ate only bread for two weeks while they chopped wood to earn their pledge money. Others gave up meat or butter to save what they could. Some managed to live on only fifty cents a week for food. Twenty students banded together and "made seventy-five cents a week for each cover all expenses, and all this in an uncomplaining and cheerful way." During all her years with the AMA Miss Phillips never saw "such examples of sacrifice for an education, both on the part of the parents and pupils."[54]

When the AMA learned of the determination of the people and the teachers to keep a school and of their willingness to sacrifice to do so, Dr. A. F. Beard telegraphed Miss Phillips that the school could continue. Miss Phillips described the community's reaction to Dr. Beard's message which "had been earnestly prayed for and eagerly watched for." The news that the Association would continue to support Lincoln "came like a ray of sunlight piercing the gloom that had enveloped our whole community. 'Old Glory' was flung to the breeze and universal joy throughout the whole neighborhood took the place of the common sorrow."[55]

After this season of trial, Lincoln School "took on new life." Marion's blacks were more aware than ever of the importance of an education and they had learned to do more for themselves. The school then grew rapidly. Children sat upon all available benches and boxes. When all the seats ran out, the teachers sometimes yielded to the pleas of parents to let their children sit on the floor if they might just have an education. It quickly became apparent that such overcrowding was harming the quality of education so the teachers and friends of the school began a campaign to raise money for a new building. In six months, the teachers, pupils, parents, and some of the school's Northern friends had raised $1,000 which they sent to the AMA with a request for a new building. The AMA matched the sum and a new canvass began. Finally the school was able to build a "fine modern brick structure, with the necessary appointments for good school work."[56]

But the school's problems were not solved when the work on the building began. The workers struck for higher wages while Miss Phillips was absent from the campus. When she returned and learned that the workers would not accept the fact that the school's funds were very limited, she called the students together and said:

> Our new building is less than half finished but we have no workers. In the last few days I have learned how to lay brick. If you will help, we can learn our lessons while mixing cement and handling the trowel. I will be your teacher, if you will construct your own building.

The students responded by helping Miss Phillips finish Van Wagenen Hall. Since then the faculty and students have proudly showed visitors the "'line of demarcation' showing the point at which experience gave way to inexperience, and a woman teacher in 1901 taught masonry."[57]

But even this building soon was crowded. Under the leadership of Miss Phillips, the enrollment of Lincoln School increased from 150 in 1897 to 400 in 1904. By the latter date, many Marion whites had become interested in the work, some contributing financially.[58]

Despite differences of location and leadership the AMA's primary, industrial, and normal schools all shared a commitment to providing equal educational opportunities for Alabama's black students. While all these schools offered industrial training, they never allowed it to displace liberal academic education, especially for future black leaders. The best example of the Association's commitment to training liberally educated black leaders, however, was the college that became the capstone of the AMA's black educational system in Alabama, Talladega College.

12

TALLADEGA COLLEGE AND CONCLUSION

Enslaved blacks built the building that later housed Talladega College; freed blacks took the initiative in establishing the school that became Talladega College. On November 20, 1865, a convention of fifty-six black men met in Mobile to discuss the implications of their new freedom. The convention passed a resolution stating, "we regard the education of our children and youths as vital to the preservation of our liberties, and true religion as the foundation of all real virtue, and shall use our utmost endeavors to promote these blessings in our common country."[1]

When Talladega's representatives at the convention, the ex-slaves, William Savery and Thomas Tarrant, returned home, they organized a society to plan and to begin a black school. Harry Knox headed the Society of Freedmen, which soon opened a school in a room of David White's house. The society chose Leonard Johnson to teach the school. Children flocked to the school in such numbers that Johnson had to use some of the better pupils to help teach the others. When the room in White's house became overcrowded, the society bought an old carpenter's shop, tore it down, and used the lumber to build a new schoolhouse near the Isbell Branch. When the society asked the aid of the Freedmen's Bureau in obtaining a more qualified teacher, the Bureau sent Mrs. Cynthia M. Hopson, from Hudson and Cleveland, Ohio.[2] Mrs. Hopson was a missionary of the Cleveland Freedman's Aid Commission, which operated the school from 1865 to 1867. The white people of Talladega shunned Mrs. Hopson, so she boarded with an elderly black couple.[3]

By 1867, the enrollment had grown so rapidly that Mrs. Hopson had to get another teacher to help her. William C. Luke soon joined the faculty and the school developed rapidly until the "terrible tragedy of his death." Although everyone at the school "who knew Mr. Luke [thought] him one of the noblest Christian workers that ever came South," a mob murdered him.[4]

Planning for another black school in Talladega began in February, 1867, when General Wager Swayne approached John Silsby, an AMA missionary, to see if the Association might be interested in establishing a school in Talladega. Swayne chose Talladega because of its healthful location and the "cheapness of living" there. He had also heard of an antebellum school that could be bought cheaply. The Coosa River Baptist Association had built this fine colonial brick building in 1852–1853 with slave labor at a cost of $30,000 to be the Talladega Baptist Male High School.[5] After the war, the Association lost the building through indebtedness. The building was to be sold for mortgage in 1867. Swayne was so interested in black education that he offered to pay half ($4,000) of the price of the building if the AMA would pay the other half, do about $2,000 worth of repairs, and establish a school in the building.[6]

While conducting negotiations with Swayne, the AMA in November, 1867, sent Rev. Henry E. Brown and his wife of Oberlin, Ohio, to begin a school in Talladega. As soon as Brown arrived, he saw the need for a large school and began looking around. The old white school "was expected to fall at any time," so it was being offered for sale at a very low figure. Late one night, Brown and William Savery took a light and examined the building. "To their surprise they found only one support decayed," so Brown wrote immediately to the AMA suggesting that they buy the building. On Brown's recommendation, the Association accepted Swayne's offer and bought the building and its thirty-four acres of land. The AMA named the building, Swayne Hall, because of his aid in securing it.[7]

When Brown began teaching in Swayne Hall, Mrs. Hopson closed her school and came to work with him. The enrollment grew quickly, so the AMA transferred two more assistants from Montgomery to help teach the 140 students who enrolled the first year. On February 17, 1869, Alabama officially incorporated Talladega College. Alabama extended the charter in 1889 to allow college work in fact as well as in name.[8]

None of the nine counties nearest Talladega had a black public school when Talladega opened. Many people in these counties asked Brown for a teacher. He did not have enough teachers for every community, so he began working toward a program of teacher training. When Brown visited one of the rundown churches and received a request for a teacher, he replied, "Pick out the best specimen of a young man you have for a teacher, and bring to church with you next Sunday all the corn and bacon you can spare for his living. I will take him into my school and make a teacher of him." On the appointed day the students came to their small country churches, bringing with them their corn, "from a handful to four quarts,—more often a handful,—in the pocket, or tied in a handkerchief, and laid it on the alter in front of the pulpit, singing as they marched around the aisle." Brown selected eight or nine young men who walked to Talladega carrying their sacks of corn and bacon on their backs.

Talladega had no accommodations for these students, but several families who lived nearby allowed students to sleep on the floors of their cabins and to bake cornbread by the fire. All the pupils from outside Talladega lived like this for the first year. They began studying the alphabet. By the end of six months, they could read in the second and third readers. By helping each other, these students learned how to teach reading. During the summer, they returned home to teach "brush" schools for those who could not come to Talladega. Despite the inconvenient "boarding" provisions, fifty more young men and women applied for the second year. They agreed to bring their rations, cornmeal for most of them, "asking only for a place to bake it and a shelter for their heads."[9]

Talladega added normal courses as the students advanced far enough to need them. By 1869, when Alabama granted the school a charter, Talladega had given some normal training to 314 public school teachers.[10]

The AMA repaired Swayne Hall at a cost of $5,000 (instead of the $2,000 originally estimated), and began using it for a library, museum, and chapel as well as for school and recitation rooms. The Association then began planning for new buildings. In August, 1869, the school laid the cornerstone of a girls' hall, which was finished in 1870 at a cost of $22,000. Foster Hall honored Rev. Lemuel Foster, of Blue Island, Illinois, who gave the largest amount for the building. In 1874 Mr. R. R. Graves of Morristown, New Jersey, gave money to build a two-story wooden house, Graves Hall, and to buy six acres of "valuable land."[11] The theological instructor lived in Graves Hall, which also contained room for a library and recitations.

Mrs. Valerie G. Stone of Malden, Massachusetts, gave the money to erect the third brick building at Talladega in 1881. Stone Hall contained a reading room and rooms for eighty young men. William Savery, the brick mason who helped build Swayne Hall while he was a slave, was the contractor for Stone Hall and for the president's house in 1881. Thus, the AMA saw Stone Hall as "not only a monument for the Christian giver of the funds for its construction, but also of the possibilities of the race for which it was erected."[12]

The college secured two instructors' houses in 1882. Seth Wadhams of Chicago, Illinois, gave the money for one of these. The college built two more faculty houses during 1891. In 1883, J. H. Cassedy of Thiels, New York, gave the money for building a two-story house for a model school for primary and intermediate students. In the following year the John F. Slater Fund contributed the money for a shop, which was soon enlarged. The college built a two-story laundry in 1890.[13]

The thirty-four acres of land which Talladega bought along with Swayne Hall soon became insufficient. Connecticut donors gave most of the money to buy the Winstead farm of 160 acres in 1877. In 1887, the school bought the Newton farm. Talladega also bought land and built two mission chapels on the outskirts of town during the 1880's. The school used these chapels for educational as well as religious purposes. By 1891, Talladega owned about 260 acres of land.[14]

Talladega organized its Normal Department in 1871, although it had been offering some normal courses before that time.[15] Fourteen students were in Talladega's first normal classes in 1871–1872. Few of these could finish the year, however, since the county schools in which they taught began before Talladega finished its school term. In 1871–1872, Talladega also established its first classes in Greek, Latin, and algebra to form the Junior Preparatory Year.

At the end of the school year, 1871–1872, Talladega invited the townspeople, many of whom had been openly critical of the school, to come to the examinations. From twenty-five to thirty of Talladega's "best representatives of [the so-called] 'superior race'" attended the exercises. The whites, many of whom had questioned whether blacks could learn, were amazed at the achievements of the students in arithmetic, geography, grammar, Latin, and Greek. From this time on, Talladega's whites had a new respect for the school.[16]

The Normal Department graduated its first class of eight in 1876. By 1899 Talladega had graduated at least 107 from the Normal Department. These normal graduates followed a very wide range of occupations, although many more became teachers (28), pastors (10), or school principals (7) than those who pursued any other professions. Only one of Talladega's normal graduates listed his occupation as farming in 1900.[17]

Although Talladega offered training for ministers since the Talladega Congregational Church began in 1868, the college first offered formal instruction in elementary theology to a class of six men from three denominations in 1872. The Theological Department formally opened in 1873 in the new Graves Hall. In 1874 Rev. George Whitfield Andrews came to Talladega from his pastorate of a Congregational Church in Montgomery to take charge of the Theological Department. Andrews stayed at Talladega until 1908 as dean and professor of the Theological Department (1875–1908), acting president (1896–1900), and president (1900–1908).[18]

George Whitfield Andrews was born on February 4, 1833 in Wayne, Ashtabula County, Ohio.[19] After growing up on his parents' farm, Andrews went to Oberlin College, receiving his B.A. in 1858 and his A.M. in 1861. After graduation Andrews served as principal of an academy in Lisbon, Illinois (1858–1860) and principal of Bloomfield Seminary in northern Ohio (1860–1865). On March 30, 1859 Andrews married Harriet West of Norwalk, Ohio, with whom he lived happily until her death in 1913.[20]

Andrews attended Andover Theological Seminary in Massachusetts from 1865 to 1867. After graduation and ordination in 1867 he served as pastor in East Hampton and Collinsville, Connecticut; Marion, Montgomery, and Talladega, Alabama. While serving as an AMA missionary in Alabama, Andrews organized the churches in Marion and Montgomery.[21] Although he taught one year at Fisk University, the Association's black college in Nashville, Tennessee, he was best known for his work at Talladega College (1874–1908). Upon retiring he remained Professor Emeritus until his death in 1931.

The one hundred black ministers Andrews helped train at Talladega loved and respected him. While he was confined to his bed (1920–1931), many of these former pupils visited him for "social, religious, and intellectual reasons." To the end of his life Andrews remained keenly interested in intellectual matters and constantly requested his nephew to read "the latest books and articles of importance" to him.

In addition to his many trips throughout the United States in the interest of Talladega, Andrews visited Europe twice. He went to London in 1891 as a member of the first International Council of Congregational Churches and then traveled through Palestine and the Near East.

Andrews received several honors in recognition of his service. The Congregational Association of Alabama elected him moderator at its organizational meeting in 1876 and reelected him in 1877, 1885, 1895, and 1896.[22] He also received the degree of Doctor of Divinity from Ripon College in 1886 and from Oberlin College in 1914.

Although Andrews could have used his "marked financial ability" in business, he chose a life of self-sacrifice, service, and small financial rewards. Having no children of his own, he managed well what little he did earn and helped many of his nieces and nephews get an education and get started in their vocations.[23]

Andrews' greatest contribution to Talladega was developing the Theological Department. Like the Normal Department, the Theological Department graduated its first class in 1876. By 1900, Talladega had some record of forty-five graduates of the Theological Department. The largest number to graduate in one year was eight in 1880.[24]

By 1876, Andrews had organized the Theological Department into a four-year course that allowed most students to pursue one course each year in the college.[25] Advanced students, however, could finish in three years. Since educated ministers were so scarce, Talladega invited all Alabama's Christian denominations to cooperate with the Theological Department by sending students and by appointing lecturers to describe the denomination's doctrines and practices. The intense denominationalism of most Alabamians rendered this a largely futile gesture, but it did indicate Talladega's desire to offer quality education across denominational lines. Talladega offered boarding accommodations in the College Boarding Hall or with private families at a cost of ten dollars per month. There was no tuition in theology, but pupils had to pay fifty cents per month for instruction in the other departments.

Theological students had the opportunity of working their way through school by doing missionary work under the direction of one of the theological instructors. The college used these theological students to establish churches and to evangelize the countryside during the summer. A theological instructor would select an area that needed a church and school, and send a student there.

The student then spent his summer holding meetings to organize a church and building a meeting house to be used as a school and church. Once a church was established, Talladega assigned a theological student as pastor to preach at regular intervals and to conduct a Sunday School. Talladega also tried to establish a day school in these meeting houses and to send a pupil to teach there at least part of the year. By 1874, Talladega had established church schools at five locations.[26]

Talladega's Theological Department could boast at least two instructors with solid academic backgrounds besides Andrews: Rev. Carroll Cutler, D.D. and Rev. J. M. P. Metcalf. Cutler was born in Windham, New Hampshire, January 31, 1829. He attended Pinkerton Academy in Derby and then Phillips Academy at Andover, where he became an assistant while preparing for college. He graduated from Yale in 1854, ranking third in scholarship out of a class of one hundred. Cutler then taught until Yale offered him a position as a tutor. While teaching at Yale in 1858, he married Susan Gallagher. The following year Cutler studied at the Universities of Berlin and Halle. In 1860 he became Professor of Mental Science and Rhetoric in Western Reserve College. After eleven years in this position, he became president of the school for the next eighteen years. Cutler believed in the higher education of women and worked for coeducation. In 1889 he accepted a theological professorship at Biddle University in North Carolina. He came to Talladega in 1891 and taught theological and college courses until he died on January 25, 1894.[27]

Rev. J. M. P. Metcalf, another excellent professor, came to Talladega in 1896 to replace Cutler. Metcalf was a graduate of Oberlin College and Union Theological Seminary and had taken a course of special studies in Berlin. He remained at Talladega for eleven years, bringing "a broad scholarship and a most earnest spirit into the theological studies." Many other theologians taught at Talladega for brief periods.[28]

The Phelps Hall Bible School at Tuskegee and the Theological Department of Talladega revealed much about the different approaches to education of the leaders of these schools. Prospective ministers or church workers at Tuskegee studied only the English Bible. Tuskegee stressed industrial training for these students to help them in their local churches. Talladega also knew that the students in its Theological Department needed industrial training. From the first Bible class in 1872 (nine years before Tuskegee opened), Talladega taught its theological students how to build meeting houses while they learned how to establish churches.

Talladega, however, realized that good ministers needed more than a familiarity with the English Bible, the focus of the other black theological departments in Alabama. Talladega's examinations in theology, the most popular examination of the school's annual commencements, revealed the extent of the theological students' training. In 1895 the professors, and those visitors who wished to do so, examined the graduates on Messianic Prophecy. Public examinations of the theological students in 1898 included questions in homiletics, church history, the prophets, Greek, and Latin.[29] Some of Talladega's graduates in theology went on to study in the Northern seminaries, yet those who did not pursue further study received theological training far superior to that offered in any other Alabama black school.

When Professor Andrews began the Theological Department at Talladega in 1872, he did not know of a single educated black preacher in Alabama. By the time he retired in 1908, graduates of Talladega's Theological Department pastored churches from Savannah to San Francisco and from Chicago to Corpus Christi, in addition to churches all over Alabama. The theological graduates most active in Alabama as pastors by 1901 included Spencer Snell (eleven years at the Talladega College Church), Fountain Gage Ragland (eleven years in Mobile, eleven years in Birmingham), and James Brown (twenty-one years in Anniston). Another theological graduate, William Harvard Holloway (Yale Divinity School, B.D.) was Director of Talladega's Extension Work in 1900.[30]

While Talladega College owed much to its early principals, Henry E. Brown (1867–1875?), Albert A. Saffold (1876), and Edwin P. Lord (1877–1879), the school made its most important gains under Rev. Henry Swift DeForest (1879–1896). In 1879, Talladega's trustees, thinking about establishing a full college course, elected DeForest to be Talladega College's first president.[31]

DeForest was born March 17, 1833 at South Edmiston, Otsego County, New York. In addition to his work on the family farm he took odd jobs to earn enough money to attend a preparatory school. He then went to Yale on a scholarship established by one of his ancestors, David Curtis de Forest. DeForest's diligence at Yale earned him a high standing in the graduating class of 1857. He then entered Yale Theological Seminary until July, 1858, when a lack of money forced him to become a mathematics tutor at Beloit College. He next studied at Union Theological Seminary in New York City for a year before returning to Yale as a Latin tutor.

When the Civil War began, DeForest was drafted and received his ordination in New Haven, Connecticut for service as Chaplain to the 11th Regiment, Connecticut Volunteers. He later told his children of the terrible hardships of the Union troops with whom he served during the Wilderness Campaign. After being mustered out of the army in December, 1865, he returned to Yale Theological Seminary, February–July, 1866.

In the summer of 1866 DeForest traveled for Congregational churches. On one of these trips he visited Grinnell, Iowa where he first saw Anna Margaret Robbins, the daughter of one of the "Iowa Band" of home missionaries from Massachusetts. DeForest quickly fell in love with Anna, but she was fourteen years his junior and at first wished he "would desist his attentions." Refusing to desist, he persuaded her to marry him on August 24, 1869 in Muscatine, Iowa with her father officiating.

From October 17, 1866 to July 1, 1870, DeForest was pastor of the Plymouth

Congregational Church in Des Moines, Iowa. He then entered Andover Theological Seminary, graduating in 1871.[32] DeForest then returned to Iowa to be pastor of Congregational churches in Council Bluffs and Waterloo before becoming financial secretary of Iowa College in Muscatine. Here DeForest received and accepted a call in 1879 to enter a new mission field as president of Talladega College where he remained until his death on January 27, 1896.[33]

For their first two years in Talladega, the DeForests lived in two small rooms on the second floor of the girls' dormitory and ate in the common dining room on the first floor. Upon learning of this, some of the DeForests' friends in Iowa and New England "contributed for the direct benefit of the DeForest family, rather than to the college itself."[34] With these gifts DeForest built a brick home for his family on a two-acre plot across from Foster Hall.

The autobiography of DeForest's son, Lee, provided a good survey of the life of missionary families in Alabama. During DeForest's early years at Talladega the native whites "totally ostracized" him and his family along with all the other teachers. Although these attitudes softened over the years as the local whites came to see the DeForests as part of the local scene and the Alabamians' conservatism triumphed over their prejudice, this ostracism was especially bitter for Mrs. DeForest and the children. One afternoon the DeForests met Colonel Hardy, a typical Southern "gentleman." When DeForest greeted Hardy, the "genial" Southerner quickly crossed to the other side of the road and "snarled, 'I don't wish to be spoken to, suh, by a damned Yankee.!' "

The DeForest children feared the local white boys and rarely went off campus unless accompanied by an adult or some of the larger black youths. But the missionaries' children were not always safe even at the college. The Lewis boys, sons of one of Talladega's richest men, frequently drove by the college in a pony cart filled with rocks to throw at children and students at Talladega. The latter usually responded in kind. Such events shut the missionaries' families off from the town and severely limited the youngsters' childhood activities, although they drove the missionary families and the black community as a whole closer together.

Lee often resented his father's severity and the inordinate amount of "religion" to which he subjected his children. But Lee admired his father's love of horses and nature, his keen sense of humor (seldom publicly displayed), his passion for orderliness, his deep, abiding affection for Latin literature, and his spirit of self-sacrifice.

DeForest knew little about music, although he "admired it in a general way." Mrs. DeForest, however, was "a skilled pianist" with a well-trained soprano voice. She enjoyed arranging community sings and recitals for the faculty members with musical ability.

During the last decade of his life, DeForest developed a chronic bronchitis because of the "sleepless nights and the strain under which he usually labored." This illness forced him to leave Talladega periodically to spend some time in the high, dry climate of New Mexico or Colorado.

In addition to running the school, DeForest had to leave his home and family every summer to tour New England and the West seeking contributions to support the school. These "fatiguing and wearisome" trips further undermined DeForest's constitution, which the campaigns of the Civil War had already weakened. Still, he "bravely and hopefully" continued making these imperative fund-raising trips. While most contributions were small, Talladega did receive $5,000 for the Cassedy School and $80,000 from Mr. Ervin (the largest single gift Talladega ever received).

Despite his poor health, DeForest remained at Talladega until his death on January 27, 1896. His death was "sudden and unexpected." After memorial services in Talladega, DeForest was buried in Sherburne, New York.[35]

Other than an honorary D.D. in 1881 from Beloit College, DeForest received little external recognition for his work at Talladega. His son later wrote that most of DeForest's reward came from experiencing "the evident ambition and consuming desire of most of those who had come to the college for aid in acquiring an education."

DeForest also received the reward of seeing substantial progress at Talladega during his presidency. Talladega was in poor enough shape in 1879 "to test the missionary zeal of even the most ardent" supporter of black education. All the buildings had broken windows and debris littered the yards. DeForest saw skinny hogs and cattle running free over the campus and primitive agriculture (farmers using "sharpened sticks for plows"). The "almost complete lack of adequate facilities" and the poor quality of the teachers were even more discouraging. Since there were few black schools in the South in 1879, Talladega had to take some Northern white men and women whose chief qualification was their missionary zeal for the freedmen. Few really good Northern teachers were willing to forsake the opportunities in the North for the meagre salaries which the poverty-stricken schools could offer. For example, DeForest received only $125 a month at Talladega.[36]

When DeForest arrived in 1879, Talladega was a normal school with a theological department and a primary and grammar division. During his administration it developed into a real college by offering theological and classical subjects to constitute a college level curriculum in addition to its continuing offerings in agriculture, industrial arts, domestic science, and nursing.[37]

Much of what DeForest was able to accomplish at Talladega was made possible by a crucial AMA educational meeting in 1881. DeForest and Andrews met with the representatives of the Association and the black schools—Berea, Atlanta, Tougaloo, Straight, LeMoyne, Hampton, and Fisk—to discuss the future of black higher education. Only Fisk and Atlanta could then justify their existence as colleges. Several felt that Talladega's location and possibilities were limited. The delegates finally decided, however, to approve college work at Talladega, Straight, and Tougaloo, as well as to continue the established programs at Fisk and Atlanta. They also decided that these former schools should seek endowments as quickly as possible. Some of the delegates felt that all other AMA schools should be organized as "feeders" of these colleges. While such a plan might have strengthened Congregationalism in the South, the conference decided that the Association's opposition to denominationalism and its primary concern with providing the best education for the most people, regardless of denomination, demanded that this suggestion be rejected.[38]

The year 1881 had great symbolic significance for black education in Alabama. In 1881 the AMA climaxed its drive for quality academic education in Alabama by allowing Talladega to begin developing a true college department. Talladega did not develop its college department haphazardly or without long and careful planning. Even after receiving the approval of the AMA in 1881, Talladega did not announce a curriculum of collegiate grade in its catalog until 1890, one year after the Alabama Legislature enlarged and confirmed Talladega's charter. Two students, Zachariah Jones and John Reuben Savage, first entered Talladega's College Department in 1892 and graduated in 1895. Two students graduated from this department in 1897 and 1899, and one graduated in 1898.[39] Thus, Talladega clearly refuted the charge that the AMA "jammed college education down the throats of illiterates just out of slavery."[40]

In 1881, the same year that Talladega began planning for collegiate education, the Alabama Legislature established Tuskegee Institute. Under the leadership of Booker T. Washington (1881–1915), Tuskegee became the symbol of primary, industrial education. The development of these two schools for the next two decades exemplified the two leading educational strategies in black schools in nineteenth-century Alabama—primary, industrial training, and liberal, higher academic education.

Washington believed that the surest way to black political and social acceptance was through economic success in the South. He repeatedly preached the message that blacks faced fewer obstacles in business in the South than in similar or other endeavors elsewhere. He constantly stressed that whites who were economically dependent upon blacks would not discriminate against blacks. Washington then concluded that industrial education was the key that would unlock the door to black economic success.

White philanthropists, foundations, and political leaders (especially on the national level) supported Washington's emphasis on industrial education for blacks. But many of these whites, operating in a basically racist, capitalistic culture, perverted Washington's plan. Whereas Washington saw his program as a first step, many of his white supporters saw it as the end of the road. These whites saw elementary, industrial education for blacks as inferior, different (training for workers, not leaders), caste education, which was all the training they intended for blacks to have.

While Washington was not fully responsible for this perversion of his plan, the contradiction between his public statements and his actions at Tuskegee implicitly supported the view that blacks needed only industrial education. Although Washington often said and wrote that black leaders needed higher education, he did little to furnish either this education or the preparation for it to the educational and religious leaders who graduated from Tuskegee. Indeed, he boasted that Tuskegee did not offer the traditional elements of a liberal education (or the preparatory course) such as Latin, philosophy, and theoretical mathematics. Washington insisted that all academic subjects be directly related to the school's industries, not that they could be taught for their own sake or to develop students' powers of abstraction and reasoning. He sometimes condemned AMA schools as alien institutions which offered the wrong kind of black education because he believed the missionaries did not understand the South or blacks.[41]

In the light of Washington's condemnation of Northern missionaries' schools it was ironic that the first school in the South to offer industrial training "as a systematic part of education" was an AMA school, Talladega College, in 1867—one year before Hampton Institute opened. While insisting that academic training was most important, Talladega's leaders realized that some industrial work would be helpful to many of their students. Along with English, Latin, Greek, history, mathematics, theology, and philosophy, Talladega also taught farming, wood-working, ironmaking, printing, and cobbling.[42]

Although Talladega insisted that industrial work was secondary, it was committed to some job-training from the first. Students worked repairing Swayne Hall and farming the land bought with it in 1867. In less than two years Talladega opened the Teachers' Home and instructed female students in housekeeping there. The first and all succeeding theological classes learned carpentry. When assigned to begin a church, the student began with a tent fly to use "as a shop by day and sanctuary by night. When the meeting house was done there were souls ready for organization, and in this way five of our Alabama churches, in the double sense of the term, were formed."[43]

Talladega acquired a press and printing materials in the spring of 1877 and some students began learning printing. That fall the students printed a paper on college affairs. The press also did some job work. "With some interruptions the [printing] department has issued a monthly paper since the year of its establishment." The Slater Shop enabled Talladega to offer more advanced work in wood-working in 1888 and in iron-work in 1899.[44]

In the 1890's, Edgar A. Bishop, a graduate of the Massachusetts Agricultural College, was the Superintendent of Talladega's Agriculture Department. In 1896, he directed the work of thirty-five students of the Junior Preparatory and Normal classes in this department. Six of the students worked by the month, saving toward their entering the day school. Talladega paid the other students by the hour. The school consumed most of the products of the farm. Bishop was careful to care for the land and to increase its value. On the farm, the students raised different varieties of fruit trees, nut trees, berries, grasses and forage plants, millet, corn, sorghum, and other vegetables and plants to learn which varieties were best for the local soil as well as to produce the food for the school. The farm also raised different varieties of hogs and cattle for the same purposes.

Bishop was also in charge of the Farmers' Convention at Talladega and in some of the beats of the county, where he sought to encourage farmers to have better homes, schools, stock, and crops. Although two of these conventions met at Talladega in 1894, by 1896 they had become annual affairs. These conventions had been meeting at Talladega since 1880, when the first such convention held by an AMA school met. This meeting was more than a decade before such conventions were established at Tuskegee, although the Talladega conventions never became so large or nationally well known as those at Tuskegee.[45]

Miss Ruth K. Kingsley supervised the laundry and cooking classes in 1896. Girls in night school did the school's washing and ironing to make money to attend day school. The cooking classes taught girls the use of modern cooking utensils in preparing, in a healthful and proper way, such foods as an average family would eat.[46]

Miss A. B. Chalfant was in charge of nursing and sewing classes in 1896. Normal students studied nursing for two years. Miss Chalfant was able to get six boys to take this course for the first time in 1896. Over two hundred girls took sewing in 1896. The sewing classes dealt with everything from hemming to mending to making garments from old clothes. Girls in these classes earned money by doing work for the school and custom work. The more advanced girls made their own dresses. In 1897 George Williamson, Instructor of the Mechanical Department, taught 137 boys the principles of wood-working, mechanical and architectural drawing (and how to make objects from these drawings), painting, glazing, and printing.[47]

While the industries were not so numerous, so well-known, or so well-developed at Talladega as they were at Tuskegee,[48] the preceding examples do show that Talladega was interested in giving its pupils the industrial training they needed. Indeed, many of the industries at Talladega, such as farming and printing, had been in operation long before Tuskegee established them. But the AMA disagreed with Washington's plan of offering only industrial and elementary training. The AMA and W. H. Councill (the other black head of a state, black, normal school in Alabama) firmly believed that black and white industrial education should be based upon and postponed until after a student acquired a thorough general education.[49]

Tuskegee, however, began this training too early in a student's course of study. Introducing industries into the grade school interfered with students' acquiring a full, basic education. Instead of training students in industrial principles which they could adapt to changing situations, Tuskegee just apprenticed them in a specific trade. This over-specialization, not just the outmoded crafts they learned, quickly rendered useless much of the industrial education Tuskegee students received.

The Association's leaders found that the industrial teachers who graduated from Tuskegee were insufficiently prepared to teach above the most elementary level. The AMA schools usually could not staff their industrial departments with Hampton and Tuskegee graduates, who were "successful craftsmen though not good teachers." These graduates could not "organize and communicate their special skill, and [were weak] in the management of men."[50]

Much more serious than the question of the efficiency of Tuskegee's or Talladega's graduates was the question of whether or not industrial training was the proper background for black *leaders.* One AMA leader wrote, "No amount of increased production through industrial efficiency could repay the loss to society if the schools should hold to lower levels men whom nature had destined for leaders."[51]

The basic issue dividing Washington and the AMA was not whether blacks in general needed industrial or liberal education, but whether black leaders needed liberal, higher academic education. John R. Savage, an 1895 graduate of Talladega's College Department, succinctly stated this true issue in an address in 1896. Pleading for "the choicest culture, the broadest scholarship" for black leaders, Savage noted that it was "here that the friends of higher education of my people are misunderstood. They clamor for the higher training, or rather the liberal training, not of the masses, but of those who would marshall the masses." He believed that schools which trained black leaders "of this character [were] . . . doing the most lasting work for the race."[52]

The AMA clearly perceived this challenge. While establishing or supporting primary, industrial, and normal schools, the Association showed its commitment to higher, liberal education for black leaders at Talladega College.[53] In 1894 Henry Swift DeForest (Talladega's president, 1879–1896) stated his and the AMA's basic educational philosophy. "We believe in the higher education, as well as in the lower . . . The schooldays of the leaders of seven millions, whose fathers were made ignorant by law, whom to teach was a crime, should not be fewer nor their opportunities less than are counted necessary to a more favored people."[54] To achieve this goal, Talladega assembled a faculty with degrees from schools like Yale and Oberlin (some with foreign study) to give its students high quality, liberal education—primary, normal, college preparatory, theological, and collegiate.[55]

It is not possible to prove that more of Tuskegee's graduates would have been better leaders had they had a different education. But nothing in Tuskegee's curriculum encouraged higher education. Washington never admitted that he was training leaders—not just "the people"; nor did he consciously shape Tuskegee's curriculum to meet the needs of two different groups—the basic students and the future upper-level leaders. True, many of Tuskegee's students did go on to get more education and many did become leaders, but this could have been owing to the native ability which they brought to Tuskegee.

Their success might have been in spite of, rather than because of, the training they received at Tuskegee.

Along with most of the heads of black schools in Alabama, many black educators (e.g., W. E. B. DuBois most notably and vociferously) rejected or openly attacked Washington's program. Washington usually replied that he did endorse higher education for black leaders (he did serve on the Board of Trustees of black universities outside Alabama). But he did nothing at Tuskegee to validate such statements except hire teachers from and send his children to black schools of higher education.

Three characteristics of the black community in Alabama further undermined Washington's argument. First, during the nineteenth century most blacks (especially up to the secondary level) in Alabama attended schools in the state. Washington's support of other schools outside Alabama did little or nothing for these students. Second, given Tuskegee's relatively large and well-equipped physical plant by the 1890's, Washington could not justly relegate all responsibility for collegiate training to Atlanta, Fisk, Howard, and Talladega. This was especially true since Alabama chartered Tuskegee as a teacher-training school and most of its graduates did become teachers. Washington had some responsibility to help train these leaders, although he avoided assuming this responsibility to appeal to rich businessmen. Washington even conspicuously bragged that he did not teach college preparatory courses (such as Latin, which he enjoyed ridiculing) at Tuskegee. His responsibility was especially serious if his exclusive emphasis on industrial training did turn some promising Tuskegee students aside from taking a higher course of study.

Finally, the socioeconomic status of most blacks in nineteenth century Alabama dictated that even allowing a child to come to school meant that a family had to be willing to sacrifice the work of a field hand. For some families living on the edge of starvation this sacrifice alone meant substantial hardship (in addition to any travel funds or money for books, clothes, or tuition they might feel impelled to give their child). So only the most dedicated, ambitious, and determined students—along with those from more well-to-do black families—could even begin to attend, much less graduate from Tuskegee and the other black schools. Although Washington refused to admit or even to face the fact, his students (and the students in the state's other black secondary schools and colleges) were the prime potential pool for the "Talented Tenth" of black leaders which DuBois so eloquently described. Washington's failure, then, was not what he did—provide industrial education for black workers—but what he failed to do—provide liberal education for black leaders to those blacks in Alabama most likely to become leaders.

Washington's neglect of liberal arts education extended beyond Tuskegee Institute to all the "little Tuskegees" established by Washington's students in the Alabama Black Belt. The letters from these teachers to Washington show both their lack of solid grammatical training at Tuskegee and their attempts to spread the Gospel of Wealth and industrial education among their students.

By 1901, Washington's national political and philanthropic connections made him increasingly influential with many blacks. But even in 1916, the year after Washington died, most black secondary schools in Alabama still followed the lead of the AMA in offering college preparatory or liberal arts education.[56]

That most black educators in Alabama did not follow Washington's lead despite all his national prominence and connections has implications for understanding race relations and black history beyond Alabama. In his public roles Washington was the representative and symbol of white interests rather than being a truly indigenous black leader. Many blacks, even in Alabama, disagreed with Washington from the first although this opposition did not receive national attention until his struggle with W. E. B. DuBois and William Monroe Trotter after 1903. This opposition often centered on principles, e.g., the importance of liberal education, not just on personalities. Even Washington's power and white patronage could not always force those who followed different strategies in trying to escape the web of subordination to adopt his program, even if this disagreement meant losing badly needed money such as the Slater Fund.

Most previous studies of race relations or black leaders and institutions have used national, regional, or political frameworks. These approaches furnish only a partial understanding of the period by overemphasizing white attempts to weave the web of subordination, the acts and ideas of the leaders of state-supported schools, the peripheral issue of industrial versus liberal, academic education, and the apparent primacy of Booker T. Washington among blacks because of his prominence in the white media.[57] A proper understanding of the late nineteenth century requires devoting more attention to the various strategies of black leaders as they tried to lead blacks through holes in the web of subordination, to the ideas and actions of leaders of black private schools which enrolled most black secondary students until after World War I,[58] to the issue of the importance of higher, liberal education for developing black leaders, and to Washington's lack of influence even among his closest counterparts, the heads of black public and private secondary schools in Alabama.

Notes

Introduction

1. For a discussion of the lack of scholarly historical studies of black colleges and universities and a list of the names of the schools that have been studied, see Frederick Chambers, "Histories of Black Colleges and Universities," LVII, *The Journal of Negro History* (July, 1972), 270–75.

2. Some of the best-known state studies would include Horace Mann Bond, *Negro Education in Alabama: A Study in Cotton and Steel* (Washington: Associated Publishers, 1939); Vernon Lane Wharton, *The Negro in Mississippi, 1865–1890* (Chapel Hill, The University of North Carolina Press, 1947); and George Brown Tindall, *South Carolina Negroes, 1877–1900* (Baton Rouge: Louisiana State University Press, 1966 [by arrangement with the University of South Carolina Press, 1952]).

3. Several recently published books do deal with developments within Alabama's black community. William Warren Rogers and Robert David Ward, *August Reckoning: Jack Turner and Racism in Post-Civil War Alabama* (Baton Rouge: Louisiana State University Press, 1973). Peter Kolchin, *First Freedom: The Responses of Alabama's Blacks to Emancipation and Reconstruction* (Westport: Greenwood Press, 1972). Louis R. Harlan, *Booker T. Washington: The Making of a Black Leader, 1856–1901* (New York: Oxford University Press, 1972). Louis R. Harlan, ed., *The Booker T. Washington Papers*, Volumes I, II, and III (Urbana: University of Illinois Press, 1972, 1974).

4. Most of the "industrial" education offered in black schools in nineteenth century Alabama would be considered "vocational" training today. There was little or no "industrial" training in the sense of preparing students to work or to assume leadership roles in modern industries. This study uses the term, "industrial education," however, both for consistency and because most of the educational leaders in Alabama's black schools in the nineteenth century used the term, "industrial education," to refer to any nonacademic job-training offered in their schools.

Most recent histories of education, blacks, Alabama, the South, or even the United States mention the Booker T. Washington-W. E. B. DuBois controversy over accommodation versus militant demands for civil rights and their quarrel over the proper type of education for blacks—industrial training for the masses versus academic, liberal, higher education for the "talented tenth." Brief statements of the Washington-DuBois dispute further give the impression that Washington represented most Southern black educators while DuBois spoke for a few critics whose cause was not to triumph for many years. If black educators in Alabama are representative of those throughout the South, however, it was Washington, not DuBois, who was outside the mainstream of black educational thought.

Chapter 1

1. The Creole residents of Mobile and Baldwin Counties quickly protested that this law violated the codicils of the treaty by which the United States ratified the Louisiana Purchase. The Alabama Legislature then allowed the education of direct descendants of the Negro Creoles who lived in and around Mobile in 1803. In 1860 one hundred and fourteen "free colored" children attended schools in Mobile. Horace Mann Bond, *Negro Education in Alabama: A Study in Cotton and Steel* (Washington: The Associated Publishers, Inc., 1939), pp. 15, 73–74.

2. Ulrich Bonnell Phillips, *American Negro Slavery* (New York: D. Appleton & Co., 1918), p. 342. Stanley M. Elkins, *Slavery: A Problem in American Institutional and Intellectual Life*, Second Edition (Chicago: University of Chicago Press, 1968). John W. Blassingame, *The Slave Community: Plantation Life in the Ante-Bellum South* (New York: Oxford University Press, 1972). Kenneth M. Stampp, *The Peculiar Institution: Slavery in the Ante-Bellum South* (New York: Random House, 1956), pp. 86–140. The active role played by many blacks in education, in politics, and in other areas of their lives immediately after the Civil War in Alabama indicates that Blassingame is correct in his insistence that blacks were able to retain meaningful identities despite the pressures of the plantation.

3. Jessie Pearl Rice, *J. L. M. Curry: Southerner, Statesman and Educator* (New York: King's Crown Press, 1949).

4. Herbert W. Gates, ed., *The Negro—A Congregational Opportunity* (New York: American Missionary Association and Congregational Church Extension Boards, [1922]), p. 19.

5. John B. Myers, "The Education of the Alabama Freedmen During Presidential Reconstruction, 1865–1867," *The Journal of Negro Education*, XL (Spring, 1971), p. 164, quoting the Selma *Morning Times*, December 30, 1865.

6. William Burns Paterson, later President of the Alabama State College [Negro] in Montgomery, began teaching blacks in such a plantation school begun for this purpose. C. M. Stanley, "A Scotch Lad's Gifts to Alabama," *The Alabama Journal*, Undated clipping. W. B. Paterson Papers. On some plantations the blacks joined in providing education for themselves by offering to build the schoolhouse and pay their teacher if the white planter would allow the teacher to board with him. Both O. O. Howard and John W. Alvord reported such plantation schools in 1866. Myers, "The Education of the Alabama Freedmen," p. 167.

7. Willis Gaylord Clark, *History of Education in Alabama*, 1702–1889. Circular of Information No. 3, 1889. Contributions to American Educational History, edited

by Herbert Adams (Washington: Government Printing Office, 1889), pp. 231–32, 270–71. Bond, *Negro Education in Alabama*, p. 84.

8. Myers, "The Education of the Alabama Freedmen," pp. 168–69.

9. Later chapters describe the work of these societies in detail. Julius H. Parmalee, "Freedmen's Aid Societies, 1861–1871," *Negro Education: A Study of the Private and Higher Schools for Colored People in the United States*, 2 volumes. Edited by Thomas Jesse Jones, Department of Interior: Bureau of Education (Washington: Government Printing Office, 1917), I, 280. Richard Bryant Drake, "The American Missionary Association and the Southern Negro, 1861–1888" (Unpublished doctoral dissertation, Emory University, 1957), pp. 18–19. C. W. Buckley to E. M. Cravath, May 17, 1867, Amistad Collection AMA Archives, Dillard University, New Orleans, Louisiana.

10. In 1866 blacks were principals of the schools in Troy and Wetumpka and of one of the schools in Tuscaloosa. Blacks also taught two classes totaling fifty students at Greenville. Elizabeth Bethel, "The Freedmen's Bureau in Alabama," *The Journal of Southern History*, XIV (February, 1948), 61–63, 70. Parmalee, "Freedmen's Aid Societies," p. 281.

11. It is impossible to distinguish "schools" from "classes" in many of the reports since the terms were often used imprecisely if not interchangeably. This total also included Sunday Schools. Bethel, "The Freedmen's Bureau," p. 70.

12. Ibid., pp. 69–70. Since the societies usually paid their teachers, many teachers reported only to their society and not to the Freedmen's Bureau. Bethel, "The Freedmen's Bureau," p. 89. With the Bureau paying more teachers in 1866 and 1867 than ever before or since, however, it is likely that more teachers reported directly to the Bureau during these years than at any other time. This circumstance probably explains some of the precipitous drop in black schools reported to the Bureau in the years after 1867. Also, most organizations, especially on the local level, kept very incomplete records during Reconstruction. The Freedmen's Bureau's reports, therefore, give only a sketchy outline of the minimum of the educational work in Alabama before 1870.

13. Bethel, "The Freedmen's Bureau," pp. 78–79, 88–90.

14. Peter Kolchin shows that the Bureau reports used by Elizabeth Bethel in her study of the Freedmen's Bureau in Alabama were grossly inaccurate and misleading after 1868. Specifically, there were many schools which did not report to the Bureau, so the decline Bethel described was more of schools reporting to the Bureau than of all black schools. Kolchin, *First Freedom: The Responses of Alabama's Blacks to Emancipation and Reconstruction* (Westport, Conn.: Greenwood Press, 1972), pp. 96–97.

15. Of this sum, $116,297.62 went for rent, repair, and construction of school buildings; $34,846.56 for teachers' salaries; $1,307.48 for teachers' transportation; $4,411.26 for superintendents' salaries; $71.87 for school books; and $6.31 for transporting school books. Bethel, "The Freedmen's Bureau," pp. 88–91.

16. Ibid.

17. Myers, "The Education of Alabama Freedmen," pp. 170–71.

18. There was no single white position on black education. As Horace Mann Bond, C. Vann Woodward, and others have pointed out, even native, Southern whites differed among themselves on most issues during this period. Still, most of Alabama's white leaders did move from opposing any black education to endorsing some form of formal, state-supported black education. Horace Mann Bond, *The Education of the*

Negro in the American Social Order [Reprinted with new material] (New York: Octagon Books, Inc., 1966), pp. 14–19. C. Vann Woodward, *Origins of the New South, 1877–1913* (Baton Rouge: Louisiana State University Press, 1951).

19. Well-known histories of Reconstruction in Alabama and education in the South incorrectly state that Alabama's whites established public schools for blacks before Congressional Reconstruction. Edgar Wallace Knight, *Public Education in the South* (Boston: Ginn & Co., 1922), p. 314. Walter Lynwood Fleming, *Civil War and Reconstruction in Alabama* (New York: Columbia University Press, 1905), pp. 607, 802. On page 892, Fleming made the patently false claim that "in education, the negro has no opportunities now [1905] that were not freely offered him in 1865–1866, and the school system is not a product of Reconstruction, but came near being destroyed by it." Significantly, Fleming did not document either claim. Two recent studies agree that black education dates from Congressional Reconstruction. Loren Schweninger, "The American Missionary Association and Northern Philanthropy in Reconstruction Alabama," *Alabama Historical Quarterly* (Fall and Winter, 1970), p. 143. Myers, "The Education of the Alabama Freedmen," p. 171. Even Willis Gaylord Clark, a Mobile educational leader and author of a history of Alabama education, admitted that Mobile—Alabama's pacesetter in public education—did not actually open schools for blacks until after Congressional Reconstruction began. Even these Mobile schools, however, were not free until after Alabama's Reconstruction Board of Education passed a bill establishing free public education for blacks and whites throughout Alabama. Willis G. Clark, *History of Education*, pp. 231–33.

20. Myers, "Education of the Alabama Freedmen," p. 170.

21. Ibid., p. 171.

22. George Arlington Hillier, "History of Educational Legislation in Alabama, 1860–1910" (Unpublished master's thesis, University of Chicago, 1924), pp. 93–94.

23. Bond, *Negro Education*, pp. 89–98.

24. Black public normal schools did not really begin to flourish until 1874–1875. Black teacher training, therefore, is a major exception to Peter Kolchin's conclusion that, "In education . . . most of the basic patterns of the new order were well established within a few years after the end of the war." Kolchin, *First Freedom*, p. 99. Black normal schools and the black normal school and university offered the only post-primary public education for nineteenth century blacks in Alabama. Excepting normal schools, the University of Alabama, and the Alabama Polytechnic Institute, the special school districts in the larger towns offered the only public high school education for white and black students in Alabama before 1907 when the state provided county high schools for white students. Even in the cities, most black public high schools began around 1900. Later chapters will describe the development of private black high schools and normal schools which enrolled most post-primary black students until after the First World War.

25. These were Mobile, Montgomery, Huntsville, and Selma (cities); Talladega, Eufaula, Athens, Tuscumbia, Marion, Evergreen, and Portersville (towns). Stephen Beauregard Weeks, *The History of Public School Education in Alabama*, Bureau of Education Bulletin No. 12, 1915 (Washington: Government Printing Office, 1915), p. 155.

26. Ibid. These classes were located in Huntsville, three; Talladega, two; Portersville, Evergreen, Montgomery, and Mobile, one each. Clark, *History of Education*, p. 254.

27. The board located these schools at Huntsville, Talladega, Marion, and Mobile.

Since there were American Missionary Association schools at each of these places, the black normal classes probably met in conjunction with the AMA schools. Clark, *History of Education*, p. 254.

28. Weeks, *Public School Education*, p. 155.

29. Clark said that Hodgson did not mention normal schools in his regular report for 1871. Clark, *History of Education*, p. 256. Bond first said that Hodgson reported sixteen classes, seven of which were for blacks, then that Hodgson reported nine classes, four of which were for blacks. Bond, *Negro Education*, p. 105.

30. The board appropriated the following amounts for these schools: Montgomery, $1,500; Marion, $1,250; Huntsville, $1,000; Sparta, $1,000. Payton Finley, the black member of the board, introduced this bill along with a bill to establish four normal schools for white teachers. The board appropriated $4,500 for the white schools. Bond, *Negro Education*, p. 106. These "schools" were usually "classes" in private schools.

31. Ibid. Clark incorrectly gave this date as 1873, instead of 1872. Clark, *History of Education*, p. 254. The sources conflicted even with themselves, about when the Montgomery and Sparta schools ceased receiving an appropriation. Weeks, *Public School Education*, p. 156. Clark, *History of Education*, pp. 253–54. Whatever the order in which the board dropped Montgomery and Sparta, only Marion and Huntsville still received appropriations after 1874.

32. Weeks, *Public School Education*, pp. 156–57. For a full discussion of Peyton Finley's political maneuvering in the Board of Education to get this normal school and university, see Bond, *Negro Education*, pp. 107–09.

33. Bond, *Negro Education*, pp. 106, 109–10. Its faculty's being white probably caused this school to get more money than the Huntsville school received.

34. Weeks, *Public School Education*, pp. 156–57.

35. H. B. Williams, "Legal Provisions for the Education of the Negro in the State of Alabama, and How They Affect the Program of Negro Education from 1873–1949" (Unpublished master's thesis, Alabama State College, Montgomery, Alabama, 1950), pp. 50–51. There is no record that this school ever opened.

36. Weeks, *History of Public School Education*, pp. 156–57.

37. The legislature did raise Huntsville's appropriation from $2,000 to $4,000 in 1885. Allen Johnston Going, *Bourbon Democracy in Alabama 1874–1890*, (University, Alabama: University of Alabama Press, 1951), pp. 159–61.

38. Bond, *Negro Education*, p. 109. Going, *Bourbon Democracy*, pp. 163–67.

39. Ibid. Unlike Mississippi which granted the black college, Alcorn, part of its land-grant money in 1878, Alabama did not give blacks any part of its land-grant money until the Second Morrill Land Grant Act of 1890 stated that the money it provided had to go to black and white schools. When the Huntsville school received this land-grant money it moved to nearby Normal to have land for its agricultural programs.

40. In 1887, Alabama dropped even the rhetoric and name of the black university as is discussed below. Going is incorrect in claiming that "After the Marion school had been moved to Montgomery in 1887, an attempt was made to change its name to the Alabama Colored People's University," Going, *Bourbon Democracy*, p. 160. This school had been the black university, in name only, since 1873.

41. Clark, *History of Education*, pp. 270–71.

42. Bond, *Negro Education*, pp. 93–94.

43. Hillier, "History of Educational Legislation," pp. 93–94.

44. William P. Vaughn, "Partners in Segregation: Barnas Sears and the Peabody Fund," *Civil War History* (September, 1964), pp. 263–64. Sears believed so strongly in segregation that he abandoned his usually nonpartisan stance to lobby actively to defeat the integration clause of the Civil Rights Act of 1875. He also pointedly penalized Louisiana public schools by refusing to give them Peabody money because they permitted integration. Perhaps the fact that Alabama's Constitution of 1868 did not require segregation caused Sears to limit Peabody grants to black schools in Alabama during Reconstruction, rather than his excuse that Alabama lacked large towns, the usual focus of Peabody grants. Ibid., pp. 260–74. In any event Alabama did receive substantially smaller grants from the Peabody Fund than did most other Southern states. See also, Lewis W. Jones, "The Agent as a Factor in the Education of Negroes in the South," *Journal of Negro Education*, XIX (1950), pp. 28–37.

45. For a fuller exposition of the limits which the American Creed placed on Southern segregation see Gunnar Myrdal, *An American Dilemma: The Negro Problem and Modern Democracy* (New York: Harper and Row, Publishers, 1944), II, 880–82. The image of a web seems to best symbolize developing white attitudes toward black education. The holes in the web then represent the options open to blacks within these restrictions. Andrew Billingsley develops the idea of opportunities within a restrictive system in his chapter, "Screens of Opportunity," in *Black Families in White America* (Englewood Cliffs: Prentice-Hall, Inc., 1968), pp. 97–121. Northern political pressure and the rise of the ideal of universal public education in the South in the late nineteenth century also helped keep Southerners from totally forbidding all education to blacks.

46. Going, *Bourbon Democracy*, p. 151. The new constitution also lowered the minimum annual appropriation for education to $100,000. Under the 1868 Constitution school revenues amounted to $484,000. Ibid. While this provision was not specifically racial, any lessening of educational funds affected the black schools more severely since their need was greater. The 1875 Constitution also struck indirectly at black private schools (many of which had received state funds during Reconstruction) by forbidding granting state funds to sectarian or denominational schools. Bond, *Negro Education*, pp. 132, 149.

47. Bond, *Negro Education*, pp. 132, 149.

48. Ibid.

49. Hillier, "History of Educational Legislation," pp. 120–23.

50. Bond wrote that this decision declared that all separate school districts with taxing powers were illegal, but the decision actually only struck down those districts which were not coterminus with municipal corporations, i.e. rural school districts or plural districts within one city. This mistake caused Bond to overestimate the seriousness of the decision and to give it too much weight as a cause of the severely discriminatory legislation of 1891. Bond, *Negro Education*, p. 137 *et passim*. Actually, from 1890–1891 to 1898–1899, the legislature created about 191 separate school districts. Most of these acts gave the district the power to levy local taxes. Hillier, "History of Educational Legislation," pp. 120–23. This local legislation also shows that all local schools were not so desperate as Bond pictured them as being.

51. While national events such as the tenth anniversary of the Compromise of 1877 ending Reconstruction or the controversy surrounding President Grover Cleveland's attempt to return captured Confederate battle flags might have contributed to an

atmosphere of tension in Alabama, the troubles of the black schools grew out of local incidents.

52. See the chapter on Councill for a full description of these events.

53. Atticus G. Haygood to Rutherford B. Hayes, June 5, 1888. Louis D. Rubin, Jr., *Teach the Freeman: The Correspondence of Rutherford B. Hayes and the Slater Fund for Negro Education* (Baton Rouge: Louisiana State University Press, 1959), II, 19–20.

54. May L. Phillips, *Lincoln Normal School, Marion, Alabama*, n.p. [1905] [p. 1]. [Montgomery] *Herald*, January 8, 1887. Huntsville *Gazette*, March 26, 1887, quoting the [Selma] *Independent*, n. d. The editor of the Huntsville *Gazette*, on March 26, 1887, claimed that the legislature "'cut off their nose to spite their faces' [when] They abolished . . . [the school] to satisfy a narrow minded denominational whim."

55. Huntsville *Gazette*, July 2, 1887.

56. Ibid., March 19, 1887 quoting the [Montgomery] *Herald*. Several of Montgomery's leading black citizens finally did agree to serve as a Board of Advisers to the trustees.

57. Interview of T. G. Jones, Montgomery *Advertiser*, August 21, 1887. Jones' vehemence against Editor Duke grew out of Duke's explanation of lynchings in terms of "the growing appreciation of white Juliets for colored Romeos." Such statements caused the white vigilantes of Montgomery to close down Duke's press and run him out of town. While the Huntsville *Gazette* condemned Duke's remarks, Booker T. Washington secretly paid him to oppose locating the school in Montgomery. Louis R. Harlan, *Booker T. Washington: The Making of a Black Leader, 1856–1901* (New York: Oxford University Press, 1972), pp. 166–67. In condemning Duke and stressing white control of the school, Jones was trying to disarm those whites who opposed locating the school in Montgomery on the grounds that it might breed other "incendiaries" like Duke.

58. Huntsville *Gazette*, June 27, 1887. [Montgomery] *Herald*, August 6, 1887. Blacks in Selma and Marion also wanted the school in their town, but the trustees never seriously considered either of the locations. M. M. Stevens to Booker T. Washington, May 24, 1887. S. Childs to Booker T. Washington, February 10, 1887. Booker T. Washington Papers. Library of Congress.

59. Louis R. Harlan's biography of Booker T. Washington described Washington's private efforts to keep the school out of Montgomery, but these private moves were only an extension of Washington's public opposition to the school. Harlan, *Booker T. Washington*, pp. 166–67.

60. "Initial," [Montgomery correspondent], Huntsville *Gazette*, July 16, 1887. [Montgomery] *Herald*, August 6, 1887. Huntsville *Gazette*, March 26, July 30, 1887.

61. Arthur L. Brooks to Booker T. Washington, [1887], Booker T. Washington Papers. T. G. Jones, Interview, Montgomery *Advertiser*, August 21, 1887.

62. T. G. Jones, Interview, Montgomery *Advertiser*, August 21, 1887. Jones carefully noted that his appointment to the board "was unexpected and undesired and not known to me until announced in the papers. I accepted as did the other members from a high sense of duty." Thus, even the leader of the fight for a black school acted only out of a sense of *noblesse oblige* and grudging paternalism.

63. Williams, "Legal Provisions," p. 17.

64. Ibid., p. 18. Going, *Bourbon Democracy*, p. 161.

65. There was one significant omission in the Montgomery school's 1889 charter. Despite T. G. Jones' remark in 1887 that it was an industrial school, Montgomery's

charter established it as a normal school although it did offer some industrial work. At the request of their presidents, the Huntsville school became a normal and industrial school in 1885 as did Tuskegee in 1893. This indicates that as late as 1889 the Alabama legislature did not believe that all black education should be industrial education. Thus, William H. Councill's and Booker T. Washington's request to make their schools legally industrial reflected more than just a desire to curry favor with the Alabama legislature.

66. Bond, *Negro Education*, pp. 153–54.

67. Going, *Bourbon Democracy*, p. 158.

68. While Alabama provided a university for whites, it offered post-primary education during the nineteenth century to blacks only in normal schools, which received their support out of the blacks' share of the state school fund. Thus, the only semblance of equality in Alabama's school system was at the level of the local primary school. Not only was the state support for the University of Alabama separate from the common school fund, but it was much larger than the amount ever allotted the black "university," (in existence on paper, 1874–1887). For example, the University of Alabama received $24,000 in 1874 while the black "university" at Marion received only $2,000. Bond, *Negro Education*, p. 110. Chapter 2 deals with the development of Alabama's black normal schools.

69. Washington attacked this newspaper story, denying emphatically that he had been bitter. He insisted that he "would have been willing for the whole legislature or all of the citizens of Tuskegee to have heard all that [he] said." Regardless of the tone or content of what he actually said, the coverage of this speech undoubtedly had much to do with Washington and Tuskegee Institute's losing the black share of the land grant money to William Hooper Councill and Alabama A. & M. College on February 13, 1891. Chapter 4, pp. 43–44 describes this conflict more fully.

70. Bond, *Negro Education*, pp. 151, 156–60. Bond's emphases.

71. Ibid., p. 160.

72. This is Bond's explanation. Ibid., p. 161.

73. Going, *Bourbon Democracy*, p. 158.

74. Weeks, *Public School Education*, p. 197. These are official figures. The actual differences might have been wider. Indeed, the greater the discrimination, the less likely a local superintendent would have been to report it.

75. Bond, *Negro Education*, p. 163.

76. Williams, "Legal Provisions," pp. 24, 26. This last provision struck at those white missionaries' children such as Lee de Forest who had been attending black schools.

77. Hillier, "History of Educational Legislation," p. 83.

78. Bond, *Negro Education*, p. 194.

Chapter 2

1. *Up From Slavery* and *Finding a Way Out* are the titles of the autobiographies of Booker T. Washington and his successor at Tuskegee, Robert Russa Moton.

2. John W. Blassingame, *The Slave Community: Plantation Life in the Ante-Bellum South* (New York: Oxford University Press, 1972).

3. This was also true for white schools in poor areas at this time, but the widespread

poverty of blacks makes this analysis especially important in understanding black schools.

4. Sometimes black parents, such as Booker T. Washington's father, were not willing to make this sacrifice and opposed their children's getting an education. Booker T. Washington, *Up From Slavery* (New York: Doubleday & Company, Inc., 1901), p. 21.

5. Of course similar activities occurred in the white schools, but there the school officials and the community supporting the school coincided. In the case of the black school, the school officials were white, whereas the community support and pressure came from blacks. Thus, to use a phrase from studies of slavery, the white superintendent was not the black teacher's sole "significant other."

6. While the figures to support such a conclusion would be virtually impossible to obtain, the local public subsidies of white education were also probably greater than those provided to black schools.

7. *Report of the United States Commissioner of Education, 1882–1883*, Bureau of Education, Interior Department (Washington: Government Printing Office, 1884), p. 7.

8. Ibid., Hillier, "Educational Legislation," p. 52.

9. Huntsville *Gazette*, 1882–1894.

10. Booker T. Washington to Major John G. Harris, February 20, 1892, *et passim*. Booker T. Washington Papers.

11. Weeks, *Public School Education*, p. 158. Hillier, "Educational Legislation," p. 52.

12. The latter resolution did have an educational as well as a political basis since poll taxes went to support education.

13. Huntsville *Gazette*, June 24, 1882; April 23, 1892; September 9, 1893; May 12, April 21, July 30, 1894; June 22, 29, November 2, 1889; July 8, 1893; May 5, June 16, 1888; June 29, August 17, 31, 1889; August 16, 30, 1890; July 4, 18, 1891; August 13, 1892.

14. This black organization preceded the reorganization of the teachers of Alabama's white schools who met in Birmingham in July, 1882, to revive the Alabama Teachers' Association, which had been inactive since the Civil War except for 1871–1872. Not wishing to be confused with the STA, the whites soon changed their name to the Alabama Education Association. Weeks, *Public School Education*, p. 159. *Report of the United States Commissioner of Education, 1882–1883*, p. 9.

15. Ibid.

16. *A Yearbook on Negro Education in Alabama, 1930–1931* (Montgomery: State Teachers Association, 1931), pp. 69–70. *Proceedings of the Congregational Association of Alabama, 1880, 1888*. Letters from G. M. Elliott to Booker T. Washington, Booker T. Washington Papers. Huntsville *Gazette*, April 21, 1887. In 1888, Edwin C. Silsby, Talladega College's Treasurer, wrote Washington that the STA had dealt with the physical and moral elements of teaching but had "not given prominence, except incidentally, to the mental element." Silsby proposed to correct this imbalance with a paper he wanted to read before the next STA convention. E. C. Silsby to Booker T. Washington, January 14, 1888. Booker T. Washington Papers.

17. Clement Richardson, editor-in-chief, *The National Cyclopedia of the Colored Race* (Montgomery: National Publishing Company, Inc., 1919), I, 420. Charles A. Brown, *Biographical Sketches of Presidents of the Alabama State Teachers Association* (n.p., [1967]), p. 4. *A Yearbook on Negro Education in Alabama, 1930–1931*, p. 70.

18. Richardson, *National Cyclopedia*, I, 42. Brown, *Biographical Sketches*, pp. 4–5.

A Yearbook on Negro Education in Alabama, 1930–1931, p. 70.

19. *A Yearbook on Negro Education in Alabama, 1930–1931*, p. 70. For a biographical sketch of Beverly see Robert G. Sherer, "John William Beverly: Alabama's First Negro Historian," *The Alabama Review*, XXVI (July, 1973), 194–208.

20. Huntsville *Gazette*, May 26, 1894. *A Yearbook on Negro Education in Alabama, 1930–1931*, p. 60. Jeremiah Barnes to Booker T. Washington, March 5, 1887; E. C. Silsby to Booker T. Washington, March 5, 1887; Peter H. Clark to Booker T. Washington, January 16, 1888; W. H. Councill to Booker T. Washington, January 11, 1888; Booker T. Washington Papers.

21. G. M. Elliott to Booker T. Washington, January 8, 1889, Booker T. Washington Papers.

22. Huntsville *Gazette*, April 16, 1887; April 21, 1888.

23. Washington to W. B. Paterson, May 4, 1892. Booker T. Washington Papers.

24. Letters to Washington, 1888. Booker T. Washington to Hon. H. S. D. Mallory, June 22, 1892. Booker T. Washington Papers.

25. Huntsville *Gazette*, May 2, June 10, July 1, 1893.

26. G. W. Andrews, "Talladega College, Ala.," *American Missionary*, LII (October, 1899, No. 4), 111.

27. None of these educational plans offered full black liberation since whites controlled the state economically and politically. But the different educational strategies did offer varying degrees of escape from the whites' attempt to subordinate blacks totally. It is important to understand the various options open to black students for achieving even limited liberation since most blacks and whites throughout our history have seen education as the best means of advancement. For a revealing exposition of America's often misplaced faith in education as a means of solving social problems see Henry J. Perkinson, *The Imperfect Panacea: American Faith in Education, 1865–1965* (New York: Random House, 1968), especially pp. 13–61, "The Negro and the Schools." Much has been written recently attacking the idea that education can solve all our social problems, most notably Christopher Jencks et al., *Inequality: A Reassessment of Family and Schooling in America* (New York: Basic Books, 1973). All such studies questioning the efficacy of education only underscore the depth and extent of America's commitment to education as a social panacea.

Chapter 3

1. For a biography of Paterson see Robert G. Sherer, "William Burns Paterson: The Pioneer as Well as Prophet of Negro Education in Alabama," *Alabama Historical Quarterly*, XXVI (Summer, 1974), 121–50.

2. Mary Frances Terrell, "William Burns Paterson, A Life Sketch," *The State Normal Courier*, II (February 7, 1924), 4. W. B. Paterson to John Paterson, May 23, 1870. Paterson Papers in a private collection. Almost all the letters in this collection are photocopies of originals in Scotland which have been lost since the copies were made in 1952.

3. W. B. Paterson to John Paterson, May 23, 1870. Paterson Papers. Paterson considered the offer of a job as a plantation overseer which would have paid him $1,200 "and perquisites, which would be 8 or 10 more." He evidently declined this job so he could return to Scotland for a visit that summer. Ibid., September 24, 1871.

4. In response to a question from his brother about James Fiske, Paterson wrote

that "thousands" were worse villains than he, "but their tact and fear of disgrace keep it hid from the public view. It is a hard matter for any one who has never been in America and especially N. York to believe how low the people have sunk in moral degradation. . . ." W. B. Paterson to John Paterson, May 6, 1872. Paterson Papers.

5. Paterson was especially concerned about violence at the time of elections. In 1871 he noted that there had already been one fight over the November election which promised "to be quite lively." American fights were more serious than those Paterson's brother, John, "used to enjoy at home for where pistols flash and bowie knives flourish in the air it is rather serious. Every man and boy goes armed [as do] most of the ladies. . . ." W. B. Paterson to John Paterson, September 24, 1871. Paterson Papers.

6. Although most people in Greensboro were afraid of the Ku Klux Klan, Paterson and several of his friends banded together to keep the Klan from rescuing one of their members from jail. One night one hundred fully armed, masked men rode into town on horses whose feet "were muffled so that they moved along as quietly as a spectre." When Paterson saw them he fired his pistol into the air, the signal for his friends to grab their pants and pistols and run to the jail. These men "were all good citizens who had sworn to resist all lawlessness and break up all secret organizations in the County." When the Klansmen prepared a battering ram to break into the jail, Paterson and his men leveled their guns. The Klan then remounted and rode off. Although the Klan had previously done "pretty much as it [had] a mind to do" in Greensboro, after this firm stand by Paterson and his friends, it was "not heard of since in this county." W. B. Paterson to John Paterson, September 24, 1871. Paterson Papers. This letter should dispel the belief that Paterson was ever in the Klan. One writer said that Paterson was in the Greensboro Klan "when it was a badge of honor to be identified with the reconstruction organization." C. M. Stanley, "A Scotch Lad's Gifts to Alabama," The Montgomery *Alabama Journal*. Undated clipping. Paterson Papers. Obviously Paterson did not consider it an honor to be in such an outlaw organization.

7. W. B. Paterson to John Paterson, July 24, 1873, May 23, November 14, 1870. Paterson Papers.

8. Stanley, "A Scotch Lad's Gifts." Paterson Papers.

9. Ibid.

10. Paterson's racial views also changed in 1870. All his letters until 1870 referred to the blacks working under his direction as "niggers." After establishing his school, he mentioned "the people" with whom he worked, who greeted him upon his return from Scotland, but he never again wrote "nigger" in any of his correspondence.

11. Terrell, "William Burns Paterson," p. 4. Walter B. Jones, "William Burns Paterson," quoting Jesse B. Hearin, *The Gulf Breeze* (New Orleans), October, 1952. Undated clipping. "Notes for Mrs. Marie B. Owen." Stanley, "A Scotch Lad's Gifts." Undated clipping. Paterson Papers.

12. W. B. Paterson to John Paterson, October 11, 1875. Paterson Papers.

13. Note that Paterson clearly emphasized both classical and modern foreign languages. He made no mention of industrial education, although he had wide experience in a variety of jobs. This would indicate that Paterson did not believe that black education should be industrial education. His adopting industrial education later in the state school must have been due to political pressure or to economic pressure—the need for funds available only by offering industrial education.

14. W. B. Paterson to John Paterson, July 24, 1873. Paterson Papers.

15. Quoted in Glenn Nolan Sisk, "The Alabama Black Belt: A Social History,

1875–1917" (Unpublished doctoral dissertation, Duke University), p. 188.

16. *The Alabama State College for Negroes, Montgomery, Alabama: Freshman Handbook, 1950–1951.* Mimeographed copy, p. 12. Hooper Councill Trenholm, *Yearbook of the Alabama State Teachers' Association, 1949* (Montgomery: State Teachers College, 1949), p. 24. Even so, Alabama gave the school only $2,000 in 1873. Hattye L. Whitney, "The Development of Public Secondary Education for Negroes in the State of Alabama, 1873 to 1945," (Unpublished master's thesis, Howard University, 1946), p. 32. The Alabama Legislature abolished the Marion school in 1887. At the urging and with the enthusiastic aid of Marion blacks, the AMA reopened a school at Marion. See the chapter on the AMA schools for the later history of this school. Actually the AMA did not own this school. Local blacks raised the money and then helped build a schoolhouse which they turned over to a board of trustees which leased it to the AMA for ten years in 1868. The AMA then provided a principal and teachers for the school. After 1870, the pastors of the local Congregational Church conducted the school until Alabama took control in 1873. *Lincoln Normal School, Marion, Alabama* (New York: American Missionary Association, n.d.), p. 1. Frederick L. Brownlee, *New Day Ascending* (Boston: Pilgrim Press, 1946), p. 124. M. L. Phillips, *Lincoln Normal School, Marion, Alabama* ([New York: American Missionary Association, 1905]), p. 1. In 1870–1871, the AMA also bought up eighty acres of land to sell to blacks in and around Marion as homesteads. This proved to be an immediate success. Brownlee, *New Day Ascending*, p. 124. This land experiment, the AMA school, and the initiative the local blacks had already showed in building the schoolhouse had far reaching consequences in the years to come. When Horace Mann Bond examined the home county of the ancestors of several leading black professionals in 1963, he discovered that by far the largest number had relatives in Perry County, where Marion is located. In citing this study in his book, *Black Families in White America*, Billingsley noted that his father was from Marion and received all his education in the Lincoln Normal School. Billingsley, *Black Families*, pp. 117–21.

17. AMA *Reports, 1872, 1874.*

18. *Freshman Handbook*, p. 12. Trenholm, *Yearbook, 1949*, pp. 15, 25. H. B. Williams, "Legal Provisions for the Education of the Negro in the State of Alabama, and How They Affect the Program of Negro Education from 1873–1949" (Unpublished master's thesis, Alabama State College for Negroes, 1950), pp. 16–17. Marion's "liberal" endowment of $2,000 compared poorly with the University of Alabama's income of $24,000 at the same time.

19. During Card's first year, 1874–1875, he was the only teacher of the thirty to forty students. In 1875 John Moore, newly appointed President of the Board of Directors of the school, reorganized the school by hiring two assistants for Card. The student body increased to seventy students during the 1875–1876 school term. These students studied reading, writing, geography, spelling, grammar, drawing, composition, arithmetic, algebra, geometry, Latin, Physiology, methods of teaching, and chemistry. Thirty of the students taught public schools during the preceding year. The school's term ran from October through June. The school day opened at 9:00 a.m. and closed at 5:00 p.m. *Report of the Alabama Superintendent of Education, 1875*, pp. 122–23. One of Card's assistants, John Silsby, was the AMA missionary who helped begin the school in 1867. *AMA Reports, 1874.*

20. Whitney, "Public Secondary Education," p. 32. Sarah H. Koyton, "State Normal's First Graduating Class," *The State Normal Courier*, II (February 7, 1924), 5.

21. Unidentified biographical sketch of W. B. Paterson. Jones, "Off the Bench," Undated clipping. *Rosemont Gardens*, Printed folder. Jones, "William Burns Paterson," quoting Hearin, *The Gulf Breeze*, Clipping. Stanley, "A Scotch Lad's Gifts," Clipping. Paterson Papers.

22. Koyton, "First Graduating Class," p. 5.

23. Williams, "Legal Provisions," pp. 16–17. The timing of the introduction of industrial work suggests that Paterson might have been primarily interested in getting money from the Slater Fund, which began providing money for schools with industrial departments in 1883.

24. A. S. Plump, "State Normal as 'The Lincoln Normal University' at Marion," *The State Normal Courier*, II (February 7, 1924), 6–7. Trenholm, *Yearbook, 1949*, p. 25.

25. See the first chapter for more details on these events.

26. "Initial," Montgomery correspondent, Huntsville *Gazette*, August 27, September 10, October 8, 1887. Feelings must have been at a fever pitch, for the *Gazette*'s editor consistently opposed emigration (even from the country to the cities of Alabama). This was one of the few times that the paper even printed an article urging emigration.

27. Terrell, "William Burns Paterson," p. 4.

28. Frances Reynolds, "Reminiscences: The First Years at Montgomery," *The State Normal Courier*, II (February 7, 1924), 7. *Alabama State College Bulletin: Montgomery, Alabama: 1967–1968*, V (July–August, 1967), 21.

29. Reynolds, "Reminiscences," p. 7. James S. Julian, "Reminiscences: The Period of 1890–1894," *The State Normal Courier*, II (February 7, 1924), 8.

30. Williams, "Legal Provisions," pp. 16–17. Reynolds, "Reminiscences," p. 7.

31. See Chapter 1 for a description of this act.

32. Julian, "Reminiscences," pp. 8–9.

33. Ibid., p. 8. Bertie L. Hall, "A Bit of History," *The State Normal Courier*, II (February 7, 1924), 8. *State College Bulletin: 1967–1968*, p. 21.

34. Huntsville *Gazette*, January 15, 1889. Alfred Billingslea was the proprietor of "a First-class Barber Shop in Exchange Hotel." Advertisement in Montgomery *City Directory, 1891*, p. 8.

35. Julian, "Reminiscences," pp. 8–9.

36. Reynolds, "Reminiscences," p. 7. Mrs. Reynolds was a member of this class.

37. *The State Normal Courier*, II (February 7, 1924), 3ff. The high school was the highest branch of the school until 1921. Ibid., p. 3. Alabama State did not award a B.A. until 1931. Trenholm, *Yearbook, 1949*, p. 28.

38. Chapter 4 contains a full description of this controversy.

39. Terrell, "Reminiscences," pp. 4–5.

40. *Report of the United States Commissioner of Education For the Year, 1882–1883* (Washington: Government Printing Office, 1884), p. 9. For a discussion of Francis W. Parker and his "Quincy Plan" see Lawrence A. Cremin, *The Transformation of the School: Progressivism in American Education, 1876–1957* (New York: Alfred A. Knopf, 1961), pp. 128–35.

41. Trenholm, *Yearbook, 1949*, p. 26.

42. *Report of the Alabama Commissioner of Education, 1902*, pp. 228–29.

43. Paterson's children did not follow him in teaching in his school, but they did continue this flower business. From a sixteen-by-fifty-foot greenhouse on a five-acre

plot in 1890, Paterson's Rosemont Gardens grew to become one of the largest florists in Montgomery. Over a half century after Paterson's death, his descendants still conduct this business. L. D. Hale, ed., *The Courier Courtesy Magazine*, IV (February, 1927), 3. Jones, "William Burns Paterson," quoting Hearin, *The Gulf Breeze*, Clipping. Jones, "Off the Bench," Clipping. Paterson Papers.

44. Terrell, "Reminiscences," p. 5. His passing was overshadowed for most of his contemporaries and most later writers by the other leader of black education who died in the same year, Booker T. Washington.

45. Hooper Councill Trenholm, *Yearbook of the Alabama State Teachers' Association, 1931* (Montgomery, State Teachers' College, 1931), p. 68.

Chapter 4

1. Walter S. Buchanan, *Founder's Day Address* (n.p., [1950]), p. 5. Reprint of June, 1950 issue of *The Normal Index*. Charles Walter Orr, "The Educational Philosophy of William H. Councill." (Unpublished master's thesis, Department of Education, Fisk University, 1939), p. 5. Buchanan, Councill's son-in-law and successor as the President of the Agricultural and Mechanical College for Negroes, wrote that the Councills were sold on the Huntsville Court House steps. H. C. Hopkins, one of Councill's first pupils, wrote that they were sold at the Green Bottom Inn near Huntsville. H. C. Hopkins, "Founder's Day Address," *The Normal Index*, [IV] (May, 1927), 155. Orr, who later taught at the school, could find no record of slaves having been sold at the Inn, although slaves were sold at the Court House. Orr insists, however, that oral tradition among Huntsville blacks maintained that Councill was sold at the Inn. Interview with Charles Walter Orr, February 26, 1969. Since the Commissioners of the school bought the land around the Inn and made the Inn into the president's home in 1891, it is possible that the oral tradition grew out of this later event as local blacks sought to elaborate the ironic image of a plantation becoming a black school.

2. Hopkins, "Founder's Day Address," p. 155.

3. Orr, "Educational Philosophy," p. 6, quoting William Hooper Councill, "From an Editorial," *The Colored American*, January 28, 1889.

4. W. H. Councill, *The Young Negro of 1864; The Young Negro of 1904* (Boston: Charles Alexander, Printer, [1904]), p. 5.

5. Ibid., pp. 4–6.

6. Hopkins, "Founder's Day Address," p. 155. Orr, "Educational Philosophy," quoting Councill, "From an Editorial," *The Colored American*, January 28, 1899.

7. Orr, "Educational Philosophy," p. 6.

8. This school did not open until 1875 "due to the diversion of the State Fund in 1873." Bond, *Negro Education*, pp. 106, 109.

9. Orr, "Educational Philosophy," p. 6. Clement Richardson, ed., *The National Cyclopedia of the Colored Race* (Montgomery: National Publishing Company, Inc., 1919), I, 460.

10. Hopkins, "Founder's Day Address," pp. 153–55. Orr, "Educational Philosophy," p. 8.

11. A. W. McKinney, "Professor W. H. Councill," *The Normal Index*, [IV, No. 7] (May, 1927), 156.

12. The 1901 Constitution of Alabama fulfilled Councill's prophecy four years early.

13. William Hooper Councill, *Bright Side of the Southern Question* (n.p., [1903]), p. 11.

14. Hopkins, "Founder's Day Address," p. 155.

15. Buchanan, *Founder's Day Address*, p. 5. Orr, "Educational Philosophy," p. 8. Peter B. Young, "The Negro Community of Huntsville, Alabama, 1881–1894" (Unpublished senior honors thesis, Louisiana State University, 1957), p. 94. On December 9, 1882, the Huntsville *Gazette* noted that Alabama State Senators Shelby and Williams had introduced bills to abolish the school.

16. Whereas Tuskegee's day began and ended with a bell, Normal's began and ended with "Taps."

17. Buchanan, *Founder's Day Address*, pp. 5, 9. Councill was an ordained African Methodist Episcopal minister and Superintendent of the Huntsville A.M.E. Church, a member of the Prince Hall Masons, and a founder of the Independent Order of Immaculates and the Pallbearers, a burial society. Interview with Charles W. Orr, February 26, 1969.

18. Richardson, *National Cyclopedia*, I, 460.

19. Ibid. Unlike Washington, Councill evidently wrote all this material himself. After 1905, Councill spent most of his time working on three more books. One described Councill's experiences in the Richmond slave pen. John Temple Graves, a Birmingham publicist, wrote a letter to be included in one of the books, and Joe Wheeler, a Confederate veteran, contributed a foreword or introduction for another. When Councill died, his secretary, Mrs. Carrie Bell Lee, prepared the manuscripts for publication but had to await the settlement of Dr. W. L. Councill's contest of the will to pay the publication costs. At this time Sidney J. Mayhew, Chairman of the school's Board of Commissioners and executor of Councill's will, decided to store the manuscripts in the vault of his bank, the Huntsville Bank and Trust Company. The bank soon burned "and the manuscripts were never found." Buchanan, *Founder's Day Address*, p. 10.

20. H. C. Hopkins, "Founder's Day Address," p. 155.

21. Buchanan, *Founder's Day Address*, p. 11.

22. W. H. Councill to Booker T. Washington, September 3, 1887. Booker T. Washington Papers, Library of Congress. Although Councill knew that the Interstate Commerce Commission would not award him any damages in his suit protesting being ejected from a first class car, he had already spent $976.70 to push the suit hoping the I.C.C. would force the railroads "to treat colored passengers as they do white ones." Councill had only received $75 in donations to help him with the suit. Ibid. Councill prophesied correctly. In its first decision, the I.C.C. did not award damages but did order equal treatment on railroads. Unfortunately for blacks, the United States government did not enforce this I.C.C. ruling.

23. Young, "The Negro Community of Huntsville," p. 96, quoting *Probate Record of Madison County*, XLIII, p. 444.

24. Buchanan, *Founder's Day Address*, p. 11.

25. Alabama first sought a white man to head Tuskegee. One white man did consider the job, but quickly rejected it when he discovered that the school had no buildings. The trustees asked Samuel Chapman Armstrong at Hampton Institute for a white nominee to conduct the school, but agreed to accept Washington instead. Basil Mathews, *Booker T. Washington: Educator and Interracial Interpreter* (Cambridge: Harvard University Press, 1948), pp. 63–64. Booker T. Washington, *Up From Slavery*

(New York: Doubleday & Co., Inc., 1901), pp. 74–75.

26. Hopkins, "Founder's Day Address," p. 155. Clark, *History of Educaton*, p. 277. *Report of the State Superintendent of Education, 1879*, pp. 8, 15.

27. Clark, *History of Education*, p. 277. Charles W. Orr claimed that Councill did teach industries at Huntsville before 1881, but he did not have any documentation to back up his claim. Interview, February 26, 1969. H. C. Hopkins, who claimed to have been a student at the school from 1875 to at least 1887, said that Councill preceded Washington in urging industrial education. Even Hopkins, however, listed no industries at the school before 1882, and he misdated a speech Councill gave supporting industrial education from 1887 to 1878. H. C. Hopkins, "Founder's Day Address," [1927], pp. 155, 165.

28. G. B. Richings, *Evidences of Progress Among Colored People* (Philadelphia: George S. Ferguson Co., 1896), p. 203. Hopkins, "Founder's Day Address," p. 155. In 1883, the Chairman of the Board of Commissioners admitted that they used $1,080 out of the state appropriation to buy the land and building. *Report of the Superintendent of Education, 1882*, p. 22. Although this was strictly illegal (only four percent of the state appropriation could legally be used for anything but teachers' salaries), there is no record of the state's taking action against the school for this purchase.

29. Clark, *History of Education*, pp. 277–78.

30. Huntsville *Gazette*, February 21, 1885.

31. Thomas McAdory Owen, *History of Alabama and Dictionary of Alabama Biography* (Chicago: The S. J. Clarke Publishing Company, 1921), I, 4. Orr, "Educational Philosophy," p. 23, quoting the Tuscaloosa *Chronicle*.

32. Hopkins, "Founder's Day Address," p. 165. Although Hopkins, one of Councill's first students when the school opened, might have been at Huntsville when these industries were introduced, his desire to praise Councill and the fact that Hopkins gave this talk forty-five years after the event raise some doubts as to the accuracy of his speech.

33. Huntsville *Gazette*, December 15, 1883. *Thirty-first Annual Report of the Superintendent of Education, 1885*, pp. 62–63.

34. Haygood to Hayes, June 5, 1888, Rubin, *Teach the Freemen*, I, 19–20. Haygood's saying "in his day" and the fact that he wrote this letter after Councill had been suspended from the school because his students had dared to sit in a "white" car on a train indicated that aid from the Slater Fund was based on not offending the sensitivities of the white South.

35. Samuel Reid Spencer, Jr., *Booker T. Washington and the Negro's Place in American Life* (Boston: Little, Brown and Company, 1955), p. 77. Huntsville *Gazette*, November 21, December 5, 1885.

36. *Report of the Commissioner of Education, 1882–1883* (Washington: Government Printing Office, 1884), p. 9.

37. Huntsville *Gazette*, May 2, 1885. Interview with Charles W. Orr, February 26, 1969. Neither Orr nor anyone who wrote on Councill's life mentioned this incident in print.

38. Huntsville *Gazette*, May 9, 16, 23, 30; July 11, August 1, 1885.

39. Louis R. Harlan, author of what most scholars believe to be the definitive biography of Booker T. Washington, and his associates overlooked the second incident which had more impact in Alabama. Louis R. Harlan, *Booker T. Washington: The Making of a Black Leader, 1856–1901* (New York: Oxford University Press, 1972),

p. 170. Louis R. Harlan, ed., *The Booker T. Washington Papers. Vol. 2, 1860–1889.* (Urbana: University of Illinois Press, 1972), pp. 307–08, footnote #2 on p. 382.

40. Hopkins, "Founder's Day Address," p. 165.

41. David Wendell Bishop, "The Attitude of the Interstate Commerce Commission Toward Discrimination on Public Carriers 1887–1910" (Unpublished master's thesis, Howard University, Washington, D.C., 1950), pp. 18, 23–24.

42. Hopkins, "Founder's Day Address," pp. 165–66. See Chapter 1 for a fuller description of these incidents.

43. Huntsville *Gazette*, December 7, 1889.

44. Orr, "Educational Philosophy," p. 56, quoting William Sanders Scarborough, "Higher Education of the Colored Race," *Addresses and Proceedings of the National Educational Association, Nashville, Tennessee, 1889* (Topeka: Kansas Publishing House, 1889), pp. 551–52.

45. Hopkins, "Founder's Day Address," p. 166.

46. The full amendment read: "Provided further: That the Legislature of any State in which institutions of a like character have been established and are now being aided by such State out of its own revenue for the education of colored students, in agriculture or the mechanical arts, whether styled colleges or not, and whether they have or not received any money heretofore under the act to which this is an amendment, may appropriate any of the portion of the fund received under this bill to such institution so established and aided by such State as a compliance with the provision in reference to separate colleges for white and colored students." Juanita Lee Williams, "Federal Legislation Relating to Negro Land Grant Colleges" (Unpublished master's thesis, Howard University, 1933), pp. 71–72, 76.

47. Ibid.

48. Harlan, *Booker T. Washington*, p. 169.

49. Bond, *Negro Education*, pp. 157–58. Bond did not relate the speech and the land grant money.

50. Booker T. Washington to Warren Logan, December 11, 1890. Washington later wrote Paterson that he knew that Councill "in speaking before the Legislative Committee used your color to prejudice the members against you." Booker T. Washington to W. B. Paterson, May 4, 1892. Booker T. Washington Papers.

51. Thomas McAdory Owen, *History of Alabama and Dictionary of Alabama Biography* (Chicago: S. J. Clarke), I, 4.

52. Richings, *Evidences of Progress*, pp. 205–06.

53. Ibid., p. 215.

54. Interview with Charles W. Orr, February 26, 1969.

55. *The Normal Index*, IV (December, 1890); IV (January, 1891). Councill even went so far as to admit that some of his graduates became domestic workers, not professionals or teachers. Thus he was conceding the contention of some critics that black industrial schools were training better cooks, maids, and handymen.

56. Ibid., VII (July 29, 1893).

57. "A Criticism" of Councill's speech in Florence, Alabama by Professor J. K. Powers, President of the Florence Normal School, quoted in *The Normal Index*, VII (September 9, 1893). Councill first amplified this position in print in an article, "The Future of the Negro," *Forum*, XXVII (July, 1899), 570–77.

58. Bond overstated the situation when he wrote that "there was much agitation to take the land-grant from Councill's school and bestow it upon Tuskegee." Bond, *Negro*

Education, pp. 204, 338. The only "agitation" came from this convention and the resolution did not mention Normal or specify that the money should go to Tuskegee rather than to Paterson's school at Montgomery. Indeed, Paterson's school would best qualify as being nearer "the centre of Negro population." This resolution was only one of five passed by the Convention petitioning the General Assembly for various reforms in the educational provisions for blacks in Alabama, not a specific attack on Councill or his school. *Proceedings of the 29th Alabama Colored Baptist State Convention, 1896* (n.p., [1896]), p. 30.

59. Mathews, *Booker T. Washington*, p. 176.

60. Normal received $18,000 from the Morrill Fund, but this was U.S. Government money, not part of the state school fund.

61. Mathews, *Booker T. Washington*, p. 141.

62. Owen, *History of Alabama*, I, 4.

63. *Report of the State Superintendent of Education* (1899–1900), pp. 14, 46, 60; (1886), pp. 71, 77; (1885), pp. 56, 61; (1899–1900), pp. 44, 63, 59, 245–55.

Chapter 5

1. Because Washington and Tuskegee are so well known, this section is more a quick summary than are the sections on Paterson and Councill. For the best biography of Washington in the nineteenth century see Harlan, *Booker T. Washington*, and Harlan, ed., *The Booker T. Washington Papers*, Vols. I, II, III.

2. Basil Mathews, *Booker T. Washington: Educator and Interracial Interpreter* (Cambridge: Harvard University Press, 1948), p. 3.

3. Booker T. Washington, *Up From Slavery* (New York: Doubleday & Co., 1901), pp. 17–18, 26, 30–31, *et passim*.

4. Ibid., pp. 5, 19, 22, 24, 29, 31, 33–37. Anson Phelps Stokes, *A Brief Biography of Booker T. Washington* (Hampton: Hampton Institute Press, 1936), p. 6.

5. Samuel R. Spencer, Jr., *Booker T. Washington and the Negro's Place in American Life* (Boston: Little, Brown and Company, 1955), p. 30. Bond, *Negro Education*, p. 196. Perhaps this educational unorthodoxy caused the AMA to turn Hampton over to an independent board of trustees in 1870. Spencer, *Booker T. Washington*, p. 30. Mathews, *Booker T. Washington*, p. 47.

6. Washington, *Up From Slavery*, pp. 47–51. Stokes, *A Brief Biography*, p. 6.

7. Washington, *Up From Slavery*, pp. 51–53. Spencer, *Booker T. Washington*, p. 40.

8. Mathews, *Booker T. Washington*, p. 55. Although Washington worked his way through Hampton as a janitor, he did learn brick-laying there. Stokes, *A Brief Biography*, p. 6. But Hampton did not tie all academic training so closely to industrial activities as did Washington at Tuskegee.

9. Spencer, *Booker T. Washington*, p. 41. Washington, *Up From Slavery*, p. 61.

10. Spencer, *Booker T. Washington*, pp. 42–47. Washington later established a successful night class at Tuskegee.

11. Washington, *Up From Slavery*, pp. 74–75.

12. Mathews, *Booker T. Washington*, pp. 62–63. Booker T. Washington, *The Story of My Life and Work* (Toronto: J. L. Nichols & Company, 1901), pp. 56–57. Washington told the whole story of Tuskegee's founding in this autobiography, but he omitted any mention of the deal in his more famous *Up From Slavery*.

13. Mathews, *Booker T. Washington*, pp. 63–64.

14. Washington, *Up From Slavery*, pp. 75–76, 78, 83, 85. Mathews, *Booker T. Washington*, p. 67.

15. Washington, *Up From Slavery*, pp. 83, 85–87. Bond, *Negro Education*, p. 197. Spencer, *Booker T. Washington*, p. 58.

16. Booker T. Washington, ed., *Tuskegee and Its People: Their Ideals and Achievements* (New York: D. Appleton and Company, 1905), p. 36.

17. Washington, *Up From Slavery*, pp. 59, 89–92, 97–98.

18. Spencer, *Booker T. Washington*, p. 73.

19. Max Bennett Thrasher, *Tuskegee: Its Story and Its Work* (Boston: Small, Maynard & Company, 1900), p. 26. Spencer, *Booker T. Washington*, pp. 73–74. Washington, *Tuskegee and Its People*, p. 39. *Annual Report of the Alabama Superintendent of Education, 1882*, pp. 23–24.

20. Mathews, *Booker T. Washington*, pp. 187–92. Spencer, *Booker T. Washington*, pp. 77, 85.

21. Mathews, *Booker T. Washington*, pp. 191–92. Spencer, *Booker T. Washington*, pp. 77, 85.

22. Thrasher, *Tuskegee*, pp. 27, 30, 42–44, 124. Spencer, *Booker T. Washington*, pp. 74, 83–84. Washington, *Up From Slavery*, pp. 125–27. Washington, *Tuskegee and Its People*, pp. 39–43, 45–49. Anson Phelps Stokes, *Tuskegee Institute: The First Fifty Years* (Tuskegee Institute Press, 1931), p. 90.

23. Mathews, *Booker T. Washington*, pp. 193–96.

24. A politician and newspaperman, Scott served as Washington's confidential secretary and Secretary of Tuskegee. He helped Washington with his correspondence, his books (actually doing the work for *Tuskegee and Its People*), his annual reports, his public relations and dealings with the press. Scott's main contributions were not at Tuskegee *per se*, but as the "Brains of the Tuskegee Machine," Washington's adviser on political and racial matters and co-organizer of the "Tuskegee Machine." Arna Bontemps, *100 Years of Negro Freedom* (New York: Dodd, Mead & Company, 1961), pp. 180–82, 220. Mathews, *Booker T. Washington*, pp. 146–48. Thrasher, *Tuskegee*, p. 190. Spencer, *Booker T. Washington*, p. 110. The use of the term "machine" here denotes informal political organization centered at Tuskegee, not corruption.

25. Carver discovered over three hundred by-products of peanuts and sweet potatoes, developed a cotton hybrid, and taught farmers the value of fertilizers and diversified farming. When measured by the traditional criterion of scholarship, publication, Carver's career was less outstanding. "He never published a single paper in a standard professional journal in his life." Richard Bardolph, *The Negro Vanguard* (New York: Vintage Books, Random House, 1961), p. 251. Writing in 1898, two years after Carver came to Tuskegee, W. H. Councill listed him as an artist instead of a scientist. W. H. Councill, *Lamp of Wisdom* (Nashville: J. T. Haley & Co., 1898), p. 99. Washington greatly limited Carver's scholarly achievement and output by insisting that the Experiment Station "should not be used for scientific experiments of interest only to experts, but should deal with the fundamental problems with which the Negro farmers of Alabama were daily confronted." Emmett Jay Scott and Lyman Beecher Stowe, *Booker T. Washington: Builder of a Civilization* (Garden City: Doubleday, Page & Co., 1916), p. 168. It is not to deny the importance of any of Carver's discoveries or to belittle the magnitude of all of them, to conclude that Carver's fame until recently in white textbooks as "the Negro scientist" rested more on his acquiescence in the "Atlanta Compromise" and the "practical" program at Tuskegee than in the intrinsic

merit of his discoveries, compared to the discoveries of other more outspoken or less-advantageously placed black scientists.

26. Thrasher, *Tuskegee*, p. 124. Penney also attended either Andover Theological Seminary, according to Thrasher, or Yale Divinity School, according to G. F. Richings, *Evidences of Progress Among Colored People* (Philadelphia: George S. Ferguson Co., 1896), p. 201. Miss Adella Hunt emphasized academics and physical development while teaching the girls' normal classes. In 1888, she married Warren Logan (Hampton, 1883) Tuskegee's Treasurer, and acting principal and "eyes" and "ears" of Washington during his absences from Tuskegee. Mathews, *Booker T. Washington*, pp. 193–96, 151. D. W. Culp, *Twentieth Century Negro Literature* (Toronto: J. L. Nichols & Co., 1902), facing pp. 199, 359. Spencer, *Booker T. Washington*, p. 82. Numerous letters from Warren Logan to Booker T. Washington, Booker T. Washington Papers, Library of Congress, Washington, D.C.

27. Scott and Stowe, *Booker T. Washington*, pp. 12–14.

28. Ibid., p. 279.

29. Washington made his service concept international when, in 1901, he sent a group of graduates and teachers to Africa to teach methods of raising cotton. Stokes, *Tuskegee Institute*, pp. 90–91.

30. In addition to preaching, one graduate of the Bible School worked as a tailor, one as a painter, several as farmers, and one became a presiding elder in his denomination. Several graduates did further work at Morris Brown College, Gammon Theological School, or Yale Divinity School. Thrasher, *Tuskegee*, pp. 123–28. Mathews, *Booker T. Washington*, p. 123. Richings, *Evidences of Progress*, p. 201.

31. Unlike the "experience" meetings the Tuskegee conferences emphasized that black farmers should raise themselves by their own efforts. One speaker in 1895 summed up this attitude when he said, "Don't set round, saying, 'I trust in God.' God ain't a-gwine to do your hoeing for you." Helen W. Ludlow, "Fourth Tuskegee Negro Conference," *The Outlook*, LI (March 9, 1895), 400.

32. Washington also sought to build unity among the delegates at the conference by having everyone attending take part in a parade featuring floats, livestock, and the delegates. Mathews, *Booker T. Washington*, p. 171.

33. Mathews, *Booker T. Washington*, pp. 168–69. Scott and Stowe, *Booker T. Washington*, p. 164. Frederick E. Drinker, *Booker T. Washington: The Master Mind of a Child of Slavery* (n.p., 1915), p. 238.

34. Scott and Stowe, *Booker T. Washington*, pp. 167–68.

35. A typical resolution passed at the first conference in 1892 urged

> all to buy land and to cultivate it thoroughly; to raise more food supplies; to build better houses with more than one room; to tax themselves to build better schoolhouses, and to extend the school year to at least six months; to give more attention to the character of our leaders, especially ministers and teachers; to keep out of debt, to avoid lawsuits, to treat our women better; and that conferences similar in aim to this one be held in every community wherever practicable.

Booker T. Washington, *Working With The Hands* (New York: Doubleday, Page & Company, 1904), p. 138.

36. Ibid.

37. Ludlow, "Fourth Tuskegee Negro Conference," p. 400.

38. Ibid.

39. Thrasher, *Tuskegee*, pp. 175–78, 182–85.

40. Stokes, *Tuskegee Institute*, p. 59. Spencer, *Booker T. Washington*, pp. 74–75.

41. Spencer, *Booker T. Washington*, pp. 73, 75. Thrasher, *Tuskegee*, pp. 31–32.

42. Drinker, *Booker T. Washington*, pp. 72, 156. Spencer, *Booker T. Washington*, p. 115. *Biennial Report of the Alabama Superintendent of Education, 1898–1899, 1899–1900*, p. 60.

43. Of this amount, $47,407.10 was for endowment, $22,916.80 for permanent improvements, and $123,845.39 for current expenses. In addition to the sources of money mentioned, Tuskegee received $800 from the Frothington Fund, $500 from the Society for Propagating the Gospel, $9,901 from students, and $361.28 interest from the Dizer Fund. The rest of the money came from "individuals, Sunday-Schools, Missionary Societies and Churches."

44. Drinker, *Booker T. Washington*, p. 72. Thrasher, *Tuskegee*, p. 186. *Biennial Report of the Alabama Superintendent of Education, 1898–1899, 1899–1900*, pp. 56–60.

Chapter 6

1. The only exceptions are one or two black high schools in Alabama cities in the late 1890's, George N. Card's presidency of Marion (1874–1878), and Peter Clark's presidency of Huntsville (1887–1888).

2. Paterson did help organize the State Teachers' Association in 1882 and served as its first president, an office Councill was never able to obtain. Paterson's educational philosophy—stressing liberal arts, higher education over industrial training—was shared by most of the black and white teachers of the private black normal schools in Alabama.

3. Councill shifted away from this position by 1893, however, as described in the chapter on Councill.

4. Booker T. Washington, *My Larger Education* (New York: Doubleday, Page & Company, 1910), p. 302.

5. William Hooper Councill, *The Young Negro of 1864: The Young Negro of 1904: The Problem Then; The Problem Now* (Boston: Charles Alexander, Printer, [1904]), p. 3.

6. Orr, "Educational Philosophy," p. 48. Orr's copy.

7. *Biennial Report of the Alabama Superintendent of Education, 1898–1899, 1899–1900*, pp. 16, 51–52.

8. William Hooper Councill, *Bright Side of the Southern Question* (n.p., [1903]), p. 17.

9. Bond, *Negro Education*, p. 204.

10. Councill, *Bright Side*, pp. 18, 15, 16.

11. William Hooper Councill, "The Future of the Negro," *Forum*, XXVII (July, 1899), 570–76.

12. Louis R. Harlan has admirably described these secret sides of Washington in *Booker T. Washington: The Making of a Black Leader, 1856–1901* (New York: Oxford University Press, 1972).

13. By 1901 Tuskegee received much more money than did Normal or Montgomery, but this money came from the Slater Fund and from Northern contributions. After 1896, Tuskegee received more indirectly from Alabama than Normal because Tuskegee and Montgomery became Agricultural Experiment Stations with a grant of $1,500 a year each. Washington got this grant primarily because he knew the Secre-

tary of Agriculture (i.e., a national, not a state contact). *Reports of the Alabama Commissioner of Education*, 1873–1901. But even here Washington only stayed even with Paterson even if he did win out over Councill. Tuskegee also received a special grant of mineral lands in the late 1890's, but again this was a national not a state grant.

14. This is not to say that Washington and Tuskegee were not powerful. But their power, even in black education in Alabama, was not absolute—nor was it so strong as has been assumed.

15. See Chapter 2 for a summary of the development of the STA.

16. Just as the Peabody Fund's founder did not require racial discrimination in the distribution of his money, the founder of the Slater Fund did not specify that only schools offering industrial education could be aided. In each case, however, the agent of the fund allowed his racial prejudices to shape the distribution of the fund. The prejudices of the Slater Fund's agent, Atticus Greene Haygood, can be seen most clearly in his denying the fund to Councill's school after Councill and his students sat in "white" railroad cars.

Chapter 7

1. When an arsonist burned the AMA school in Quitman, Georgia, two of its teachers came to Montgomery to establish a school for black girls. Frederick Leslie Brownlee, *New Day Ascending* (Boston: Pilgrim Press, 1946), p. 108. This school might have been either the Langridge Academy or the Montgomery Industrial School. It was probably the former since most AMA schools did not ignore academic education to focus on industrial training.

2. This building had been a slave pen before the war.

3. Notes of J. T. Alexander from an interview with Gertrude Campbell, the daughter of Mr. and Mrs. Henry Campbell, who attended the school. The interview took place at Miss Campbell's home in Montgomery in 1961, shortly before her death.

4. *Montgomery City Directories, 1898–1901*.

5. Beatrice Bowen Butcher, "The Evolution of Negro Women's Schools in the United States" (Unpublished master's thesis, Howard University, 1936), p. 33.

6. Tuskegee Institute printed the paper for these years. Letters of Misses White and Beard to Booker T. Washington, 1886–1894. Booker T. Washington Papers.

7. Huntsville *Gazette*, April 28, 1894.

8. In 1916, Montgomery Industrial was a "well-managed elementary day school for girls," whose 10 white teachers taught 325 pupils. Although it was an industrial school, it had eight academic and only two industrial teachers. Its total income in 1916 was $7,500. Jones, *Negro Education*, II, 310–13. When Misses Beard and White had to close the school "because of physical disability," they gave the building to the AMA which then sold it to Montgomery. The building later became part of the Booker T. Washington Junior High School. E. S. Thompson, Sr. (ed.), *A Century of Negro Progress in Montgomery City and County, Centennial Edition, 1863–1963* (Montgomery: Southeastern Publishing Company, [1963]), p. 46. The school might have received some aid from the AMA, but the AMA reports before 1901 and the AMA pamphlets and histories never mentioned Miss Beard and White or their school.

9. *Industrial Missionary Association of Alabama* (n.p., n.d.), p. 3.

10. Ibid., pp. 1–5. *Kind Words* [an IMA pamphlet] (n.p., n.d.), Jones, *Negro Education*, II, 42.

11. This effort to put evangelism on a financially profitable basis had largely failed by 1913. Curtis and his wife managed the entire association. A board of directors composed of local blacks had little influence. Only one-fourth of the land bought by the IMA in 1888 had been sold; tenants farmed the rest. The IMA's secretary, a local black man, managed the store and mills as private enterprises. Jones, *Negro Education*, II, 42. The paternalistic, pietistic, externally imposed structure of the IMA had much to do with its failure. Most successful enterprises grew out of the needs of local blacks as they perceived them and gave local blacks more responsibility in developing and maintaining the program.

12. This was more than land cost near Tuskegee, but Bell said that the price was so high because the land was near the railroad. Booker T. Washington must have been in charge of raising money for the new school since he wrote the $250 check to pay for the additional ten acres which the school bought in 1892. He also hired Augustus Perdue to build the schoolhouse in 1892. Mabel W. Dillingham to Washington, August 15, 1891; Washington to W. F. Crockett [a black lawyer in Montgomery], February 14, 1892; Augustus Perdue to Washington, February 25, 1892; Booker T. Washington Papers.

13. Miss Dillingham died October 14, 1896. Maggie to Washington, October 14, 1896. Booker T. Washington Papers.

14. William L. McDavid, "Calhoun Land Trust: A Study of Rural Resettlement in Lowndes County, Alabama" (Unpublished master's thesis, Fisk University, 1943), p. 43. Glenn Nolan Sisk, "Alabama Black Belt: A Social History, 1875–1917" (Unpublished doctoral dissertation, Duke University, 1951), 191. Richardson, *National Cyclopedia*, I, 28.

Calhoun's community activities in 1915 included parents' meetings, farmers' conferences and an agricultural fair, county teachers' meetings, and several clubs devoted to improving homes and farms. The school also maintained two "outpost" schools nearby. Jones, *Negro Education*, II, 59. Calhoun was primarily responsible for the development of the community "which is described by standard books on the South as exceptionally moral, intelligent, and progressive, with far-reaching influence, and intimately cooperative with all the work of the school."

Miss Thorn was still Calhoun's principal in 1917. An independent board of trustees, presided over by Hollis B. Frissell, President of Hampton Institute, owned the school. Calhoun's income from an endowment and contributions totaled $73,236.26 in 1916–1917. Calhoun then offered work from the first to the tenth grade to 405 pupils, 92 of whom boarded at the school. Calhoun's thirty-five salaried workers were nearly equally divided between whites and blacks. Richardson, *National Cyclopedia*, I, 28–29.

15. In 1937, Will W. Alexander, head of the Farm Security Administration, highly complimented Calhoun. "The program which has been carried on for a number of years (at Calhoun) is the most successful demonstration that has been made of a thing which the Resettlement Administration is now attempting to do on a nation-wide basis." McDavid, "Calhoun Land Trust," pp. 44–51, 56, 73. McDavid described the transactions of the land company in detail.

16. Richardson, *National Cyclopedia*, I, 58–59.

17. Ibid. This schoolhouse was located on Murdock's Place, an old plantation which had been the site of a white school before the Civil War. Richard Stephen Jordan, Jr., "An Historical Study of the Georgia Washington High School, Mount

Meigs, Alabama, From 1893–1958, as to the Faculty, School Plant, Enrollment and its Influence on the Community" (Unpublished master's thesis, Alabama State College, 1959), pp. 26–28.

18. Before the Civil War, blacks worshipped in a segregated part of this church, which they reached through a separate entrance. After the war, the white members died or moved away until only Dr. J. C. Nicholson, a white physician, was left. He gave the church to the blacks of Mt. Meigs. Jordan, "Georgia Washington High School," pp. 28–32.

19. Ibid., pp. 28–32, 34.

20. To allay this confusion, the names of the schools became: People's Village School (Miss Washington's) at the Mt. Meigs Post Office; and Mt. Meigs Colored Institute (Miss Bowen's) at the Waugh Post Office. Booker T. Washington to Miss Georgia Washington, 1896, Booker T. Washington Papers.

21. Jordan, "Georgia Washington High School," pp. 40–48.

22. By 1958, the community had renamed the People's Village School, the Georgia Washington High School. Ibid. pp. 32–34.

23. Richardson, *National Cyclopedia*, I, 22–23.

24. William E. Peck to Booker T. Washington, June 21, 1893; J. H. Michael to Booker T. Washington, July 6, 1893; March 14, 1895, Booker T. Washington Papers.

25. Letterhead of a letter to Booker T. Washington, February 23, 1895, and several letters of Robert Charles Bedford to Washington, Booker T. Washington Papers.

26. Edwards' mother had named him Ulysses Grant, but his grandmother, who had worked for whites since the Civil War, changed his name to William. Edwards' acquiescence in this name change indicated a basically accommodationist stance toward whites. Edwards later added James, his grandfather's name, to make his full name, William James Edwards. Perhaps Edwards got some of his interest in education from this grandfather he chose as a namesake. James Carmichael had been an educated preacher during slavery. Whites trusted him enough to allow him to travel eight or ten miles to preach. William James Edwards, *Twenty-five Years in the Black Belt* (Boston: The Cornhill Company, 1918), pp. 2–4.

27. Edwards, *Twenty-five Years*, pp. 2–4, 6–11, 13–15.

28. William J. Edwards to Booker T. Washington, September 5, 1894, Booker T. Washington Papers.

29. Emphasis added. Edwards, *Twenty-five Years*, pp. 36–38.

30. His largest contribution—$10,000—came from Andrew Carnegie after Carnegie heard Edwards speak at the twenty-fifth anniversary of Tuskegee on April 5, 1906. Ibid., pp. 38–48. The Washington Papers contain several endorsements of Edwards and Snow Hill.

31. In 1897 Edwards claimed that there were no black schools which ran for more than three months within thirty miles of Snow Hill, and no black industrial school within seventy-five or one hundred miles of Snow Hill. Printed, circular letter from Edwards, 1897, Booker T. Washington Papers. This was not true. Calhoun School was only about thirty miles away and all the Wilcox County Schools later supported by the Board of Missions for Freedmen of the Presbyterian Church (See Chapter 8) were within thirty miles.

Snow Hill continued to grow, and by 1916, the total enrollment reached 293. The all black faculty of twenty-nine included fourteen academic instructors, five boys' industries' instructors, two girls' industries' instructors, one matron, one agricultural instructor, and six executive and office workers. Snow Hill's main concern was agricultural training, but it also offered some academic work and training in several industries—carpentry, blacksmithing, printing, leather work, masonry, tailoring, and a commercial course. In 1915, Snow Hill owned two thousand acres of land and twenty-one buildings and industrial equipment. The entire physical plant was worth about $90,000. Richardson, *National Cyclopedia*, I, 41.

32. The school took this name in 1904. The earlier name was the Snow Hill Colored Literary and Industrial Institute. Joseph Davis, "A Historical Study of Snow Hill Normal and Industrial Institute and Its Contributions to the Educational Program of the State of Alabama," (Unpublished master's thesis, Alabama State College, 1954), p. 16.

33. Ibid., p. 32.

34. See Edwards, *Twenty-five Years*, pp. 63–76, for stories of the graduates of Snow Hill. All of those Edwards described graduated after 1901.

Chapter 8

1. During Reconstruction the FAS also established freedmen's schools in Decatur (1867–1872), Bluffton (1867–1871), Montgomery, Evergreen (1869), Jonesboro (1872), and Dadeville (1879). Of these schools, only those in Huntsville and Dadeville remained open between 1874 and 1901. *Annual Report of Freedmen's Aid Society of the Methodist Episcopal Church, 1867, 1866–1880, 1888–1892.* Mason Crum, *The Negro in the Methodist Church* (New York: Editorial Department of the Board of Missions and Church Extension of the Methodist Church, 1951), p. 66.

2. *Freedmen's Aid Society Reports, 1877.*

3. Ibid., *1875, 1868–1869, 1877.*

4. Huntsville *Gazette*, January 16, December 18, 1886; *Freedmen's Aid Society Reports, 1866–1880, 1888–1892.* The FAS also changed its name to the Freedmen's Aid and Southern Education Society in 1888 to reflect the fact that it had begun to aid white as well as black schools. Ibid., *1888–1889.* For continuity FAS is retained as the society's name.

5. *Freedmen's Aid Society Reports, 1872, 1873, 1875.*

6. Ibid., *1879.* Much of what Brandon wrote might be true. Although the AMA had a school in Huntsville immediately after the Civil War, it was not a normal school. Since the AMA school did not survive the end of Reconstruction and Rust did, perhaps Rust was the best school for blacks in North Alabama after the Civil War.

7. Ibid. For more specific information on these two men and other Huntsville black leaders, see the Huntsville *Gazette*, 1881–1894 and Peter B. Young, "The Negro Community in Huntsville, Alabama, 1881–1894" (Unpublished B.A. honors thesis, Louisiana State University, 1957). One should remember this tie of Hendley and Binford to Rust in reading the glowing praise of Rust in the Huntsville *Gazette*, e.g., "Rust Institute has done more than all others towards enlightening, cultivating, and improving colored society in this section." Huntsville *Gazette*, editorial, May 6, 1882. Hendley and Binford championed academic training and led those blacks in north Alabama who opposed W. H. Councill's and Booker T. Washington's stressing industrial training for blacks at the expense of academic instruction.

8. *Freedmen's Aid Society Report, 1879.* Since most black children had to work in the fields during the summer and early fall, most normal school students had to leave

their school after the first term and go to teach a school to finance their education. These circumstances had the double disadvantage of having many partly educated teachers in the field teaching for severely limited periods of time, and of either stretching out the normal student's study over many years or of tempting him to drop out to teach full time with partial preparation. This situation worsened when the state began cutting into the blacks' share of the school fund in earnest in the 1890's.

9. Huntsville *Gazette*, 1883. After Misses Hindman and Lakin, Miss M. M. Harrington, Mr. C. W. Munson and Miss M. C. Owen, Mr. J. F. Blunt, and Mrs. Mary L. Raines served as Principal of Rust. In 1881, Miss O. L. Smith was Rust's Principal. Mr. D. S. Brandon, acting principal in 1879 became principal by 1882. In 1882, Dr. Rust chose Reverend J. H. Owens of Cottage City, Massachusetts, to succeed Brandon. In 1883, Mrs. Mary L. Raines again became principal. In 1885, Mrs. Raines resigned when her family decided to move to Missouri. Reverend A. W. McKinney succeeded her as Rust's Principal. The rapid turnover of principals ceased with McKinney, who remained principal from 1885 to 1901. *Freedmen's Aid Society Report, 1879, 1901*, p. 18. Huntsville *Gazette*, September 2, 1882; August 18, September 22, 1883.

10. *Freedmen's Aid Society Report, 1877*.

11. Huntsville *Gazette*, September 19, October 17, November 17, 1885. Rust's reading room, containing books and maps, opened at the same time as did the boarding department.

12. Ibid., December 18, 1886; February 5, 12, 1887, *et passim*.

13. Ibid., May 28, 1887. *Freedmen's Aid Society Report, 1888*.

14. *Freedmen's Aid Society Report, 1891;* Huntsville *Gazette*, September 3, 1892.

15. *Freedmen's Aid Society Report, 1891*. Richardson, *National Cyclopedia*, I, 375. After a fire destroyed Central's main building around 1928, the school closed—never to reopen. *The Christian Educator* (May, 1928), p. 6; 1928–1931.

16. Elliott died in January, 1920 at the Richard Allen Presbyterian Academy in Pine Bluff, Arkansas. "While no buildings or memorials mark his work, his influence was written invisibly but indelibly [*sic*] in the life fiber of hundreds whom he touched." *Minutes of the Congregational Association of Alabama, 1880*. Letters in the Washington Papers from G. M. Elliott, 1885, 1894. Research memorandum prepared by Charles A. Brown, Research Secretary of the Alabama State Teachers' Association, for a history of the ASTA, 1969.

By 1916, Knox enrolled 705 students, 28 of whom were in secondary grades. Seven of the school's seventeen teachers were white. Knox received $7,300 in 1916 and its plant was worth $52,500. Jones, *Negro Education*, II, 320–44.

17. While pastor of this church he led the Alabama and Mississippi Synods in their mission project of buying Harrison W. Ellis from a Eutaw slaveowner and sending Ellis to Africa as a missionary. William Marion Sikes, "The Historical Development of Stillman Institute" (Unpublished master's thesis, University of Alabama, 1930), pp. 17–18, 29, 32–33, 35.

18. The Alabama Synod's Memorial Resolution honoring Stillman after his death in 1895, stressed his work in black education. "The great work of his life, outside of his pastoral duties, was given to the Church in connection with the Institute at Tuscaloosa for training colored ministers, of which he was the superintendent from its origin up to a few months previous to his death. Of this Institute it might almost be said that he was the founder and father. . . . In gratitude for his services to it the

General Assembly at the time of his retirement from the office of superintendent named it the Stillman Institute for Training Colored Ministers."

19. He also helped blacks organize their Salem Presbyterian Church in 1880. As soon as the church finished its building, the school used it for a chapel. In 1881, the Sunday School, "which for nearly twenty-five years had been conducted for the colored people in the lecture room of the First Presbyterian Church, was removed to Salem Church." Ibid., pp. 36–37, 40–41, 80.

20. The father of Judge William G. Cochrane built the house in 1840. It was "one of the most perfect examples of Greek architecture in Corinthian style found anywhere in this country." The builder imported the capitals on each of the six columns from Italy at a cost of $600 each. Ibid., pp. 40–50, 80–83, 52.

21. No girls lived on the campus until the 1920's. Until then, only girls who lived in Tuscaloosa and attended the day school were allowed in the Institute. Ibid., p. 50.

22. Little grew up in Tuscaloosa in close contact with the teachers of the Institute. After receiving his A.B. and M.A. degrees from the University of Alabama, he went to the Louisville Theological Seminary in Louisville, Kentucky to get his B.D. While in Louisville, Little showed the influence of his Tuscaloosa boyhood by beginning the Hancock Street Mission for blacks in that city. Ibid., pp. 50, 52–53, 83, 85.

23. Ibid., pp. 52–54, 84.

24. Stillman was truly a school for all Southern Presbyterian blacks. Of the school's forty-one graduates by 1898, only twelve came from Alabama Presbyteries. Ibid., pp. 130–32.

25. Some Southern Presbyterians did not support black education. As late as Snedecor's administration, 1903–1916, he frequently encountered Presbyterian ministers who would not even allow him into their pulpits to make a plea for money for Stillman Institute. Ibid., pp. 14–15, 54, 93–95, 109–10. Such treatment of Snedecor, who shifted Stillman's emphasis from academic to theological training, revealed why Southern Presbyterians and their school, Stillman Institute, did not appeal to or influence many black Alabamians.

26. George Freeman Bragg, *History of the Afro-American Group of the Episcopal Church* (Baltimore: Church Advocate Press, 1922), p. 151. *Down Where the Need is Greatest: A Record in the Field of Negro Education* (New York: American Church Institute for Negroes, n.d.), pp. 39–41.

27. In 1906, St. Mark's became one of the five Southern black schools supported by the American Church Institute for Negroes, an auxiliary of the National Council of the Episcopal Church. In 1916, Brooks was still principal. Although St. Mark's was still largely elementary, it did have some secondary pupils and a small boarding department in 1916. Ibid., Alabama Historical Records Survey Project, *Inventory of Church Archives of Alabama: Protestant Episcopal Church* (Birmingham: Alabama Historical Records Survey Project, 1939), p. 61. Jones, *Negro Education*, II, 52.

28. Leilafred Ballard, "The American Negro 1880–1895 as Portrayed in the Huntsville *Gazette*" (Unpublished master's thesis, Howard University, 1952), p. 20. Trenholm, *Yearbook, 1949*, p. 26.

29. By 1916, I. C. Franklin was the principal over seven workers. A local board of trustees owned the school, which then received aid from the Christian Women's Board of Missions. Most of its students were in the elementary grades, although a few pupils studied secondary subjects. Lum also offered some industrial work. On its sixty acres of ground, Lum was "attempting to do a rural work in a plantation

section where conditions were very primitive." Richardson, *National Cyclopedia*, I, 567. Jones, *Negro Education*, II, 60; Richings, *Evidences of Progress*, p. 480.

30. Jones lists the Camden Academy, the Canton Bend Mission School, the Millers Ferry Normal and Industrial School, and the Prairie Institute as black schools which the Board of Missions for Freedmen of the Presbyterian Church established in Alabama before 1901. None of the reports of the board up to 1901, however, mentioned these schools. The board either took on the support of these schools, which had been in existence for some time, between 1901 and 1916 or these schools might have been among the small, parochial schools which the BMF did not list individually. All of these schools were in Wilcox County. The Camden Academy, W. G. Wilson, Principal, was an elementary school with a small secondary enrollment (18) in 1916. It began in 1895. The Canton Bend Mission School began in 1896. By 1916, it was an elementary day school with 194 pupils. Although the BMF controlled the school, it had a local board of trustees (all blacks), who advised the board running the school. Reverend J. N. Cotton was the principal. The Millers Ferry Normal and Industrial School began in 1884. In 1916, the principal, I. H. Bonner, supervised 211 elementary and 22 secondary pupils. The Prairie Institute began in 1895. In 1916, T. M. Elliott was principal of the school's 112 elementary pupils. Jones, *Negro Education*, II, 90–93.

31. *Annual Report of the Board of Missions for Freedmen of the Presbyterian Church in the United States of America* (North) *1893–1901*. Since Miller Memorial was one of the denomination's smaller schools, the annual reports never included a detailed report on it. Jones did not include the school in his list of black schools in Alabama in 1916. Since the enrollment in 1901 was only seven above the enrollment in 1894, the year of its founding, Miller Memorial must have been an experiment that did not work.

32. Beatrice Bowen Butcher, "The Evolution of Negro Women's Schools in the United States" (Unpublished master's thesis, Howard University, 1936), p. 35.

33. *Board of Missions for Freedmen Report, 1896, 1897*.

34. Ibid., *1898–1901*.

35. Butcher, "Negro Women's Schools," p. 35.

36. In 1930, Barber merged with Scotia Women's College in Concord, North Carolina, to become Barber-Scotia College. All Barber's movable goods came to Concord with the merger. In 1932, Barber-Scotia merged with Johnson C. Smith University, but it remained Barber-Scotia Junior College in Concord under its own dean. Dwight Oliver Wendell Holmes, *The Evolution of the Negro College*, Contribution to Education No. 609 (New York: Bureau of Publications, Teachers College, Columbia University, 1934), p. 134.

Chapter 9

1. Many of the letters in the Booker T. Washington Papers tell of the denominational pressures on teachers. Among the schools described in this study, Tuskegee, Normal, and Snow Hill came under attack from black denominations. For example, after attacking W. H. Councill for not hiring one of their denomination to teach at Normal in 1889, the Huntsville Primitive Baptists tried to establish a "Central College" to take students from primary schools established by each church in the association. W. H. Gaston, who had taught a primary day and night school in his church for some time, built "a very neat school house" on the church's property and led the denomination in establishing a Primitive Baptist Institute there in 1894. Evidently

this school did not succeed since Jones did not list it in his survey of black colleges in 1916. Huntsville *Gazette*, September 3, 1887; June 23, 1888; September 7, 28, October 5, December 7, 1889; October 6, 20, 27, November 3, 1894.

2. James Beverly Ford Shaw, *The Negro in the History of Methodism* (Nashville: Parthenon Press, 1954), p. 117. Dwight Oliver Wendell Holmes, *The Evolution of the Negro College*, Contribution to Education No. 609 (New York: Bureau of Publications, Teachers College, Columbia University, 1934), p. 149.

3. The school's name honored Bishop Lomax, who had been interested in beginning such a school, and Mr. Hannon, whose contributions helped it get started. A Board of Trustees, composed primarily of AMEZ members, owned and controlled the school. By 1916 J. R. Wingfield was principal of Lomax-Hannon, which then had 8 black teachers, 118 elementary pupils, and 24 secondary pupils. Rufus E. Clement, "The Educational Work of the African Methodist Episcopal Zion Church, 1820–1920" (Unpublished master's thesis, Northwestern University, 1922), pp. 76, 83, 98. Jones, *Negro Education*, II, 37, 137.

4. Many A.M.E. leaders felt that there was no need for a school in Alabama since the district already had a school, Morris Brown College, in Atlanta. Winfield Henry Mixon, *History of the African Methodist Episcopal Church in Alabama* (Nashville: A.M.E. Church Sunday School Union, 1902), pp. 86–87.

5. Charles L. Harris preached the first educational sermon of which there is any record at these meetings. He later joined the Congregational Church which, through the AMA, had the largest number of black schools in Alabama. Ibid., p. 44.

6. Ibid., pp. 47–49, 54, 62, 86–88.

7. Ibid., pp. 96, 114. Richings, *Evidences of Progress*, p. 142.

8. In 1916, twelve of Payne's thirteen teachers were in its academic department. By 1919, Payne had a well-developed College or Normal course which included work in Latin (four years), Greek (one year), German (one year), English (four years), mathematics (seven years), history (two years), and economics, psychology, education, physiology, and elementary science (one year each). In 1923, the school moved to Montgomery as Bethel College; and, in 1939, it reopened in Birmingham as the greater Payne University, where it long remained. Richings, *Evidences of Progress*, p. 142. Jones, *Negro Education*, II, 348. Richardson, *National Cyclopedia*, I, 320. Trenholm, *1949 Association Yearbook*, pp. 28–29.

9. Since most black Christians in Alabama were Baptists, a study of the educational work of the Baptist convention is especially important in understanding black religious leaders' attitudes toward education.

10. Alabama black Baptists lost Avery's services soon after the Civil War when he became a Methodist and moved to Mississippi. Charles Octavius Boothe, *The Cyclopedia of The Colored Baptists of Alabama* (Birmingham: Alabama Publishing Company, 1895), pp. 33–34. Boothe might have underestimated the number of educated, slave preachers. W. J. Edwards, for example, claimed that his grandfather was an educated, slave preacher. See the section on Edwards and Snow Hill School.

11. Only three of these men—William Henry McAlpine, Holland Thompson, and C. O. Boothe—could write. *Minutes of the Colored Missionary Baptist Convention, 1897*, p. 3.

12. Ibid., *1868*.

13. Ibid., *1869*, p. 21.

14. Ibid., *1870*, pp. 10–11.

15. Ibid., *1872*, p. 6.

16. McAlpine's resolution stated,

> *Whereas*, We are desirous to promulgate the Word of God, and to instruct our people more thoroughly in doctrine, discipline and Gospel truths; therefore be it
>
> *Resolved* . . . That we plant in the State of Alabama a Theological School to educate our young men.
>
> *Be it also resolved*, That every Baptist Church, Association or private member be requested to raise all the money in their power to aid in building this school. Each member of a Baptist Church in Alabama is requested to give one dollar ($1) a year.

17. A 1903 history of Selma University stated that the exact reply was, "The white Baptists are very much interested in seeing the colored brethren supplied with a competent pastorate. If your convention has any money to put on the education of young men, and any young men to send to school; we would gladly take the money and send them to some school already established. But to attempt such [as] is contemplated by the resolution would be folly." *Twenty-Sixth Annual Catalogue of the Alabama Baptist University, Selma, Alabama, 1903–1904* (Selma: Selma University Print., [1904]), p. 26. McAlpine's daughter remembered still another version of the story. McAlpine "got a committee to go to the white preachers' convention to ask their permission to start a school. They turned him down saying it was too soon after the closing of slavery. He went back the next day telling them that the colored preachers were not prepared to preach. So they decided to get rid of him by asking him what could he do toward helping to establish the school. He said that he could go out on the field and raise money. They told him if he could raise the money they would grant him permission. The next year he went back with $500, and in 1878 the school was started. . . ." Research notes of J. T. Alexander, Montgomery, Alabama, from an interview with a daughter of McAlpine. Alexander did not identify the daughter, nor did he give the date of the interview [before 1968].

18. *C.M.B.C.A. Minutes, 1873*, p. 11.

19. *Selma University Catalog, 1903–1904*, p. 26.

20. *C.M.B.C.A. Minutes, 1876*, p. 10.

21. Ibid., *1874*, pp. 16–17, 22.

22. Ibid., *1875*, pp. 6, 9, 13, 16. Boothe's emphasis.

23. Ibid., pp. 13–14, 16.

24. Ibid., *1917*, p. 106.

25. The officers of the convention each year held the one-year positions. The following men were on the first board of trustees; one-year, M. Tyler, B. Burke, C. O. Boothe, C. Casby, Thomas Smith; two-year, J. Ware, J. Shorter, J. Blevens, P. Underwood, W. H. McAlpine; three-year, B. Burk, A. Butler, J. Dozier, H. Stephens, C. Blunt. Ibid., *1875*, p. 14.

26. Ibid., p. 12.

27. Ibid., p. 5. This was one of the very few mentions of the "menace" of Roman Catholicism in the Minutes of the convention. It is interesting that the Alabama black Baptists saw Roman Catholicism as less a threat, or selling point for their school, than did such liberal, white mission boards as the AMA and the FAS of the Methodist Episcopal Church (North).

28. Ibid.

29. *C.M.B.C.A. Minutes, 1876*, p. 10.

30. Ibid., *1876*, pp. 6–8, 18.
31. Ibid., *1877*, pp. 17–18.
32. Ibid., *1879*, p. 15.
33. *The Selma University Chronicle*, XI (January, 1950), 5.
34. Henry Lyman Morehouse, *Baptist Home Missions in North America* (New York: Baptist Home Mission Rooms, 1883), p. 70.
35. *C.M.B.C.A. Minutes, 1876*, pp. 12, 16.
36. Ibid., *1917*, p. 106.
37. Ibid., *1876*, pp. 15–16, 18.
38. Ibid., *1877*, p. 25. These institutes continued throughout the nineteenth century with the aid of the Northern and Southern white Baptists. Their main aim, however, was teaching doctrine, not training preachers in even elementary subjects. Thus, these institutes were really more evangelistic than didactic.
39. Boothe, *Cyclopedia*, p. 54.
40. William Cathcart, *Baptist Encyclopedia* (Philadelphia: Evarts Publishing Co., 1881), pp. 1274–75.
41. *C.M.B.C.A. Minutes*, 1877, pp. 19–20, 26–27.
42. Boothe, *Cyclopedia*, p. 43.
43. *C.M.B.C.A. Minutes, 1878*, p. 10.
44. *Selma University Catalog, 1903–1904*, p. 27.
45. Pettiford, for example, in the Summer of 1878, served as Colporteur and Bible reader for the American and Foreign Bible Society. While traveling for the society, he also collected over $100 for the school above his expenses.
46. *C.M.B.C.A. Minutes, 1878*, pp. 10–15, 21. While the school's teachers were not this successful every summer, they constantly had to seek funds to keep the school open. This strenuous fund raising was a major drain on the strength and health of the leaders of all the black schools in Alabama.
47. Ibid., pp. 11, 13.
48. Ibid., *1879*, pp. 12–15.
49. Ibid., *1880*, p. 18; *1881*, p. 16.
50. Boothe, *Cyclopedia*, p. 166.
51. Ibid. Thus, in a sense, Selma University was established through the influence of the AMA through Talladega College. According to McAlpine's daughter, he went from Talladega to Marion, where he served as pastor for four years before going to Selma to work for the school. Alexander, Research Notes.
52. McAlpine was also active in church work. He served as pastor of churches in Talladega, Jacksonville, Marion, Anniston, and Montgomery (Dexter Avenue Baptist Church). He also helped write the constitution and was elected the first President of the National Baptist Convention in 1880.

McAlpine first married Miss Mary Rivers in Talladega. When she died, two or three years later, he married her sister, Emma. They had two daughters while they were in Talladega and one after they moved to Selma.

At a meeting in 1905, McAlpine caught a cold when someone took his luggage, which contained his overcoat. He also got some mosquito bites which gave him malaria. Although he was sick, McAlpine went to Chicago to speak at the Twenty-Fifth Anniversary of the National Baptist Convention, which he had helped establish. On this trip, his cold turned into pneumonia and he died on November 3, 1905, a few days after returning home. A tribute to McAlpine which appeared in Cathcart's *Baptist*

Encyclopedia in 1883, was as true when McAlpine died as it was when it was originally written. "No man has done more for the elevation of the colored people in Alabama." Booth, *Cyclopedia*, pp. 166–67. Alexander, Research Notes. Cathcart, *Baptist Encyclopedia*, p. 764. *The Selma University Chronicle*, XI (January, 1950), 2–3.

53. *C.M.B.C.A. Minutes, 1881*, pp. 16–17; *1882*, p. 47.

54. Ibid., *1882*, pp. 12–13, 24–27, 46.

55. Upon resigning the presidency of Selma, Woodsmall reentered the service of the ABHMS taking charge of the work in Alabama, Tennessee, Mississippi, and Arkansas. While engaged in this work he died in 1888. The Committee on Deceased Ministers of the 1888 black Baptist convention wrote that Woodsmall "did us a great deal of good in this state. The work he did in helping to lay the foundation of the Selma School, in building up our paper and in giving shape to the mission work in the state can never be forgotten." Ibid., *1888*, p. 19.

56. Selma must have meant "Slater" instead of "State" Fund since the 1875 constitution forbade giving state money to private schools. The decision to begin an industrial department in 1883 (the first year of the Slater Fund) showed that the Baptists began their industrial work as another means of getting badly needed funds, not because they basically endorsed industrial training. There was never even any serious debate in the convention about emphasizing industrial training over academic and theological education as Washington did at Tuskegee.

57. Ibid., *1883*, pp. 20–22.

58. The ABHMS's decision to support only Selma's Normal Department forced the board of trustees to find someone who would serve as both president and theological instructor. Ibid. Evidently this money shortage, rather than any disagreement, caused Woodsmall and McAlpine to resign.

59. After three years at Selma, Brawley resigned in 1886 to become the American Baptist Publication Society's District Secretary for the South. In 1890, he left the society to become the pastor of the First Baptist Church of Petersburg, Virginia; but he soon returned to work for the society "at its earnest solicitation." Brawley was also pastor of churches in Greenville, South Carolina; Darien, Georgia; and Palatka, Florida.

In conjunction with his church work, he worked with several newspapers and wrote several books and pamphlets "along race and denominational lines." This experience helped him become Editorial Secretary of the National Baptist Publishing Board in Nashville, Tennessee at the end of the nineteenth century. Culp, *Negro Literature*, facing p. 255. George Brown Tindall, *South Carolina Negroes, 1877–1900* (Columbia: University of South Carolina Press, 1952), pp. 188–89.

60. *C.M.B.C.A. Minutes, 1885*, pp. 7, 13.

61. *The Selma University Chronicle*, XI, 3.

62. *C.M.B.C.A. Minutes, 1883*, p. 15; *1886*, p. 18. Boothe, *Cyclopedia*, p. 47.

63. Ibid., *1887*, p. 36. *The Selma University Chronicle*, XI, 3.

64. *C.M.B.C.A. Minutes, 1886*, p. 18; *1887*, pp. 13, 20–21. Boothe, *Cyclopedia*, p. 48. Although he was a Presbyterian, Paterson was quite interested in the affairs of the black Baptists. He attended several of the conventions (joining as an annual member when he did so), and he served on Selma's Board of Trustees. Paterson would have opposed locating the Baptist school in Montgomery in 1887 since he was then in the process of moving his school there.

65. *C.M.B.C.A. Minutes, 1887*, unnumbered page; *1888*, p. 36.

66. Ibid., *1890*, p. 32.

67. Ibid., *1888*, p. 25; *1889*, p. 24; *1890*, p. 33; *1891*, pp. 25–26; *1892*, p. 37. *The Selma University Chronicle*, XI, 3.

68. *C.M.B.C.A. Minutes, 1889*, p. 25.

69. Ibid., Booth, *Cyclopedia*, pp. 41–52.

70. *C.M.B.C.A. Minutes, 1892*, pp. 38–39. Purce's emphasis.

71. There were no hard feelings against Purce personally; for on February 22, 1894, the Negro State Mission Board and Sunday-School Board appointed Purce General Missionary to work under the joint appointment of the ABHMS and the Baptists of Alabama. Later in the year, Purce resigned this position to become the president of a university in Kentucky. Ibid., *1894*, pp. 23, 32.

72. For some reason, however, McAlpine retained his joint appointment by the Southern and Alabama Baptist Conventions (white) as, ironically enough, "Theological Instructor of ministers in Selma University and the State." The Board of Trustees also reelected Pettiford as Selma's Financial and Corresponding Secretary. Ibid., *1892*, p. 48; *1893*, pp. 34–35. So the convention's acts must have resulted from a grass roots revolt on the floor of the convention.

73. Ibid., *1893*, p. 19.

74. By 1897, the Baptists had found the new name "ungrammatical and clumsey," so they petitioned the legislature to allow the school to become Selma University again. The legislature did not approve this request until 1908. Ibid., *1897*, p. 20; *1917*, p. 107.

75. Ibid., *1895–1899*.

76. Ibid., *1890*, p. 21.

77. In September, 1881, he married Miss Pauline E. Fears (also a Roger Williams graduate) in Roger Williams University in Nashville. They had two boys and three girls. His son, William H. Dinkins, later also served as Selma's president.

Dinkins also served as pastor of the York Street Church and on the faculty of the State University of Kentucky in Louisville, Kentucky; language instructor at Selma University; pastor of the Marion Baptist Church of Marion, Alabama; and General Sunday-School Missionary of Alabama for the American Baptist Publication Society. In 1890, the State University of Kentucky awarded Dinkins the D.D. degree.

78. Boothe, *Cyclopedia*, pp. 134–35, 137–38. Boothe's emphasis.

79. *C.M.B.C.A. Minutes, 1894*, pp. 14–15, 39–40.

80. Emphasis added. Ibid., *1895*, pp. 39, 43.

81. Ibid., *1897*, pp. 11, 15.

82. Ibid., *1893–1899*.

83. Boothe, *Cyclopedia*, pp. 49, 51.

84. *C.M.B.C.A. Minutes, 1896*, p. 31; *1898*, pp. 27–28, 37; *1899*, pp. 8–9.

85. By 1916, there were twelve small Baptist schools in Alabama in addition to the Selma University, Livingstone Academy, and the Union Springs Normal School. Jones, *Negro Education*, II, 96.

86. *C.M.B.C.A. Minutes, 1899*, p. 43, *et passim, 1897–1899*.

87. Ibid., *1895*, pp. 40–41.

88. Selma named the chapel in honor of Dinkins when it was ready for use in 1904. Ibid., *1897*, pp. 35–36; *1898*, pp. 52–53; *1899*, p. 50. *The Selma University Chronicle*, XI, 3.

89. *C.M.B.C.A. Minutes, 1899*, p. 49. Throughout Dinkins' administration, girls'

sewing classes were the primary (and some years the only) industrial opportunities offered to the students. Ibid., *1893–1899*.

90. *Selma University Catalog, 1903–1904*, pp. 38, 40.

Chapter 10

1. Richard Bryant Drake, "The American Missionary Association and the Southern Negro, 1860–1888" (Unpublished doctoral dissertation, Emory University, 1957), pp. 1, 9–11, 154–55.

2. Ibid., pp. 26–29. Drake lists the denominations and the dates of their cooperation with the AMA on pp. 26–27.

3. Ibid., pp. 37–75.

4. Although Alabama was under Cravath's jurisdiction, Jacob R. Shipherd of the Chicago office went into Alabama to help establish Emerson Institute in Mobile. This venture caused trouble for the AMA, Shipherd, and Emerson Institute. In January, 1868, Shipherd wrote Whipple to brag "about his triumph over General [Wager] Swayne, [Head of the Freedmen's Bureau in Alabama] on the property at Mobile, and of how much he had saved the Association." Actually, Shipherd's "browbeating the Bureau for a few extra dollars" caused Swayne to complain to General Howard and to refuse to work with any AMA agent except Cravath. Shipherd had to resign later in the year when another AMA missionary pointed out that Shipherd had diverted $271 intended for Topeka, Kansas into Emerson Institute. Shipherd also antagonized the Mobile whites and laid the foundation for much of the school's later trouble. Ibid., pp. 78–96.

5. Ibid., pp. 99–103. Drake emphatically denied the earlier writers' contention that the K.K.K. had forced the AMA to resort to normal schools. It was not fear, but economic necessity that caused this shift in emphasis. Ibid., p. 160.

6. Harlan Paul Douglass, *Christian Reconstruction in the South* (Boston: Pilgrim Press, 1909), p. 224.

7. Frederick Leslie Brownlee, *New Day Ascending* (Boston: Pilgrim Press, 1946), pp. 118–19.

8. Drake, "The American Missionary Association," p. 112.

9. Drake estimated that seventy percent of the AMA's funds went to support work with the freedmen under Whipple, but only fifty percent under Strieby. Ibid., pp. 104–05.

10. Ibid., pp. 104–05, 232, 235–36.

11. Ibid., pp. 236–43, 245–46.

12. Augustus Field Beard, *A Crusade of Brotherhood* (Boston: The Pilgrim Press, 1901), pp. 230–31.

13. Drake correctly noted that Booker T. Washington's influence on the formation of policy by the Slater Fund was "negligible." Drake, "American Missionary Association," p. 205. If anything, the influence was more the other way.

14. Ibid., p. 211.

15. In 1916, Thomas Jesse Jones, an intense partisan of Booker T. Washington, admitted in his survey of black schools and colleges in Alabama that Talladega College then offered the only real college-level work available in any black school in the state. While there were no other outside surveys of black schools in Alabama prior to that of Jones, Talladega evidently had held this honorable position for two decades since

it began college work in the 1890's.

Chapter 11

1. The AMA established at least one other primary school in Alabama. Swayne School in Montgomery survived and flourished as a public school after Reconstruction. In 1865, General Wager Swayne,* head of the Freedmen's Bureau in Alabama, secured a grant of $10,000 from the Bureau to build a black school in Montgomery. Swayne himself gave one acre of ground for the school. In 1867 the AMA purchased one and one-half acres and began operating the school with white teachers. By 1872, J. M. McPherson of Tabor, Iowa, was superintendent over 6 teachers, 612 pupils in day school, 150 in Sabbath School, and 150 in the Mission Sabbath School. McPherson reported that attendance, punctuality, and (especially) deportment of the students had greatly improved during the year. In 1874, the city of Montgomery took over the school from the AMA, but McPherson remained the principal. There were still only six teachers, including McPherson's wife, but the school had acquired a matron, Mrs. George Whitfield Andrews, the wife of the local Congregational minister (later President of Talladega College). Yellow fever delayed opening the school, but 477 enrolled in the day school and 164 in the Sabbath School. B. S. Thompson, Sr., editor, *A Century of Negro Progress in Montgomery City and County* (Montgomery: n.p. [1963]), p. 43. *AMA Annual Report, 1872*, p. 51; *1874*, p. 46. Drake, "The American Missionary Association," p. 299.

In 1883–1884, F. W. Eveleth was principal, assisted by five teachers. A Fisk University graduate, Charles A. Duncan, the first black principal, was at Swayne in 1888. In 1895, Joseph D. Bibb was principal over five teachers, one supernumerary teacher, and a janitor. Under Bibb, the school grew until it needed more room, so black citizens formed the Swayne School Association, Dr. William Washington, Chairman. With Montgomery's aid, the Association bought two lots on the southeast corner of Union and Grove Streets. James H. Phillips became principal in 1898 and remained until after 1901. Phillips' staff consisted of eight teachers and a janitor, 1898–1899; nine teachers, 1900; and five teachers, 1901. Thompson, *Century of Progress*, p. 43. *Montgomery City Directories, 1883–1884*, p. 4; *1888*, p. 16; *1895*, p. 46; *1897*, p. 51; *1898*, p. 79; *1899*, pp. 260–61; *1900*, p. 59; *1901*, p. 41. For a brief biographical sketch of Joseph D. Bibb and his controversial stand that black state schools should employ only blacks whenever possible (an indirect attack on his former employer and current competitor, W. B. Paterson) see Louis R. Harlan, ed., *The Booker T. Washington Papers*, Volume III (Urbana: University of Illinois Press, 1974), pp. 242–43.

*For an intensely pro-Southern white interpretation of Swayne and the Freedmen's Bureau in Alabama, see Walter Lynwood Fleming, *Civil War and Reconstruction in Alabama* (New York: Columbia University Press, 1905), pp. 407, 424, 492–93, 498. Even Fleming admitted that Swayne did much to improve relations between the races and "long enjoyed the confidence of the best [white] men." But Fleming bitterly condemned Swayne's participation in politics in Alabama. Ibid., pp. 492–93. For a much more sympathetic presentation of Swayne, see William S. McFeely, *Yankee Stepfather: General O. O. Howard and the Freedmen* (New Haven: Yale University Press, 1968), pp. 66, 77–78, 245, 259–60, 282, 317.

2. *History of the American Missionary Association* (New York: American Missionary Association, 1874), p. 42. *Holding the Fort at Athens, Alabama* ([New York: American

Missionary Association,] n.d.), n.p. Miss Mary F. Wells to Rev. Edw'd F. Smith, February 26, 1867, Amistad Collection.

3. *Trinity School, Athens, Ala. After 15 Years' Experience and First Impressions* (New York: American Missionary Association, [1903–1904]), p. 1. *History of the American Missionary Association, 1891*, p. 43.

4. *Trinity School*, p. 2.

5. Brownlee, *New Day Ascending*, p. 121. *Congregational Milestones* (New York: Congregational National Home Missionary Societies, n.d.), pp. 54–55.

6. Miss Mary F. Wells to Rev. Edw'd P. Smith, February 18, 1867, Amistad Collection.

7. *Congregational Milestones*, pp. 54–55.

8. *History of the AMA, 1891*, p. 43.

9. *AMA Annual Report, 1892*, p. 3; *1893*, p. 50; *1896*, p. 41; *1899*, p. 57; *1900*, p. 65; *1901*, p. 64.

10. *Trinity School*, p. 2.

11. *Where Cotton is King and the People are Poor: Cotton Valley School, Fort Davis, Alabama* (New York: American Missionary Association, n.d.), n.p. In 1906, "Aunt or Grandmother Boyd" was ninety-three years old and had over 125 direct descendants living in the small community. E. M. T. Cottin, *Cotton Valley School* (New York: American Missionary Association, [1906]), n.p. Mrs. Boyd was so proud that the teacher had lived with her that she left in the ceiling of her house the nails that held the curtain which separated Miss Davis from the Boyd family. *Does Cotton Valley Pay?* (New York: Congregational Rooms, [1905]), n.p.

12. Cottin, *Cotton Valley School*, n.p.

13. Brownlee, *New Day Ascending*, pp. 128–29.

14. Douglass, *Christian Reconstruction*, pp. 222–23.

15. *Where Cotton is King*, n.p.

16. "Cotton Valley, Ala.," *American Missionary*, L (May, 1896), 156–57.

17. *Does Cotton Valley Pay?*, n.p. *AMA Annual Report, 1898*, p. 48; *1899*, p. 57; *1901*, p. 64.

18. Douglass, *Christian Reconstruction*, pp. 221–22.

19. Perhaps the school at Talladega first gave Benson the idea of establishing his school.

20. A. F. Beard, "Samples and Examples," *American Missionary*, LII (June, 1898), 61–65. Clinton J. Calloway to Booker T. Washington, November 9, 30, 1895, Booker T. Washington Papers, Library of Congress. Evidently Washington approved of the project for he donated a typewriter at the request of Calloway. Ibid.

21. *AMA Annual Report, 1901*, p. 64. By 1916 the elder Benson formed the Dixie Industrial Company to coordinate all his enterprises. It was capitalized at $100,000 and owned 10,000 acres of land, a store, a turpentine still, a cottonseed-oil mill, cotton gin, and fifty tenant farms, totaling 1,800 acres. The trustees of the school and the company overlapped, but they were separate organizations. Northern men and women and local blacks composed the Board of Trustees which ran the school. Thomas Jesse Jones, *Negro Education: A Study of the Private and Higher Schools for Colored People in the United States*, 2 volumes, Bureau of Education, Department of Interior (Washington: Government Printing Office, 1917), II, 48.

22. Richardson, *Cyclopedia*, I, 79.

23. *History of the AMA, 1891*, p. 39. Hattye L. Whitney, "The Development of

Public Secondary Education for Negroes in the State of Alabama" (Unpublished master's thesis, Howard University, 1946), pp. 17–18.

24. *AMA Annual Report, 1872*, p. 53. AMA missionaries frequently gave undue credence to "leading [white] Southerners' expressions of support."

25. Ibid., *1874*, p. 46.

26. *Report of the Alabama Superintendent of Education, 1875*, p. 115.

27. *AMA Annual Report, 1876*, p. 71.

28. *History of the AMA, 1891*, p. 40.

29. *AMA Annual Report, 1891*, p. 57. A. T. Burnell, "Burrell School, Selma, Alabama," *American Missionary*, XLIX (August, 1895, No. 18), 260–61.

30. Ibid. XLVIII (July, 1894), 260–61; L (August, 1896), 253–54; LI (April, 1897), 127–28; LI (September, 1897), 226.

31. *AMA Annual Report, 1894*, pp. 54–55; *1898*, p. 48.

32. George N. White, *Burrell Normal School* (New York: American Missionary Association, [1907]), n.p.

33. J. Silsby to Rev. Whipple, November 2, 1865; to Rev. M. E. Strieby, February 26, 1866. Amistad Collection.

34. Mr. Kelsey, Mr. Kimbell, and Miss M. Waterbury later served as Emerson's principal. A. T. Burnell, "Emerson Normal Institute," *American Missionary*, LV (April–June, 1901), 93. *AMA Annual Report, 1872*, p. 51.

35. Since they lived in Illinois, the Emersons chose to work through Jacob R. Shipherd instead of E. M. Cravath, who was in charge of the AMA's work in Alabama. Shipherd's maneuverings to establish and build up the school led to his resignation from the AMA. Drake, "The American Missionary Association," pp. 78–96. For a fuller discussion of the Shipherd incident, see Chapter 10. Harlan Paul Douglass, *The Story of Emerson Institute* (New York: American Missionary Association, 1909), p. 4.

36. Douglass, *The Story of Emerson Institute*, pp. 4–5. *History of the American Missionary Association With Illustrative Facts and Anecdotes* (New York: American Missionary Association, 1891), p. 38.

37. *AMA Annual Report, 1874*, p. 45.

38. Ibid., *1876*, pp. 70–71, quoting the school's paper, the Emerson *Sentinel.*

39. Ibid. One of these graduates, Mrs. M. E. Jones, conducted a successful school in her home for many years. Another, Professor W. A. Caldwell served as Principal of Mobile's Broad Street Academy, one of the few municipal public high schools for blacks (if not the first) in Alabama from its founding in 1886 until after 1900. Burnell, "Emerson Normal Institute," p. 96. *History of the AMA, 1891*, p. 38.

40. *History of the AMA, 1891*, p. 38.

41. Ibid., p. 39. Burnell, "Emerson Normal Institute," p. 98. Clark, *History of Education*, p. 280.

42. The wives of G. W. Andrews and H. S. DeForest of Talladega also served as special missionaries. Evidently this was necessary for a family to make a living wage as missionaries. *AMA Annual Report, 1886*, p. 47.

43. Ibid., Douglass, *The Story of Emerson Institute*, pp. 7–9. Clark, *History of Education*, p. 280.

44. *History of the AMA, 1891*, p. 39. A. T. Burnell, *Emerson Normal Institute* (New York: Congregational Rooms, n.d.) unnumbered pages. Tuition in 1888 ranged from $.80 per month in the primary grades to $1.20 per month in the normal grades. Music

lessons cost from $1.75 to $2.00 per month. Clark, *History of Education*, p. 280.

45. While living in Birmingham he was the historian of the Medical Society of Alabama.

46. Clark, *History of Education*, p. 280. Burnell, *Emerson Normal Institute*, unnumbered pages. Douglass, *The Story of Emerson Institute*, pp. 6, 9.

47. Burnell, *Emerson Normal Institute*, unnumbered pages.

48. The story of this school from its beginning in 1867, through its being taken over by Alabama in 1873, appears in the section of this book which describes the development of Alabama State College. The following section deals with Lincoln School from 1888, when the AMA resumed work at the initiative of local blacks in Marion, until 1901. When the Association turned Lincoln School over to the state on Alabama's pledge to give the school $4,000 a year, "the persons in charge of the state school misappropriated many funds, although [John] Silsby, who was retained on the faculty, seems not to have been involved in them." Drake, "The American Missionary Association," p. 299.

49. The relevant portions of the laws were in Sections IV and VIII.

> The trustees shall take charge of all the property of the State of Alabama near Marion, Perry County, upon which is located the State Normal School and University, . . . but shall not allow said property, or any part thereof, to be used for a school or college of any kind after the first day of August, 1887, except as hereinafter provided.
>
> The governor shall appoint two commissioners . . . who, with the county shall have power to select so much of the land now belonging to the State of Alabama lying near Marion, and used for a Normal School and colored or Lincoln Institute, by whatever name called, as will be sufficient for a common public school for the colored children of that township only, and to designate the same, and to select a building thereon one suitable for a school house. . . . Thereupon the governor shall sell all the remaining land and buildings and have the proceeds thereof applied to the building or equipment of the Alabama Colored University. . . . Whenever the governor sells any of said land, he shall have power to convey a fee simple title to said land to the purchaser, upon his condition expressed in the deed that it shall never be used for school purposes of any kind, and if this condition is broken said land shall revert to the State of Alabama. Williams, "Legal Provisions," pp. 44–46.

50. *Lincoln Normal School, Marion, Alabama* (New York: American Missionary Association, n.d.), p. 1. Brownlee, *New Day Ascending*, p. 125.

51. *AMA Annual Report, 1893*, p. 50; *1894*, p. 54; *1896*, *1897*, p. 51; *1898*, p. 48; *1899*, p. 57 listed Miss M. A. E. Sanborn of Alaban, Vermont, as principal; but Miss Phillips was listed for 1900 and 1901; *1900*, p. 65; *1901*, p. 64.

52. M. E. Wilcox, "Lincoln Normal Institute, Marion, Ala.," *American Missionary*, XLVIII (September, 1894), 318–19.

53. M. L. Phillips, *Lincoln Normal School, Marion, Ala.* ([New York: American Missionary Association, 1905]), pp. 1–2. Brownlee, *New Day Ascending*, p. 125.

54. Phillips, *Lincoln Normal School*, pp. 2–3.

55. Ibid., p. 2.

56. Ibid., p. 3. In 1901, Miss Phillips had seven assistants to help her with the 274 pupils. *AMA Annual Report, 1901*, p. 64.

57. Brownlee, *New Day Ascending*, p. 125.
58. Phillips, *Lincoln Normal School*, p. 3.

Chapter 12

1. Herbert Wright Gates, ed., *The Negro—A Congregational Opportunity* [New York]: American Missionary Association, [1922], p. 19.

2. Ibid. Jereline Ryus Bell, "A Limited Study of the Contributions of the American Missionary Association to Negro Education in Alabama" (Unpublished master's thesis, The State College for Negroes at Montgomery, Alabama, 1949), p. 32. Beard, *A Crusade of Brotherhood*, p. 174. Henry Lee Swint, *The Northern Teacher in the South* (Nashville: Vanderbilt University Press, 1941), p. 187. According to Cicely Savery, daughter of one of the founders of the school that became Talladega College, the first teacher was Miss Hopkins from "somewhere in Illinois." Miss Savery probably did not remember the exact spelling of the teacher's name. Both Miss Savery and Swint could have been correct about the teacher's home since missionary teachers sometimes belonged to a church in a town other than that in which their family lived. Cicely Savery, *Two Girls' Work* (New York: American Missionary Association, n.d.), p. 2.

3. Savery, *Two Girls' Work*, p. 2. J. Silsby to E. M. Cravath, February 26, 1867, Amistad Collection.

4. Savery, *Two Girls' Work*, p. 2. Luke was an independent missionary and a member of the Talladega Congregational Church. The mob murdered him at Patona, Alabama in 1870. *American Missionary*, XIV (October, 1870), 285.

5. During the Civil War, the Confederates used the building as a prison. One of the Union inmates scratched "Prisoners of War" on one of the windowpanes. The school later highly prized this windowpane.

6. John Silsby to E. M. Cravath, February 26, 1867, and to Edward P. Smith, March 25, 1867, Amistad Collection. Gates, *The Negro*, p. 19. William Cathcart, *Baptist Encyclopedia* (n.p., 1881), p. 17. Brownlee, *New Day Ascending*, p. 194.

7. Brownlee, *New Day Ascending*, p. 194. Savery, *Two Girls' Work*, p. 2.

8. Gates, *The Negro*, p. 21. Brownlee, *Heritage of Freedom*, p. 32.

9. Beard, *A Crusade of Brotherhood*, pp. 173–74.

10. Brownlee, *New Day Ascending*, pp. 194–95.

11. *History of the AMA, 1891*, p. 29. A. F. Beard said that Graves was from Brooklyn. Augustus Field Beard, *Talladega College* (New York: American Missionary Association, [1907]), p. 9.

12. Beard, *Talladega College*, p. 12. *History of the AMA, 1891*, p. 29. Savery Library, built in 1939, commemorated the ex-slave, William Savery, who contributed so much to Talladega College. A tablet in the library summarized some of his contributions.

"This building was named in honor of William Savery:
1852—A carpenter in bondage, he labored to build Old Swayne Hall.
1865—A free man, with others he organized the first school for Negroes in this county.
1867—A man of faith, he led the American Missionary Association in the purchase of Old Swayne Hall and the founding of Talladega College.
1869—An incorporator and original trustee of the college, he builded for the generation to come."

Brownlee, *New Day Ascending*, p. 196. Savery lived to see three of his daughters graduate from Talladega; Cicely, Louise, and Mary Elizabeth. These also taught at

Talladega. Another daughter, Katie Lord, graduated in 1899. Beard, *A Crusade of Brotherhood*, p. 176. *AMA Annual Report, 1891, 1893, 1894.*

13. *History of the AMA, 1891*, pp. 29–30.

14. Ibid., p. 30.

15. Ibid.

16. In *Our Mountain Home*, Talladega's white paper, G. T. McAfee wrote: "I have resided in this city since March 1, 1833, and have been for the most part connected, as a trustee, with the principal schools in this place, . . . and I will content myself by saying that no institution of learning since that time to the present equals this College. . . ." *AMA Annual Report, 1872*, pp. 45–56; *1874*, pp. 39–40.

17. *The Graduates of Talladega College and What They Are Doing* (Talladega: Press of *Our Mountain Home*, 1900), pp. 5–8, 65. *AMA Annual Report, 1876*, p. 65. In 1900, the other normal graduates were employed as follows: two medical students, missionaries, and nurses; one lawyer, merchant, farmer, engineer, soldier, doctor, school treasurer, agricultural school student, preacher and teacher, bank cashier, clerk, college professor, pastor and President of a Normal and Industrial School, pharmacist and dentist, worker in the U.S. Pension Office, post office mailing clerk, post office mail carrier, pastor and school principal, mechanic. Most of the women were housewives. Talladega was especially proud of its former students who became missionaries to Africa (under the Southern Presbyterian Board of Missions); Miss Lucy Gantt (Mrs. William Shepherd), Miss Lillian M. Thomas, and Miss Maria Fearing. All these went to the Congo Free State. Ibid.

18. Beard, *Talladega College*, p. 9. *The Yearbook of the Congregational and Christian Churches, 1931 Statistics*, p. 60.

19. George W. Andrews, "Reverend George Whitfield Andrews, D.D." A two page typed biographical sketch by Andrews' nephew and namesake, Oberlin College Archives.

20. Upon his wife's death, Andrews went to live with his nephew and niece in Oberlin, Ohio. During the last eleven years of his life (1920–1931) Andrews was confined to his bed because of a fall. Andrews, "Reverend George Whitfield Andrews, D.D."

21. Andrews' wife also served as a special AMA missionary in Alabama for several years. *AMA Annual Report, 1874–1901.*

22. Andrews was an outstanding leader in all the meetings of the Association. His other offices on committees and as representative for the Association are too numerous to list here. *Proceedings of The Congregational Association of Alabama, 1876–1901.*

23. Andrews, "Andrews." Oberlin *News Tribune*, April 4, 1931, Oberlin College Archives. "Andrews, George Whitfield, 1833–1931," *The Yearbook of the Congregational and Christian Churches, 1931 Statistics*, p. 60.

24. *The Graduates of Talladega College*, pp. 3–4.

25. A student who elected to follow the four year program took the following courses.

First Year. Introduction to the Bible; Biblical Geography; Harmony of the Gospels; Rhetoric; Homiletics.

Second Year. Old Testament History; Ceremonial Law; Acts of the Apostles; Church History; Psychology; Moral Philosophy.

Third Year. Systematic Theology; Selections from Pauline Epistles, Psalms, and Isaiah; Church Polity.

Fourth Year. Systematic Theology; Homiletics; Selections from the Minor Prophets; Revelation; Biblical Theology; Progress of Doctrine in the Old and New Testaments; Revivals.

Rhetorical Exercises, Plans of Sermons or Preaching Exercises weekly each year. *Talladega College: Theological Department* (n.p., n.d.). Amistad Collection. This was by far the most advanced black theological program in nineteenth century Alabama.

26. Ibid. *AMA Annual Report, 1874*, p. 21.

27. *American Missionary*, XLVIII (March, 1894), 129–30.

28. Beard, *Talladega College*, pp. 12–13.

29. See the chapter on Tuskegee for a more complete discussion of Tuskegee's Bible School. *History of the AMA, 1891*, pp. 30–31. *American Missionary*, XLIX (August, 1895), 255; LII (September, 1898), 118.

30. Beard, *Talladega College*, p. 10. *Talladega College: Theological Department*, n.p.

31. Soon after reaching Talladega, DeForest described his reasons for accepting this position:

> *First*, I am needed. This is a great work and the workmen are few. . . . We have more of a field than we can occupy. . . . I am often weary on Saturday, and poorly enough prepared for Sunday, but I am spared the anguish of not knowing where to go or what to do. Few would care for my shoes, but I hope to wear them myself and wear them here.
>
> *Second*, there is here perhaps an unsurpassed opportunity for influencing men. I am not only a "home missionary," but also a foreign missionary to Africa, and that last with special facilities. I am master of the language, and do not work at the disadvantage of a half-learned and half-mastered tongue. Without the honors of a foreign missionary, I am also without many of his disadvantages. . . .
>
> *Third*, the most pressing work in our own country is here. As surely as in 1861 our national peril is in the South. Patriotism as well as humanity and Christianity keep me here, and no campaigning in our recent war seemed more of a duty of loyalty than that in which I am now engaged. Certainly just now I would rather be here than in any other part of the universe of God. Tell our friends at the North that we do not need their sympathy but we do need their help. Beard, *A Crusade of Brotherhood*, pp. 214–15.

32. Lee de Forest, *Father of Radio: The Autobiography of Lee de Forest* (Chicago: Wilcox and Follett Co., 1950), pp. 10–13. *American Missionary*, XLVIII (February, 1894), 79. Lee adopted the original spelling of his family name, "de Forest," instead of DeForest as his father wrote the name.

33. de Forest, *Father of Radio*, pp. 7, 10–14, 79. *Yale Obituary Record, 1890–1900*, p. 28, Yale University Archives. *American Missionary*, L (March, 1896), 88–89; XLVIII (February, 1894), 79.

34. Booker T. Washington received similar contributions, especially for the care of his children after the death of his second wife, Olivia A. Davidson.

35. de Forest, *Father of Radio*, pp. 6, 9–14, 16–19, 21–23, 30–31, 37–38, 41, 46–49, 51, 79. *Yale Obituary Record, 1890–1900*, p. 28, Yale University Archives. *American Missionary*, L (March, 1896), 88–89; XLVIII (February, 1894), 79.

36. Even this low salary was over twice what Booker T. Washington was able to offer his teachers (in addition to board) during the 1890's. Harlan, *Washington Papers, Volume 3*.

37. de Forest, *Father of Radio*, pp. 6, 9–10, 16–19, 21–23, 30–31, 37–38, 41, 46–49, 51.

38. Brownlee, *New Day Ascending*, pp. 178–79.

39. Hooper Councill Trenholm, *Yearbook of the Alabama State Teachers' Association, 1949* (Montgomery: State Teachers' College, 1949), p. 26. *The Graduates of Talladega College*, p. 5. In 1916, Talladega College was "the only institution in Alabama equipped to give education of college grade to colored people." Talladega enrolled forty-five in the College Department that year. Jones, *Negro Education*, II, 83.

40. Brownlee, *New Day Ascending*, p. 197. Brownlee was quoting the charge to refute it, not making it.

41. Even here Washington could be devious. When addressing the New York Congregational Club on January 16, 1893, he had little but praise for the work of the Congregationalists in the South.

42. *American Missionary*, XLVIII (August, 1894), 288–89. Brownlee, *New Day Ascending*, p. 179.

43. *American Missionary*, XLVIII (August, 1894), 289.

44. *Industrial Training at Talladega College—Many Departments* (New York: American Missionary Association, n.d.), n.p.

45. *American Missionary Association Calendar* (New York: Bible House, 1897), July, 1897. *American Missionary*, XLVIII (August, 1894), 289; L (April, 1896), 125–26; LI (September, 1897), 220.

46. *American Missionary*, L (April, 1896), 126–27.

47. Ibid., 127–29; LI (September, 1897), 220.

48. Talladega did not get nearly so much money from the Slater Fund for establishing industries as did Tuskegee; nor did Talladega get an appropriation from Alabama for an Agricultural Experiment station. Talladega's connection with the Congregational Church through the AMA probably alienated some of the businessmen attracted by Tuskegee's nondenominational if not secular orientation. Of course, neither Talladega nor any other black school had so efficient a fund-raiser as Washington.

49. Harlan Paul Douglass, *Christian Reconstruction in the South* (Boston: Pilgrim Press, 1909), p. 294. Councill stated his agreement with this philosophy in 1893. See the chapter on Councill.

50. Ibid., pp. 289–90.

51. Ibid., p. 292.

52. "Address of Mr. J. R. Savage," *The American Missionary*, L (March, 1896), 405.

53. Although Thomas Jesse Jones, personally, believed in industrial education in black schools (as is shown in his section on industrial schools and by his devoting so many pages to a detailed, laudatory description of Tuskegee), he admitted that in 1916 Talladega was the only school offering college level work (and a theological course at the college level) to blacks in Alabama. Jones, *Negro Education*, II, 32.

54. *The American Missionary*, XLVIII (August, 1894), 288–89.

55. At least one of Talladega's graduates did influence the liberal arts orientation of another Alabama black college. W. H. McAlpine helped the Baptists establish Selma University and served as its first black president (1881–1883). *The Selma University Chronicle*, XI (January, 1950), 2–3. Charles Octavius Boothe, *The Cyclopedia of Colored Baptists of Alabama* (Birmingham: Alabama Publishing Company, 1895), p. 166.

56. Jones, *Negro Education*, II, p. 32.

57. The best example of this distorted overemphasis on Washington is a thesis which labels Talladega, Normal, and the "other [black] colleges" in Alabama as the result of "The Leaven of Tuskegee Institute." James Benson Sellers, "Negro Education in Alabama" (Unpublished master's thesis, University of Alabama, 1924), [ii].

58. In 1916 Alabama's black, private secondary schools enrolled 1,220 students—the black public schools, 778 students—in secondary classes. All forty-five black college students in the state were then at Talladega. Jones, *Negro Education*, II, p. 32.

Bibliography

I. PRIMARY SOURCES

A. *Manuscripts*

American Missionary Association Archives. Letters and pamphlets describing the work of the association and its missionaries in Alabama. Amistad Collection. Dillard University, New Orleans, Louisiana.

"George Whitfield Andrews, D.D." Two-page typed biography by Andrews' nephew, George Whitfield Andrews. Oberlin College Archives, Oberlin, Ohio.

John William Beverly necrology information in Brown University Archives, Providence, Rhode Island.

Winfield Henry Mixon Papers. Diary and clippings of a Presiding Elder in the Alabama African Methodist Episcopal Church. Duke University, Durham, North Carolina.

William Burns Paterson Papers. Photostats of letters in Scotland, typed family history, clippings. Private collection of Paterson's descendants, Montgomery, Alabama.

Booker Taliaferro Washington Papers. Letters to and from Washington, pamphlets, speech manuscripts. Library of Congress, Washington, D.C.

B. *Official Records and Documents*

1. Publications of the United States Government

Alabama Historical Records Survey Project. *Inventory of Church Archives of Alabama: Protestant Episcopal Church*. Birmingham: Alabama Historical Records Survey Project, 1939.

Clark, Willis Gaylord. *History of Education in Alabama, 1702–1889*. Circular of Information No. 3, 1889. Contributions to American Educational History, edited by

Herbert Baxter Adams. Washington: Government Printing Office, 1889.
Jones, Thomas Jesse, ed. *Negro Education: A Study of the Private and Higher Schools for Colored People in the United States.* Bureau of Education Bulletin No. 38, 1916, 2 volumes. Washington: Government Printing Office, 1917.
Report of the United States Commissioner of Education, 1866–1901. Washington: Government Printing Office.
Weeks, Stephen Beauregard. *The History of Public School Education in Alabama.* Bureau of Education, Bulletin No. 12, 1915. Washington: Government Printing Office, 1915.
Works Projects Administration: Writers Program of the Works Projects Administration in the State of Alabama. *Alabama: A Guide to the Deep South.* American Guide Series. New York: Richard R. Smith, 1941.

2. Publications of the Alabama State Government and Subordinate Agencies

City Directory of Birmingham, 1887–1901.
City Directory of Mobile, 1866–1901.
City Directory of Montgomery, 1866–1901.
Report of the Alabama Commissioner of Education, 1866–1901.

C. *Reports of Nongovernmental Organizations*

Alabama A & M College, Normal, Alabama Catalog, 1907–1908, 1959–1960. Alabama State College Bulletin: Montgomery, Alabama: 1967–1968, V (July–August, 1967).
Alabama State Teachers Association. *Yearbook and Convention Program, 1921–1964.*
American Missionary Association. *Annual Report, 1866–1901.*
Board of Missions for Freedmen of the Presbyterian Church in the United States of America. *Annual Report, 1893–1901.*
Convention of the Colored Missionary Baptists of Alabama. *Minutes, 1868–1901.*
Conference of Congregational Churches of the State of Alabama. *Minutes, 1877–1898.*
Freedmen's Aid Society of the Methodist Episcopal Church. *Annual Report, 1866–1901.*
The Normal Index. December, *1890*–September, *1893*, scattered issues.

D. *Newspapers and Periodicals*

American Missionary, 1866–1901.
Huntsville *Gazette, 1882–1894.*

E. *Books and Pamphlets*

Barnes, E. A. *How the Problem Is Solved at Talladega College.* New York: American Missionary Association, [1903].
Beverly, John William. *History of Alabama.* Montgomery: Alabama Printing Co., 1901.
Boothe, Charles Octavius. *The Cyclopedia of the Colored Baptists of Alabama.* Birmingham: Alabama Publishing Co., 1895.
Burnell, A. T. *Emerson Normal Institute.* New York: Congregational Rooms, n.d.
Cooper, James Wesley. *The American Missionary Association in Alabama.* New York: American Missionary Association, 1900.
Councill, William Hooper. *Bright Side of the Southern Question.* n. p. [1903].

______. *Lamp of Wisdom or Race History Illuminated.* Nashville: J. T. Haley & Co., Publishers, 1898.

______. *The Young Negro of 1864; The Young Negro of 1904; The Problem Then; The Problem Now.* Boston: Charles Alexander, Printer, 1904.

Culp, Daniel Wallace. *Twentieth Century Negro Literature.* Toronto: J. L. Nichols & Co., 1902.

de Forest, Lee. *Father of Radio: The Autobiography of Lee de Forest.* Chicago: Wilcox and Follett Co., 1950.

Edwards, William James. *Twenty-Five Years in the Black Belt.* Boston: The Cornhill Company, 1918.

Haley, James T. *Afro-American Encyclopedia.* Nashville: Haley & Florida, 1895.

Harlan, Louis R. et al., eds. *The Booker T. Washington Papers.* Volumes I, II, III, Urbana: University of Illinois Press, 1972, 1974.

History of the American Missionary Association. New York: American Missionary Association, 1875.

History of the American Missionary Association with Illustrative Facts and Anecdotes. New York: American Missionary Association, 1891.

Hood, James Walker. *One Hundred Years of the African Methodist Episcopal Zion Church.* New York: African Methodist Episcopal Zion Book Concern, 1895.

Mixon, Winfield Henry. *History of the African Methodist Episcopal Church in Alabama.* Nashville: A.M.E. Church Sunday School Union, 1902.

Morehouse, Henry Lyman. *Baptist Home Missions in North America.* New York: Baptist Home Mission Rooms, 1883.

Payne, Daniel Alexander. *History of the African Methodist Episcopal Church.* Nashville: Publishing House of the A.M.E. Sunday School Union, 1891.

Phillips, May L. *Lincoln Normal School, Marion, Alabama.* n.p.: [1905].

Pipkin, James Jefferson. *The Story of a Rising Race.* n.p.: Thompson Publishing Co., 1902.

Richings, G. B. *Evidences of Progress Among Colored People.* Philadelphia: George S. Ferguson Co., 1896.

Rubin, Louis D., Jr., ed. *Teach the Freeman: The Correspondence of Rutherford B. Hayes and The Slater Fund For Negro Education.* 2 volumes. Baton Rouge: Louisiana State University Press, 1959.

Savery, Cicely. *Two Girls' Work.* New York: American Missionary Association, n.d.

Scott, Emmett Jay and Lyman Beecher Stowe. *Booker T. Washington: Builder of a Civilization.* Garden City: Doubleday, Page & Co., 1916.

Sheppard, Lucy Gant. *From Talladega College to Africa.* New York: American Missionary Association, n.d.

Silsby, Edwin C. *Congregationalism in Alabama.* [New York: American Missionary Association, 1900].

Simmons, William J. *Men of Mark.* Cleveland: G. M. Rewell & Co., 1887.

Trinity School, Athens, Alabama: After Fifteen Years Experience and First Impressions. New York: American Missionary Association, [1904].

Washington, Booker Taliaferro. *The Future of the American Negro.* Boston: Small, Maynard & Co., 1899.

______. *My Larger Education.* New York: Doubleday, Page & Co., 1910.

______. *Story of My Life and Work.* Toronto: J. L. Nichols & Co., 1901.

______. *The Story of the Negro: The Rise of the Race From Slavery.* 2 volumes. New York: Peter Smith, 1940 [1909].

———. *Tuskegee and Its People: Their Ideals and Achievements*. New York: D. Appleton & Co., 1905.
———. *Up From Slavery*. New York: Doubleday & Co., Inc., 1901.
———. *Working with the Hands*. New York: Doubleday, Page & Co., 1904.
——— and William Edward Burghardt DuBois. *The Negro in the South*. Philadelphia: George W. Jacobs & Co.
———, N. B. Wood, and Fannie Barrier Williams. *A New Negro for a New Century*. Chicago: American Publishing House, [1900–1901].
Washington, Ernest Davidson, ed. *Selected Speeches of Booker T. Washington*. Garden City: Doubleday, Doran & Co., Inc., 1932.

F. *Articles*

Andrews, G. W. "Talladega College, Ala." *American Missionary*, LIII (October, 1899), 112–13.
Calloway, Thomas J. "Booker Washington and the Tuskegee Institute." *The New England Magazine*, XVII (October, 1897), 131–46.
Councill, William Hooper. "The Future of the Negro." *Forum*, XXVII (July, 1899), 570–76.
———. "Kindness a Necessary Element in Leadership." *The Colored American Magazine*, XI (December, 1906), 403.
Forde, Florence T. Johnson, [Mrs.] "The Founder As I Knew Him." *The Normal Index*, XXII (May, 1940), 3–4.
Hopkins, H. C. "Founder's Day Address." *The Normal Index* (May, 1927), 153–55, 165–68.
Julian, James S. "Reminiscences: The Period of 1890–1894." *The State Normal Courier*, II (February 7, 1924), 8–9.
Kobbe, Gustav. "Slave—Now Teacher." *Harpers Weekly*, XXXVI (May 21, 1892), 500–01.
Koyton, Sarah H. "State Normal's First Graduating Class." *The State Normal Courier*, II (February 7, 1924), 5–6.
Ludlow, Helen Wilhelmina. "Fourth Tuskegee Negro Conference." *The Outlook*, LI (March 9, 1895), 400–01.
McKinney, Dr. A. W. "Professor William H. Councill as I Knew Him and I Knew Him Well." *The Normal Index* (May 8, 1920), n.p.
———. "Professor W. H. Councill." *The Normal Index*, IV (May, 1927), 156.
Plump, A. S. "State Normal as 'The Lincoln Normal University' at Marion." *The State Normal Courier*, II (February 7, 1924), 6–7.
Reynolds, Frances. "Reminiscences: The First Years at Montgomery." *The State Normal Courier*, II (February 7, 1924), 7.

II. SECONDARY WORKS

A. *Manuscripts*

J. T. Alexander Research Notes. Information about Alabama Black Baptists, primarily from Alexander's interviews with descendants of early Baptist leaders. Private Collection, Montgomery, Alabama.
Research memorandum prepared by Charles A. Brown, Research Secretary of the

Alabama State Teachers Association for a history of the association, 1969 [typed, one page].

B. *Books and Pamphlets*

A Continuing Service. Reprinted from the Annual Report for 1938 of the Board of Home Missions of the Congregational and Christian Churches covering the work of the American Missionary Association for the year ending May 31, 1938. New York: American Missionary Association, 1938.

"The Alabama State College for Negroes, Montgomery, Alabama: Freshman Handbook, 1950–1951." Mimeographed. Alabama State College.

The American Church Institute for Negroes. *Down Where the Need Is Greatest*. New York: American Church Institute for Negroes, n.d.

Armes, Ethel. *The Story of Coal and Iron in Alabama*. Birmingham: Chamber of Commerce, 1910.

Barber, Jesse Belmont. *Climbing Jacob's Ladder*. New York: Board of National Missions, Presbyterian Church in the United States of America, 1952.

Bardolph, Richard. *The Negro Vanguard*. New York: Vintage Books, 1961.

Beard, Augustus Field. *A Crusade of Brotherhood*. The Pilgrim Press, Boston, 1901.

______. *Talladega College*. New York: American Missionary Association, 1907.

Billingsley, Andrew. *Black Families in White America*. Englewood Cliffs: Prentice-Hall, Inc., 1968.

Binford, Pearl A. *Cotton Valley School, Alabama*. New York: American Missionary Association, n.d.

Blassingame, John W. *The Slave Community: Plantation Life in the Ante-Bellum South*. New York: Oxford University Press, 1972.

Bond, Horace Mann. *The Education of the Negro in the American Social Order* [Reprinted with new material]. New York: Octagon Books, Inc., 1966.

______. *Negro Education in Alabama: A Study in Cotton and Steel*. Washington: The Associated Publishers, Inc., 1939.

Bontemps, Arna. *100 Years of Negro Freedom*. New York: Dodd, Mead & Co., 1961.

Bragg, George Freeman. *History of the Afro-American Group of the Episcopal Church*. Baltimore: Church Advocate Press, 1922.

Brooks, Arthur A. *The History of Unitarianism in the Southern Churches*. Boston: American Unitarian Association, n.d.

Brown, Charles A. *Biographical Sketches of the Presidents of the Alabama State Teachers Association*. Montgomery: Alabama State Teachers Association, [1967].

Brown, J. N. *Lincoln Normal School, Marion, Alabama*. New York: American Missionary Association, n.d.

Brownlee, Frederick Leslie. *Heritage of Freedom*. Philadelphia: United Church Press, 1963.

______. *New Day Ascending*. Boston: Pilgrim Press, 1946.

Bullock, Henry Allen. *A History of Negro Education in the South: From 1619 to the Present*. Cambridge, Massachusetts: Harvard University Press, 1967.

Cathcart, William. *Baptist Encyclopedia*. Philadelphia: Evarts, 1881.

Congregational Milestones. New York: Congregational National Home Mission Societies, n.d.

Cooper, James Wesley. *Alabama*. New York: American Missionary Association, n.d.

Cottin, E.M.T. *Cotton Valley School.* New York: American Missionary Association, [1906].

Cotton Valley School for Negro Youth: Fort Davis, Alabama. New York: American Missionary Association, [1918].

Cremin, Lawrence A. *The Transformation of the School: Progressivism in American Education, 1876–1957.* New York: Alfred A. Knopf, 1961.

Crum, Mason. *The Negro in the Methodist Church.* New York: Editorial Department of the Board of Missions and Church Extension of the Methodist Church, 1951.

Dabney, Charles William. *Universal Education in the South.* 2 volumes. Chapel Hill: University of North Carolina Press, 1936.

Does Cotton Valley Pay? New York: Congregational Rooms, [1905].

Douglass, Harlan Paul. *Christian Reconstruction in the South.* Boston: Pilgrim Press, 1909.

———. *The Story of Emerson Institute.* New York: [American Missionary Association], 1909.

Drewes, Christopher F. *Half a Century of Lutheranism Among Our Colored People.* St. Louis: Concordia Publishing House, 1927.

Drinker, Frederick E. *Booker T. Washington: The Master Mind of a Child of Slavery.* Philadelphia: National Publishing Company, 1915.

DuBois, William Edward Burghardt. *Black Reconstruction.* New York: Russell & Russell, 1935.

Elkins, Stanley M. *Slavery: A Problem in American Institutional and Intellectual Life.* Second edition. Chicago: University of Chicago Press, 1968.

Factor, Robert L. *The Black Response to America: Men, Ideals, and Organization from Frederick Douglass to the NAACP.* Reading, Massachusetts: Addison-Wesley Publishing Co., 1970.

Fleming, Walter Lynwood. *The Churches of Alabama During the Civil War and Reconstruction.* Montgomery: W. M. Rogers & Co., 1902.

———. *Civil War and Reconstruction in Alabama.* New York: Columbia University Press, 1905.

———. *A Documentary History of Reconstruction.* 2 volumes. Cleveland: A. H. Clark & Co., 1907.

Gallagher, Buell Gordon. *Let My People Come.* Talladega: Talladega College, 1940.

Gates, Herbert Wright, ed. *The Negro—A Congregational Opportunity.* [New York]: American Missionary Association, [1922].

Going, Allen Johnston. *Bourbon Democracy in Alabama 1874–1890.* University of Alabama: University of Alabama Press, 1951.

The Graduates of Talladega College and What They Are Doing. Talladega: Press of *Our Mountain Home*, 1900.

Harlan, Louis R. *Booker T. Washington: The Making of a Black Leader, 1856–1901.* New York: Oxford University Press, 1972.

Holding the Fort at Athens, Alabama. [New York: American Missionary Association], n.d.

Holmes, Dwight Oliver Wendell. *The Evolution of the Negro College.* Contribution to Education No. 609. New York: Bureau of Publications, Teachers College, Columbia University, 1934.

Hyatt, Oscar W. *The Development of Secondary Education in Alabama Prior to 1920.* Nashville: George Peabody College for Teachers, 1933.

Industrial Training at Talladega College—Many Departments. New York: American Missionary Association, n.d.

Industrial Training in the Institutions of the American Missionary Association on the Prairie—In the South. New York: American Missionary Association, n.d.

Jencks, Christopher, et al. *Inequality: A Reassessment of the Effect of Family and Schooling in America.* New York: Basic Books, 1973.

Jenkins, Frank Edwin, ed. *Anglo-Saxon Congregationalism in the South.* Atlanta: The Franklin-Turner Co., 1908.

Jones, Lance George Edward. *Negro Schools in the Southern States.* New York: Oxford University Press, 1928.

Jordan, Lewis Garnett. *Negro Baptist History, U. S. A., 1875–1930.* Nashville: The Sunday School Publishing Board, National Baptist Convention, 1931.

Kolchin, Peter. *First Freedom: The Responses of Alabama's Blacks to Emancipation and Reconstruction.* Westport: Greenwood Press, 1972.

Knight, Edgar Wallace. *Public Education in the South.* Boston: Ginn & Co., 1922.

Leavell, Ullim Whitney. *Philanthropy in Negro Education.* Nashville: George Peabody College for Teachers, 1930.

Lincoln Normal School, Marion, Alabama. New York: American Missionary Association, n.d.

Lincoln Normal School for Negro Youth, Marion, Alabama. New York: American Missionary Association, [1918].

Logan, Rayford Whittingham. *The Betrayal of the Negro from Rutherford B. Hayes to Woodrow Wilson.* New York: The Macmillan Co., 1967.

McFeely, William S. *Yankee Stepfather: General O. O. Howard and the Freedmen.* New Haven: Yale University Press, 1968.

McMillan, Malcolm Cook. *Constitutional Development in Alabama, 1798–1901: A Study in Politics, the Negro, and Sectionalism.* Chapel Hill: University of North Carolina Press, 1955.

Mathews, Basil. *Booker T. Washington: Educator and Interracial Interpreter.* Cambridge: Harvard University Press, 1948.

Meier, August. *Negro Thought in America, 1880–1915: Racial Ideologies in the Age of Booker T. Washington.* Ann Arbor: University of Michigan Press, 1963.

Miller, Kelly, et al. *From Servitude to Service.* Boston: American Unitarian Association, 1905.

Missionaries from Talladega College in Africa. New York: American Missionary Association, [1908].

Moore, Albert Burton. *History of Alabama and Her People.* 3 volumes. New York: American Historical Society, 1927.

Moorman, Joseph H. and E. L. Barrett, eds. *Leaders of the Colored Race in Alabama.* Mobile: The News Publishing Co., Inc., 1928.

Murray, Andrew E. *Presbyterians and the Negro.* Philadelphia: Presbyterian Historical Society, 1966.

Myrdal, Gunnar. *An American Dilemma: The Negro Problem and Modern Democracy.* 2 volumes. New York: Harper & Row, Publishers, 1944.

Owen, Marie Bankhead. *Alabama: A Social and Economic History of the State.* Montgomery: Dixie Book Co., Inc., 1927.

———. *The Story of Alabama, A History of the State.* New York: Lewis Historical Publishing Co., [1949].

Owen, Thomas McAdory. *History of Alabama and Dictionary of Alabama Biography,* 4 volumes. Chicago: S. J. Clarke, 1924.

Pelt, Owen D. and Ralph Lee Smith. *The Story of the National Baptists*. New York: Vantage Press, 1960.

Perkinson, Henry J. *The Imperfect Panacea: American Faith in Education, 1865–1965*. New York: Random House, 1968.

Phillips, Charles Henry. *The History of the Colored Methodist Episcopal Church in America*. Jackson, Tennessee: Publishing House C.M.E. Church, 1925.

Phillips, Ulrich Bonnell. *American Negro Slavery*. New York: D. Appleton & Co., 1918.

Rice, Jessie Pearl. *J. L. M. Curry: Southerner, Statesman, and Educator*. New York: King's Crown Press, 1949.

Richardson, Clement, editor-in-chief. *The National Cyclopedia of the Colored Race*. Montgomery: National Publishing Co., 1919.

Riley, Benjamin Franklin. *The Life and Times of Booker T. Washington*. New York: Fleming H. Revell Co., 1916.

———. *A Memorial History of the Baptists of Alabama*. Philadelphia: Judson Press, 1923.

Rogers, William Warren and Robert David Ward. *August Reckoning: Jack Turner and Racism in Post-Civil War Alabama*. Baton Rouge: Louisiana State University Press, 1973.

Shaw, James Beverly Ford. *The Negro in the History of Methodism*. Nashville: Parthenon Press, 1954.

Silberman, Charles E. *Crisis in the Classroom: The Remaking of American Education*. New York: Vintage Books, A Division of Random House, 1971.

Singleton, George A. *The Romance of African Methodism*. New York: Exposition Press, 1952.

Spencer, Samuel Reid, Jr. *Booker T. Washington and the Negro's Place in American Life*. Boston: Little, Brown & Co., 1955.

Stampp, Kenneth. *The Peculiar Institution: Slavery in the Ante-Bellum South*. New York: Random House, 1956.

Stokes, Anson Phelps. *A Brief Biography of Booker Washington*. Hampton: Hampton Institute Press, 1936.

———. *Tuskegee Institute: The First Fifty Years*. Tuskegee: Tuskegee Institute Press, 1931.

Stone, Alfred Holt. *Studies in the American Race Problem*. New York: Doubleday, Page & Co., 1908.

Street, T. Watson. *The Story of Southern Presbyterians*. Richmond: John Knox Press, 1960.

Sumner, F. A. *Talladega College, Talladega, Alabama*. New York: American Missionary Association, n.d.

Swint, Henry Lee. *The Northern Teacher in the South*. Nashville: Vanderbilt University Press, 1941.

Talladega College. New York: American Missionary Association, n.d.

Talladega College. New York: American Missionary Association, [1927].

Talladega College Alumni Are Making Good: Our Graduates in Educational Work. Talladega: The College Press, n.d.

Talladega College Alumni Are Making Good: Pastors. Talladega: The College Press, [1921].

Talladega College: Catalog and Announcements, 100th Anniversary Issue. March, 1967.

Talladega College, Talladega, Alabama: Three Questions. n.p., n.d.

Talladega College: Theological Department. n.p., n.d.

Terry, Paul Washington and Tennent Lee. *A Study of Stillman Institute.* University, Alabama: University of Alabama Press, 1947.

34 Year's [sic] *Investment in Lincoln Normal School, Marion, Alabama.* New York: American Missionary Association, n.d.

Thomas, Isaac Lemuel, ed. *Methodism and the Negro.* New York: Eaton & Mains, 1910.

Thompson, E. S., Sr., ed. *A Century of Negro Progress in Montgomery City and County, Centennial Edition, 1863–1963.* Montgomery: Southeastern Publishing Co., [1963].

Thompson, Ernest Trice. *Presbyterian Missions in the Southern United States.* Richmond: Whittet & Shepperson, 1934.

Thrasher, Max Bennett. *Tuskegee: Its Story and Its Work.* Boston: Small, Maynard & Co., 1900.

Tindall, George Brown. *South Carolina Negroes, 1877–1900.* Baton Rouge: Louisiana State University Press, 1967.

Walker, Anne Kendrick. *Tuskegee and the Black Belt.* Richmond: Dietz Press, Inc., 1944.

Wharton, Vernon Lane. *The Negro in Mississippi, 1865–1890.* Chapel Hill: University of North Carolina Press, 1947.

Where Cotton Is King and the People Are Poor: Cotton Valley School, Fort Davis, Alabama. New York: American Missionary Association, n.d.

White, Charles Lincoln. *A Century of Faith.* Philadelphia: The Judson Press, 1932.

White, George N. *Burrell Normal School.* New York: American Missionary Association, [1907].

Woodson, Carter Godwin. *The History of the Negro Church.* Washington: Associated Publishers, 1921.

Woodward, Comer Vann. *Origins of the New South.* Baton Rouge: Louisiana State University Press, 1951.

Wright, Richard Robert, ed. *Centennial Encyclopedia of the African Methodist Episcopal Church.* Philadelphia: Book Concern of the A.M.E. Church, 1916.

C. *Unpublished Works*

Baker, Robert Andrew. "The American Baptist Home Mission Society and the South, 1832–1894." Unpublished doctoral dissertation, Yale University, 1947.

Ballard, Leilafred. "The American Negro, 1880–1895 as Portrayed in the Huntsville *Gazette.*" Unpublished master's thesis, Howard University, 1952.

Bell, Jereline Ryus. "A Limited Study of the Contributions of the American Missionary Association to Negro Education in Alabama." Unpublished master's thesis, The State College for Negroes at Montgomery, Alabama, 1949.

Bishop, David Wendell. "The Attitude of the Interstate Commerce Commission Toward Discrimination on Public Carriers, 1887–1910." Unpublished master's thesis, Howard University, 1950.

Bowling, Eugene Burgess. "A Historical Study of the Religious Motive in Secondary Education from 1607–1938." Unpublished master's thesis, Howard University, 1940.

Brown, Charles A. "George Milton Elliott." Research memorandum for a history of the Alabama State Teachers Association, 1969. Typed copy received from Brown, Statistical-Secretary of the Alabama State Teachers Association and President of the Alabama branch of the Association for the Study of Negro Life and History, Birmingham, Alabama.

Butcher, Beatrice Bowen. "The Evolution of Negro Women's Schools in the United

States." Unpublished master's thesis, Howard University, 1936.

Church, Zelmera. "The Participation of Negro Land-Grant Colleges and Universities in Federal Emergency and Regular Educational Funds." Unpublished master's thesis, Howard University, 1939.

Clement, Rufus E. "The Educational Work of the African Methodist Episcopal Zion Church, 1820–1920." Unpublished master's thesis, Northwestern University, 1922.

Davis, Joseph. "A Historical Study of Snow Hill Normal and Industrial Institute and Its Contributions to the Educational Program of the State of Alabama." Unpublished master's thesis, Alabama State College, 1954.

DeBoer, John James. "The Influence of Reconstruction on Education in Alabama." Unpublished master's thesis, University of Chicago, 1927.

Drake, Richard Bryant. "The American Missionary Association and the Southern Negro, 1860–1888." Unpublished doctoral dissertation, Emory University, 1957.

Fisher, Charles C. "A Study of the Educational Contributions of the Presbyterian Church, U. S. to Negro Education in Alabama from 1876–1952." Unpublished master's thesis, Alabama State College, 1953.

Galloway, Gladys Gordon. "The Education of the Negro During Reconstruction." Unpublished master's thesis, Howard University, 1924.

Hillier, George Arlington. "History of Educational Legislation in Alabama, 1860–1910." Unpublished master's thesis, University of Chicago, 1924.

Jones, Lee A. "The Influence of Tuskegee Institute on the Education of Negroes in Macon County, Alabama, 1881–1946." Unpublished master's thesis, Tuskegee Institute, 1947.

Jones, William Marquette. "A History of the Burrell Normal School." Unpublished master's thesis, Fisk University, 1936.

Jordan, Lawrence Ferrill. "The Development of Public Education for Negroes in the State of Alabama." Unpublished master's thesis, Howard University, 1931.

Jordan, Richard Stephen, Jr. "An Historical Study of the Georgia Washington High School, Mount Meigs, Alabama, From 1893–1958, as to the Faculty, School Plant, Enrollment and Its Influence on the Community." Unpublished master's thesis, Alabama State College, 1959.

Lacey, Marguerite Dobbins. "The Social, Economic, and Political Life of the Negro in Madison County from 1880–1900." Unpublished master's thesis, Alabama A & M College, 1963.

McCain, Virgil Bowden. "Private Philanthropy in Negro Education in Alabama." Unpublished master's thesis, University, Alabama: University of Alabama, 1939.

McDavid, William L. "Calhoun Land Trust: A Study of Rural Re-settlement in Lowndes County, Alabama." Unpublished master's thesis, Fisk University, 1943.

Miles, Esmie E. "Amory D. Mayo, Northern Promoter of Southern Education." Unpublished master's thesis, Howard University, 1955.

Orr, Charles Walter. "The Educational Philosophy of William H. Councill." Unpublished master's thesis, Fisk University, 1939.

Perry, Grace Naomi. "The Educational Work of the African Methodist Episcopal Church Prior to 1900." Unpublished master's thesis, Howard University, 1948.

Pickens, James D. "The Significance of the John F. Slater Fund in the Development of Public Education in Alabama." Unpublished master's thesis, Alabama State College, 1953.

Raymond, Thelma. "The Development of Secondary Education for Negroes Prior to

1920." Unpublished master's thesis, Howard University, 1941.
Reed, Ernest Ellsworth. "The Educational Philosophy of Booker T. Washington." Unpublished master's thesis, University of Cincinnati, 1928.
Sellers, James Benson. "Negro Education in Alabama." Unpublished master's thesis, University of Alabama, 1924.
Sikes, William Marion. "The Historical Development of Stillman Institute." Unpublished master's thesis, University of Alabama, 1930.
Sisk, Glenn Nolan. "Alabama Black Belt; A Social History, 1875–1917." Unpublished doctoral dissertation, Duke University, 1930.
Turner, Willie Lovell. "Federal Aid to Negro Education." Unpublished master's thesis, Howard University, 1930.
Venable, Thelma C. "Decisions of the State Courts Involving the Rights of Negroes, 1877–1900." Unpublished master's thesis, Howard University, 1948.
Whitney, Hattye L. "The Development of Public Secondary Education for Negroes in the State of Alabama, 1873 to 1945." Unpublished master's thesis, Howard University, 1946.
Williams, Arthur. "The Participation of Negroes in the Government of Alabama, 1867–1874." Unpublished master's thesis, Atlanta University, 1946.
Williams, H. B. "Legal Provisions for the Education of the Negro in the State of Alabama, and How They Affect the Program of Negro Education from 1873–1949." Unpublished master's thesis, Alabama State College for Negroes, 1950.
Williams, Juanita Lee. "Federal Legislation in Relation to Negro Land Grant Colleges." Unpublished master's thesis, Howard University, 1933.
Wiman, David Wayne. "A History of the Colored Cumberland Presbyterian Church." Unpublished B.D. thesis, Cumberland Presbyterian Theological Seminary, 1936.
Young, Peter Beeken. "The Negro Community of Huntsville, Alabama, 1881–1894." Unpublished senior honors thesis, Louisiana State University, 1957.

D. *Periodicals and Articles*

Alabama State College Bulletin, V (July–August, 1967), 21.
"Andrews, G. W." Oberlin *News Tribune*, April 4, 1931.
"Andrews, George Whitfield, 1835–1931." *The Yearbook of Congregational and Christian Churches*, LX (1932).
Bethel, Elizabeth. "The Freedman's Bureau in Alabama." *The Journal of Southern History*, XIV (February, 1948), 49–92.
Buchanan, Walter S. "Founder's Day Address," reprinted from *The Normal Index*, (June, 1950).
Chambers, Frederick. "Histories of Black Colleges and Universities." *The Journal of Negro History*, LVII (July, 1972), 270–75.
"DeForest, Henry Swift." *Yale Obituary Record, 1890–1900*, p. 28.
Hale, L. D., ed. *The Courier Courtesy Magazine*, IV (February, 1927), 3.
Hall, Bertie L. "A Bit of History." *The State Normal Courier*, II (February 7, 1924), 7–8.
Jones, Lewis W. "The Agent as a Factor in the Education of Negroes in the South." *Journal of Negro Education*, XIX (1950), 28–37.
Lewis, Agnes J. "A Sketch of Professor J. W. Beverly." *The State Normal Courier*, II (February 7, 1924), 11–12.
Myers, John B. "The Education of the Alabama Freedmen During Presidential Reconstruction, 1865–1867." *The Journal of Negro Education*, XL (Spring, 1971), 163–71.

Orr, Charles Walter. "Founder's Day Address." *The Normal Index*, XXII (May, 1940), 4–8.

Schweninger, Loren. "The American Missionary Association and Northern Philanthropy in Reconstruction Alabama." *Alabama Historical Quarterly* (Fall and Winter, 1970), 129–56.

The Selma University Chronicle, XI (January, 1950), 2–3.

"Silsby Memorial Number." *The Talladegan*, XLI (January, 1923).

Terrell, Mary Frances. "William Burns Paterson; A Life Sketch." *The State Normal Courier*, II (February 7, 1924), 4–5.

Thorpe, Earl Endris. "William Hooper Councill." *The Negro History Bulletin*, XIX (January, 1956), 85–86.

Vaughn, William P. "Partners in Segregation: Barnas Sears and the Peabody Fund." *Civil War History* (September, 1964), 260–74.

Index